The Reference Shelf

The Power of the Press

Edited by Beth Levy
and Denise M. Bonilla

The Reference Shelf
Volume 71 • Number 1

The H.W. Wilson Company
New York • Dublin
1999

The Reference Shelf

The books in this series contain reprints of articles, excerpts from books, addresses on current issues, and studies of social trends in the United States and other countries. There are six separately bound numbers in each volume, all of which are usually published in the same calendar year. Numbers one through five are each devoted to a single subject, providing background information and discussion from various points of view and concluding with a subject index and comprehensive bibliography that lists books, pamphlets, and abstracts of additional articles on the subject. The final number of each volume is a collection of recent speeches, and it contains a cumulative speaker index. Books in the series may be purchased individually or on subscription.

Visit H.W. Wilson's Web site: www.hwwilson.com

Library of Congress Cataloging-in-Publication data

The power of the press
        p. cm—(Reference shelf; v. 71, no. 1)
    Includes bibliographical references and index
    ISBN 0-8242-0962-1 (pbk. : alk. paper)
1. Press and politics   2. Journalism—political aspects. 3. Government and the press.
4. Freedom of the press.5. Journalistic ethics.   I. Bonilla, Denise M.   II. Levy, Beth
III. Series
PN4751 .P69   1999   99-21172
070.4—dc21   CIP

Printed in the United States of America

Contents

Preface

Before there was anything known as a "press," there was news. Before the emergence of writing, our ancestors passed along news in the form of the spoken word—sometimes as a whisper in a cave, other times as a call from a hilltop. Over the centuries, as civilizations have risen and fallen, humans have relied on this information for survival—and so news media have developed from their most primitive forms into high-tech, rapidly transmissible forms.

Since their earlist days, news reporters have had critics. People have formed opinions of their news sources, and have frequently taken issue with the practices and priorities of the people behind the news. Each nation's press has a different relationship with its government, businesses, institutions, and public. It has been critical and criticized.

The past century has seen the greatest broadening of the term "press" to include many media, including radio, television, and the Internet, but for many people, newspapers represent the most official and reliable reports on record. This represents a massive change in the role of newspapers since their establishment in this country, when most newspapers were mouthpieces for political parties. At another stage, around the turn of the century, newspapers made it their mission to provide a sense of community for ethnic groups, which led to a peak in the number of newspapers nationwide. Immigrants represented an array of political stripes and reading interests, thus heightening the diversity of newspapers. Today, the number of newspapers has dropped, in large part because they must compete with other media, but readers most often look to them for objective reporting. Press objectivity is a relatively modern phenomenon, prized by Americans in particular, and there is constant debate over what reporting is truly objective, or "the truth." Over the years, journalists have been labeled muckrakers and gossip-mongers, troublemakers, peacemakers, and freedom fighters. Their critics often challenge the notion of truth, and the stories of their struggles reflect greater struggles in our culture as a whole.

This book is intended to provide an introduction to recent issues of importance in news reporting. In an effort to provide a diversity of writing styles, we have tried to include news stories as well as opinion pieces. When reading, please keep in mind that for every opinion that appears on paper in this volume, there are many more opinions out there—on the Web, in magazines, on TV, on the radio. This book's contents represent only a selection, but we hope that the articles included here spark your interest in exploring the topics further.

In the first chapter, "Defining the Media," we begin with some observations on the composition and values of the press today, including the media's ties to business, a tendency toward reporting on human-interest stories, and the role of the World Wide Web in news reporting. The chapters that follow explore current issues for the media. One issue that has both guided the news and been the subject of reports in the past few years is the relationship between celebrity and journalism. The articles included in the second chapter, "The Marriage of Celebrity and Journalism," are meant to critique the judgment of journalists when it comes to dealing with celebrities and with their own celebrity.

An extremely important, and often most controversial, journalistic value is ethics. The third chapter, "Spotlight on Ethics," explores some timely ethical issues of journalism, including responsible reporting, selective use of information, and story retraction. Ethics have not only influenced the news in the past few years, professional ethics have become the news in many cases. Thus, in "When Journalism Fails," the following chapter, we have assembled some accounts and criticism of recent ethics cases that have affected both large and small publications, among them CNN and *Time*, the *Boston Globe*, and the *New Republic*.

We close with a discussion of press freedom. Following an overview of attacks on the press, the articles in chapter five, "Press Freedom at Home and Abroad," explore the press's entanglements with governments in Hong Kong and Nigeria. This chapter also provides an introduction to issues of press freedom in the United States.

The editors wish to thank the following individuals who helped make this book possible: Sarah Swart and Helen Mazarakis, proofreaders; and Mary Tomaselli, indexer. Thanks also go to the following members of the H. W. Wilson General Reference department staff: Hilary Claggett, senior editor; Sandra Watson, editorial assistant; Geoffrey Orens, editorial assistant; Gray Young, managing editor; and Michael Schulze, vice president of General Reference.

Denise M. Bonilla
Beth Levy

March 1999

I. Defining the Media

Editors' Introduction

Today's news media are powerful, but different critics identify the source of their power in different ways. Is it the ability to broadcast widely? A reporter's decision to report a story can change the lives of everyone involved in a given incident, and let the whole world know in the process. To some, this is a good thing, encouraging broad coverage of current events. Is the media's power linked to corporate power? Some see today's media as overly selective in what they will cover, choosing only stories that will garner high ratings or win them high readership. This chapter pays particular attention to TV news programs and commentary, and takes into account the growth of cable television and the Internet, as well.

Whatever someone's individual perceptions may be, news organizations must constantly consider how their reporting will be perceived by their owners and audiences alike. The first article in this chapter, "Why Americans Hate the Media," by James Fallows, analyzes several clear disconnects between what Americans idealize in journalism and how it is actually practiced, particularly in televised political commentaries and talk shows. Fallows also criticizes the media for not always recognizing what elements of a story might resonate positively with viewers, using President Clinton's 1995 State of the Union address as an example.

In the late 1990s, many news organizations and nearly all television networks have become parts of much larger corporate entities. The second two articles in this chapter, "Does Big Mean Bad," by Tom Goldstein, and "Money Lust: How Pressure for Profit Is Perverting Journalism," by Neil Hickey, explore the concerns critics have regarding corporate consolidation of the media. While the first of these two articles is primarily an introduction to the subject, asking readers to consider both the pros and cons of media concentration, the second unquestioningly points to this trend as the triggering event in what the author sees as the media's downfall, in which objective hard news stories have been replaced by tabloid-style stores to enhance commercial success.

The fourth article in this chapter, "News Lite," by James McCartney, questions the prevalence of human-interest stories in the news, and takes it one step further by asking how this reflects democracy. Some are concerned that coverage of government has been sacrificed in favor of human-interest stories, thus leading to a poorly informed electorate and an erosion of democracy. Others, however, believe that by covering lighter news, more media ensure their own survival. Some also believe that there is less "hard news" to report at this point in history.

The final article in this chapter, "The Web Made Me Do It," by Jack Shafer, analyzes the reliability and prominence of the Internet as a news source. He writes that currently many critics feel that the Web allows people to believe unfiltered reporting and rumors rather than thoroughly fact-checked stories. He also writes, however, that people may have less to fear from new technology than they might think. To give readers some perspective, he offers up the reminder that a century ago, fear of how the telephone might affect the news was rampant. He articulates the hope that news audiences will be able to distinguish between rumor and fact.

Why Americans Hate the Media[1]

In the late 1980s public-television stations aired a talking-heads series called *Ethics in America*. For each show more than a dozen prominent citizens sat around a horseshoe-shaped table and tried to answer troubling ethical questions posed by a moderator. The series might have seemed a good bet to be paralyzingly dull, but at least one show was riveting in its drama and tension.

The episode was taped in the fall of 1987. Its title was "Under Orders, Under Fire," and most of the panelists were former soldiers talking about the ethical dilemmas of their work. The moderator was Charles Ogletree, a professor at Harvard Law School, who moved from panelist to panelist asking increasingly difficult questions in the law school's famous Socratic style.

During the first half of the show Ogletree made the soldiers squirm about ethical tangles on the battlefield. The man getting the roughest treatment was Frederick Downs, a writer who as a young Army lieutenant in Vietnam had lost his left arm in a mine explosion.

Ogletree asked Downs to imagine that he was a young lieutenant again. He and his platoon were in the nation of "South Kosan," advising South Kosanese troops in their struggle against invaders from "North Kosan." (This scenario was apparently a hybrid of the U.S. roles in the Korean and Vietnam wars.) A North Kosanese unit had captured several of Downs's men alive—but Downs had also captured several of the North Kosanese. Downs did not know where his men were being held, but he thought his prisoners did.

And so Ogletree put the question: How far would Downs go to make a prisoner talk? Would he order him tortured? Would he torture the prisoner himself? Downs himself speculated on what he would do if he had a big knife in his hand. Would he start cutting the prisoner? When would he make himself stop, if the prisoner just wouldn't talk?

Downs did not shrink from the questions or the implications of his answers. He wouldn't enjoy doing it, he told Ogletree. He would have to live with the consequences for the rest of his life. But yes, he would torture the captive. He would use the knife. Implicit in his answers was the idea that he would do the cutting himself and would listen to the captive scream. He would do whatever was necessary to try to save his own men. While explaining his decisions Downs sometimes gestured with his left hand for emphasis. The hand was a metal hook.

Ogletree worked his way through the other military officials, asking all how they reacted to Frederick Downs's choice. William Westmoreland, who had commanded the whole U.S. force in Vietnam when Downs was serving there, deplored Downs's deci-

1. Article by James Fallows, excerpted from *Breaking the News: How the Media Undermine American Democracy* (1996). First printed in *Atlantic Monthly* Feb. 1996. Copyright © James Fallows. Reprinted with permission.

sion. After all, he said, even war has its rules. An Army chaplain wrestled with how he would react if a soldier in a morally troubling position similar to Downs's came to him privately and confessed what he had done. A Marine Corps officer juggled a related question: What would he do if he came across an American soldier who was about to torture or execute a bound and unarmed prisoner, who might be a civilian?

The soldiers disagreed among themselves. Yet in describing their decisions they used phrases like "I hope I would have the courage to . . ." and "In order to live with myself later I would . . ." The whole exercise may have been set up as a rhetorical game, but Ogletree's questions clearly tapped into discussions the soldiers had already had about the consequences of choices they made.

Then Ogletree turned to the two most famous members of the evening's panel, better known even than Westmoreland. These were two star TV journalists: Peter Jennings, of *World News Tonight* and ABC, and Mike Wallace, of *60 Minutes* and CBS.

Ogletree brought them into the same hypothetical war. He asked Jennings to imagine that he worked for a network that had been in contact with the enemy North Kosanese government. After much pleading Jennings and his news crew got permission from the North Kosanese to enter their country and film behind the lines. Would Jennings be willing to go? Of course, he replied. Any reporter would—and in real wars reporters from his network often had.

But while Jennings and his crew were traveling with a North Kosanese unit, to visit the site of an alleged atrocity by U.S. and South Kosanese troops, they unexpectedly crossed the trail of a small group of American and South Kosanese soldiers. With Jennings in their midst the Northern soldiers set up an ambush that would let them gun down the Americans and Southerners.

What would Jennings do? Would he tell his cameramen to "Roll tape!" as the North Kosanese opened fire? What would go through his mind as he watched the North Kosanese prepare to fire?

Jennings sat silent for about 15 seconds. "Well, I guess I wouldn't," he finally said. "I am going to tell you now what I am feeling, rather than the hypothesis I drew for myself. If I were with a North Kosanese unit that came upon Americans, I think that I personally would do what I could to warn the Americans."

Even if it meant losing the story? Ogletree asked.

Even though it would almost certainly mean losing my life, Jennings replied. "But I do not think that I could bring myself to participate in that act. That's purely personal, and other reporters might have a different reaction."

Ogletree turned for reaction to Mike Wallace, who immediately replied. "I think some other reporters *would* have a different reaction," he said, obviously referring to himself. "They would regard it simply as another story they were there to cover." A moment later Wallace said, "I am astonished, really." He turned toward Jennings and began to lecture him: "You're a reporter. Granted you're an American" (at least for purposes of the fictional example; Jennings has actually retained Canadian citizenship). "I'm a little bit at a loss to understand why, because you're an American, you would not have covered that story."

Ogletree pushed Wallace. Didn't Jennings have some higher duty to do something other than just roll film as soldiers from his own country were being shot?

"No," Wallace said flatly and immediately. "You don't have a higher duty. No. No. You're a reporter!"

Jennings backtracked fast. Wallace was right, he said: "I chickened out." Jennings said that he had "played the hypothetical very hard." He had lost sight of his journalistic duty to remain detached.

As Jennings said he agreed with Wallace, several soldiers in the room seemed to regard the two of them with horror. Retired Air Force General Brent Scowcroft, who would soon become George Bush's National Security Advisor, said it was simply wrong to stand and watch as your side was slaughtered. "What's it *worth*?" he asked Wallace bitterly. "It's worth 30 seconds on the evening news, as opposed to saving a platoon."

After a brief discussion between Wallace and Scowcroft, Ogletree reminded Wallace of Scowcroft's basic question. What was it worth for the reporter to stand by, looking? Shouldn't the reporter have said *something*?

Wallace gave a disarming grin, shrugged his shoulders, and said, "I don't know." He later mentioned extreme circumstances in which he thought journalists should intervene. But at that moment he seemed to be mugging to the crowd with a "Don't ask me!" expression, and in fact he drew a big laugh—the first such moment in the discussion. Jennings, however, was all business, and was still concerned about the first answer he had given.

"I wish I had made another decision," Jennings said, as if asking permission to live the past five minutes over again. "I would like to have made his decision"—that is, Wallace's decision to keep on filming.

A few minutes later Ogletree turned to George M. Connell, a Marine colonel in full uniform. Jaw muscles flexing in anger, with stress on each word, Connell said, "I feel utter contempt."

Two days after this hypothetical episode, Connell said, Jennings or Wallace might be back with the American forces—and could be wounded by stray fire, as combat journalists often had been before. When that happens, he said, they are "just journalists." Yet they would expect American soldiers to run out under enemy fire and drag them back, rather than leaving them to bleed to death on the battlefield.

"I'll do it!" Connell said. "And that is what makes me so contemptuous of them. Marines will die going to get . . . a couple of journalists." The last words dripped disgust.

Not even Ogletree knew what to say. There was dead silence for several seconds. Then a square-jawed man with neat gray hair and aviator glasses spoke up. It was Newt Gingrich, looking a generation younger and trimmer than he would when he became speaker of the House, in 1995. One thing was clear from this exercise, Gingrich said. "The military has done a vastly better job of systematically thinking through the ethics of behavior in a violent environment than the journalists have."

One thing was clear from this exercise, Gingrich said. "The military has done a vastly better job of systematically thinking through the ethics of behavior in a violent environment than the journalists have."

That was about the mildest way to put it. Although Wallace and Jennings conceded that the criticism was fair—if journalists considered themselves "detached," they could not logically expect American soldiers to rescue them—nevertheless their reactions spoke volumes about the values of their craft. Jennings was made to feel embarrassed about his natural, decent human impulse. Wallace seemed unembarrassed about feeling no connection to the soldiers in his country's army or considering their deaths before his eyes "simply a story." In other important occupations people sometimes face the need to do the horrible. Frederick Downs, after all, was willing to torture a man and hear him scream. But Downs had thought through all the consequences and alternatives, and he knew he would live with the horror for the rest of his days. When Mike Wallace said he would do something horrible, he barely bothered to give a rationale. He did not try to explain the reasons a reporter might feel obliged to remain silent as the attack began—for instance, that in combat reporters must be beyond country, or that they have a duty to bear impartial witness to deaths on either side, or that Jennings had implicitly made a promise not to betray the North Kosanese when he agreed to accompany them. The soldiers might or might not have found such arguments convincing; Wallace didn't even make them.

Not Issues But the Game of Politics

A generation ago political talk programs were sleepy Sunday-morning affairs. The Secretary of State or the Senate majority leader would show up to answer questions from Lawrence Spivak or Bob Clark, and after 30 minutes another stately episode of *Meet the Press* or *Issues and Answers* would be history.

Everything in public life is "brighter" and more "interesting" now. Constant competition from the weekday trash-talk shows has forced anything involving political life to liven up. Under pressure from the Saturday political-talk shows—*The McLaughlin Group* and its many disorderly descendants—even the Sunday-morning shows have put on rouge and push-up bras.

Meet the Press, moderated by Tim Russert, is probably the meatiest of these programs. High-powered guests discuss serious topics with Russert, who worked for years in politics, and with veteran reporters. Yet the pressure to keep things lively means that squabbling replaces dialogue.

The discussion-shows that are supposed to enhance public understanding may actually reduce it, by hammering home the message that issues don't matter except as items for politicians to fight over. Some politicians in Washington may indeed view all issues as mere tools to use against their opponents. But far from offsetting this view of public life, the national press often encourages it. As Washington-based talk shows have become more popular in the past decade, they have had a trickle-down effect in cities across the country. In Seattle, in Los Angeles, in Boston, in Atlanta, journalists gain notice and influence by appearing regularly on talk shows—and during those appearances they mainly talk about the game of politics.

In the 1992 presidential campaign candidates spent more time answering questions from "ordinary people"—citizens in town-hall forums, callers on radio and TV talk shows—than they had in previous years. The citizens asked overwhelmingly about the what of politics: What are you going to do about the health-care system? What can you do to reduce the cost of welfare? The reporters asked almost exclusively about the how: How are you going to try to take away Perot's constituency? How do you answer charges that you have flip-flopped?

After the 1992 campaign the contrast between questions from citizens and those from reporters was widely discussed in journalism reviews and postmortems on campaign coverage. Reporters acknowledged that they should try harder to ask questions about things their readers and viewers seemed to care about—that is, questions about the differences that political choices would make in people's lives.

In January of last year there was a chance to see how well the lesson had sunk in. In the days just before and after Bill Clinton delivered his State of the Union address to the new Republican-controlled Congress, he answered questions in a wide variety of forums in order to explain his plans.

On January 31, a week after the speech, the President flew to Boston and took questions from a group of teenagers. Their questions concerned the effects of legislation or gov-

The discussion-shows that are supposed to enhance public understanding may actually reduce it, by hammering home the message that issues don't matter except as items for politicians to fight over.

ernment programs on their communities or schools. These
were the questions (paraphrased in some cases):

- "We need stronger laws to punish those people who are
  caught selling guns to our youth. Basically, what can you
  do about that?"
- "I notice that often it's the media that is responsible for
  the negative portrayal of young people in our society."
  What can political leaders do to persuade the media that
  there is good news about youth?
- Apprenticeship programs and other ways to provide job
  training have been valuable for students not going to college. Can the Administration promote more of these programs?
- Programs designed to keep teenagers away from drugs
  and gangs often emphasize sports and seem geared
  mainly to boys. How can such programs be made more
  attractive to teenage girls?
- What is it like at Oxford? (This was from a student who
  was completing a new alternative-school curriculum in
  the Boston public schools, and who had been accepted at
  Oxford.)
- "We need more police officers who are trained to deal
  with all the other different cultures in our cities." What
  can the government do about that?
- "In Boston, Northeastern University has created a model
  of scholarships and other supports to help inner-city kids
  get to and stay in college. . . . As President, can you urge
  colleges across the country to do what Northeastern has
  done?"

Earlier in the month the President's performance had been
assessed by the three network-news anchors: Peter Jennings,
of ABC; Dan Rather, of CBS; and Tom Brokaw, of NBC. There
was no overlap whatsoever between the questions the students asked and those raised by the anchors. None of the
questions from these news professionals concerned the
impact of legislation or politics on people's lives. Nearly all
concerned the struggle for individual advancement among
candidates.

Peter Jennings, who met with Clinton as the Gingrich–Dole
Congress was getting under way, asked whether Clinton had
been eclipsed as a political leader by the Republicans. Dan
Rather did interviews through January with prominent politicians—Senators Edward Kennedy, Phil Gramm, and Bob
Dole—building up to a profile of Clinton two days after the
State of the Union address. Every question he asked was
about popularity or political tactics. He asked Phil Gramm to
guess whether Newt Gingrich would enter the race (no) and
whether Bill Clinton would be renominated by his party
(yes). He asked Bob Dole what kind of mood the President
seemed to be in, and whether Dole and Gingrich were, in
effect, the new bosses of Washington. When Edward

Kennedy began giving his views about the balanced-budget amendment, Rather steered him back on course: "Senator, you know I'd talk about these things the rest of the afternoon, but let's move quickly to politics. Do you expect Bill Clinton to be the Democratic nominee for re-election in 1996?"

The *CBS Evening News* profile of Clinton, which was narrated by Rather and was presented as part of the series *Eye on America*, contained no mention of Clinton's economic policy, his tax or budget plans, his failed attempt to pass a health-care proposal, his successful attempt to ratify NAFTA, his efforts to "reinvent government," or any substantive aspect of his proposals or plans in office. Its subject was exclusively Clinton's handling of his office—his "difficulty making decisions," his "waffling" at crucial moments. If Rather or his colleagues had any interest in the content of Clinton's speech as opposed to its political effect, neither the questions they asked nor the reports they aired revealed such a concern.

Tom Brokaw's questions were more substantive, but even he concentrated mainly on politics of the moment. How did the President feel about a poll showing that 61 percent of the public felt that he had no "strong convictions" and could be "easily swayed"? What did Bill Clinton think about Newt Gingrich? "Do you think he plays fair?" How did he like it that people kept shooting at the White House?

When ordinary citizens have a chance to pose questions to political leaders, they rarely ask about the game of politics. They want to know how the reality of politics will affect them—through taxes, programs, scholarship funds, wars. Journalists justify their intrusiveness and excesses by claiming that they are the public's representatives, asking the questions their fellow citizens would ask if they had the privilege of meeting with presidents and senators. In fact they ask questions that only their fellow political professionals care about. And they often do so—as at the typical White House news conference—with a discourtesy and rancor that represent the public's views much less than they reflect the modern journalist's belief that being independent boils down to acting hostile.

Reductio Ad Electionem: The One-Track Mind

The limited curiosity that elite reporters display in their questions is also evident in the stories they write once they have received answers. They are interested mainly in pure politics and can be coerced into examining the substance of an issue only as a last resort. The subtle but sure result is a stream of daily messages that the real meaning of public life is the struggle of Bob Dole against Newt Gingrich against Bill Clinton, rather than our collective efforts to solve collective problems.

The natural instinct of newspapers and TV is to present every public issue as if its "real" meaning were political in the meanest and narrowest sense of that term—the attempt by parties and candidates to gain an advantage over their rivals. Reporters do, of course, write stories about political life in the broader sense and about the substance of issues— the pluses and minuses of diplomatic recognition for Vietnam, the difficulties of holding down the Medicare budget, whether immigrants help or hurt the nation's economic base. But when there is a chance to use these issues as props or raw material for a story about political tactics, most reporters leap at it. It is more fun—and easier—to write about Bill Clinton's "positioning" on the Vietnam issue, or how Newt Gingrich is "handling" the need to cut Medicare, than it is to look into the issues themselves.

The natural instinct of newspapers and TV is to present every public issue as if its "real" meaning were political in the meanest and narrowest sense of that term.

Examples of this preference occur so often that they're difficult to notice. But every morning's newspaper, along with every evening's newscast, reveals this pattern of thought.

- Last February, when the Democratic President and the Republican Congress were fighting over how much federal money would go to local law-enforcement agencies, one network-news broadcast showed a clip of Gingrich denouncing Clinton and another of Clinton standing in front of a sea of uniformed police officers while making a tough-on-crime speech. The correspondent's sign-off line was "The White House thinks 'cops on the beat' has a simple but appealing ring to it." That is, the President was pushing the plan because it would sound good in his campaign ads. Whether or not that was Clinton's real motive, nothing in the broadcast gave the slightest hint of where the extra policemen would go, how much they might cost, whether there was reason to think they'd do any good. Everything in the story suggested that the crime bill mattered only as a chapter in the real saga, which was the struggle between Bill and Newt.

- Last April, after the explosion at the federal building in Oklahoma City, discussion changed quickly from the event itself to politicians' "handling" of the event. On the Sunday after the blast President Clinton announced a series of new anti-terrorism measures. The next morning, on National Public Radio's *Morning Edition*, Cokie Roberts was asked about the prospects of the proposals' taking effect. "In some ways it's not even the point," she replied. What mattered was that Clinton "looked good" taking the tough side of the issue. No one expects Cokie Roberts or other political correspondents to be experts on controlling terrorism, negotiating with the Syrians, or the other specific measures on which Presidents make stands. But all issues are shoehorned into the area of expertise the most-prominent correspondents do have: the struggle for one-upmanship among a handful of political leaders.

- When health-care reform was the focus of big political battles between Republicans and Democrats, it was on the front page and the evening newscast every day. When the Clinton Administration declared defeat in 1994 and there were no more battles to be fought, health-care news coverage virtually stopped too—even though the medical system still represented one seventh of the economy, even though HMOs and corporations and hospitals and pharmaceutical companies were rapidly changing policies in the face of ever-rising costs. Health care was no longer political news, and therefore it was no longer interesting news.

- After California's voters approved Proposition 187 in the 1994 elections, drastically limiting the benefits available to illegal immigrants, the national press ran a trickle of stories on what this would mean for California's economy, its school and legal systems, even its relations with Mexico. A flood of stories examined the political impact of the immigration issue—how the Republicans might exploit it, how the Democrats might be divided by it, whether it might propel Pete Wilson to the White House.

- On August 16 last year Bill Bradley announced that after representing New Jersey in the Senate for three terms he would not run for a fourth term. In interviews and at the news conferences he conducted afterward Bradley did his best to talk about the deep problems of public life and economic adjustment that had left him frustrated with the political process. Each of the parties had locked itself into rigid positions that kept it from dealing with the realistic concerns of ordinary people, he said. American corporations were doing what they had to do for survival in international competition: they were downsizing and making themselves radically more efficient and productive. But the result was to leave "decent, hardworking Americans" more vulnerable to layoffs and the loss of their careers, medical coverage, pension rights, and social standing than they had been in decades. Somehow, Bradley said, we had to move past the focus on short-term political maneuvering and determine how to deal with the forces that were leaving Americans frustrated and insecure.

That, at least, was what Bill Bradley said. What turned up in the press was almost exclusively speculation about what the move meant for this year's presidential race and the party lineup on Capitol Hill. Might Bradley challenge Bill Clinton in the Democratic primaries? If not, was he preparing for an independent run? Could the Democrats come up with any other candidate capable of holding on to Bradley's seat? Wasn't this a slap in the face for Bill Clinton and the party he purported to lead? In the aftermath of Bradley's announcement prominent TV and newspaper reporters competed to come up with the shrewdest analysis of the political impact of the move. None of the country's major papers or networks used Bradley's announcement as a news peg for an analysis of the real issues he had raised.

The day after his announcement Bradley was interviewed by Judy Woodruff on the CNN program *Inside Politics*. Woodruff is a widely respected and knowledgeable reporter, but her interaction with Bradley was like the meeting of two beings from different universes. Every answer Bradley gave was about the substance of national problems that concerned him. Every one of Woodruff's responses or questions was about short-term political tactics. Woodruff asked about the political implications of his move for Bill Clinton and Newt Gingrich. Bradley replied that it was more important to concentrate on the difficulties both parties had in dealing with real national problems.

Midway through the interview Bradley gave a long answer to the effect that everyone involved in politics had to get out of the rut of converting every subject or comment into a political "issue," used for partisan advantage. Let's stop talking, Bradley said, about who will win what race and start responding to one another's ideas.

As soon as he finished, Woodruff asked her next question: "Do you want to be President?" It was as if she had not heard a word he had been saying—or *couldn't* hear it, because the media's language of political analysis is utterly separate from the terms in which people describe real problems in their lives.

The effect is as if the discussion of every new advance in medicine boiled down to speculation about whether its creator would win the Nobel Prize that year. Regardless of the tone of coverage, medical research will go on. But a relentless emphasis on the cynical game of politics threatens public life itself, by implying day after day that the political sphere is nothing more than an arena in which ambitious politicians struggle for dominance, rather than a structure in which citizens can deal with worrisome collective problems.

Pointless Prediction: The Political Experts

On Sunday, November 6, 1994, two days before the congressional elections that swept the Republicans to power, *The Washington Post* published the results of its "Crystal Ball" poll. Fourteen prominent journalists, pollsters, and all-around analysts made their predictions about how many seats each party would win in the House and Senate and how many governorships each would take.

One week later many of these same experts would be saying on their talk shows that the Republican landslide was "inevitable" and "a long time coming" and "a sign of deep discontent in the heartland." But before the returns were in, how many of the 14 experts predicted that the Republicans would win both houses of Congress and that Newt Gingrich would be speaker? Exactly three.

What is interesting about this event is not just that so many experts could be so wrong. Immediately after the election even Newt Gingrich seemed dazed by the idea that the 40-year reign of the Democrats in the House had actually come to an end. Rather, the episode said something about the futility of political prediction itself—a task to which the big-time press devotes enormous effort and time. *Two days* before the election many of the country's most admired analysts had no idea what was about to happen. Yet within a matter of weeks these same people, unfazed, would be writing articles and giving speeches and being quoted about who was "ahead" and "behind" in the emerging race for the White House in 1996.

As with medieval doctors who applied leeches and trepanned skulls, the practitioners cannot be blamed for the limits of their profession. But we can ask why reporters spend so much time directing our attention toward what is not much more than guesswork on their part. It builds the impression that journalism is about what's entertaining—guessing what might or might not happen next month—rather than what's useful, such as extracting lessons of success and failure from events that have already occurred. Competing predictions add almost nothing to our ability to solve public problems or to make sensible choices among complex alternatives. Yet such useless distractions have become a specialty of the political press. They are easy to produce, they allow reporters to act as if they possessed special inside knowledge, and there are no consequences for being wrong.

Spoon-feeding: The White House Press Corps

In the early spring of last year, when Newt Gingrich was dominating the news from Washington and the O. J. Simpson trial was dominating the news as a whole, the *Washington Post* ran an article about the pathos of the White House press room. Nobody wanted to hear what the President was doing, so the people who cover the President could not get on the air. Howard Kurtz, the *Post*'s media writer, described the human cost of this political change:

> Brit Hume is in his closet-size White House cubicle, watching Kato Kaelin testify on CNN. Bill Plante, in the adjoining cubicle, has his feet up and is buried in the *New York Times*. Brian Williams is in the corridor, idling away the time with Jim Miklaszewski.
>
> An announcement is made for a bill-signing ceremony. Some of America's highest-paid television correspondents begin ambling toward the pressroom door.
>
> "Are you coming with us?" Williams asks.
>
> "I guess so," says Hume, looking forlorn.

The White House spokesman, Mike McCurry, told Kurtz that there was some benefit to the enforced silence: "Brit Hume has now got his crossword puzzle capacity down to record time. And some of the reporters have been out on the lecture circuit."

The deadpan restraint with which Kurtz told this story is admirable. But the question many readers would want to scream at the idle correspondents is *Why don't you go out and do some work?*

Why not go out and interview someone, even if you're not going to get any airtime that night? Why not escape the monotonous tyranny of the White House press room, which reporters are always complaining about? The knowledge that O. J. will keep you off the air yet again should liberate you to look into those stories you never "had time" to deal with before. Why not *read a book*—about welfare reform, about Russia or China, about race relations, about anything? Why not imagine, just for a moment, that your journalistic duty might involve something more varied and constructive than doing standups from the White House lawn and sounding skeptical about whatever announcement the President's spokesman put out that day?

What might these well-paid, well-trained correspondents have done while waiting for the O. J. trial to become boring enough that they could get back on the air? They might have tried to learn something that would be of use to their viewers when the story of the moment went away. Without leaving Washington, without going farther than 10 minutes by taxi from the White House (so that they could be on hand if a sudden press conference was called), they could have prepared themselves to discuss the substance of issues that affect the public.

For example, two years earlier Vice President Al Gore had announced an ambitious plan to "reinvent" the federal government. Had it made any difference, either in improving the performance of government or in reducing its cost, or was it all for show? Republicans and Democrats were sure to spend the next few months fighting about cuts in the capital-gains tax. Capital-gains tax rates were higher in some countries and lower in others. What did the experience of these countries show about whether cutting the rates helped an economy to grow? The rate of immigration was rising again, and in California and Florida it was becoming an important political issue. What was the latest evidence on the economic and social effects of immigration? Should Americans feel confident or threatened that so many foreigners were trying to make their way in? Soon both political parties would be advancing plans to reform the welfare system. Within a two-mile radius of the White House lived plenty of families on welfare. Why not go and see how the system had affected them, and what they would do if it changed? The federal government had gone further than most private industries in trying to open opportunities to racial minorities and women. The Pentagon had gone furthest of all. What did people involved in this process—men and women, blacks and whites—think about its successes and failures? What light did their experience shed on the impending affirmative-action debate?

There is no longer any such thing as an accusation too embarrassing to be printed if it seems to bear on a politician's "character."

The list could go on for pages. With a few minutes' effort—about as long as it takes to do a crossword puzzle—the correspondents could have drawn up lists of other subjects they had never before "had time" to investigate. They had the time now. What they lacked was a sense that their responsibility involved something more than standing up to rehash the day's announcements when there was room for them on the news.

Glass Houses: Journalists and Financial Disclosure

Half a century ago reporters knew but didn't say that Franklin D. Roosevelt was in a wheelchair. A generation ago many reporters knew but didn't write about John F. Kennedy's insatiable appetite for women. For several months in the early Clinton era reporters knew about but didn't disclose Paula Jones's allegation that, as governor of Arkansas, Bill Clinton had exposed himself to her. Eventually this claim found its way into all the major newspapers, proving that there is no longer any such thing as an accusation too embarrassing to be printed if it seems to bear on a politician's "character."

It is not just the President who has given up his privacy in the name of the public's right to know. Over the past two decades officials whose power is tiny compared with the President's have had to reveal embarrassing details about what most Americans consider very private matters: their income and wealth. Each of the more than 3,000 people appointed by the President to executive-branch jobs must reveal previous sources of income and summarize his or her financial holdings. Congressmen have changed their rules to forbid themselves to accept honoraria for speaking to interest groups or lobbyists. The money that politicians do raise from individuals and groups must be disclosed to the Federal Election Commission. The information they disclose is available to the public and appears often in publications, most prominently the *Washington Post.*

No one contends that every contribution makes every politician corrupt. But financial disclosure has become commonplace on the "Better safe than sorry" principle. If politicians and officials are not corrupt, the reasoning goes, they have nothing to fear from letting their finances be publicized. And if they are corrupt, public disclosure is a way to stop them before they do too much harm. The process may be embarrassing, but this is the cost of public life.

How different the "Better safe than sorry" calculation seems when journalists are involved! Reporters and pundits hold no elected office, but they are obviously public figures. The most prominent TV-talk-show personalities are better known than all but a handful of congressmen. When politicians and pundits sit alongside one another on Washington talk shows and trade opinions, they underscore the essential similarity of their political roles. The pundits have no vote in Congress, but the overall political impact of a word from George Will, Ted Koppel, William Safire, or any of their colleagues who run the major editorial pages dwarfs anything a third-term congressman could do. If an interest group had the choice of buying the favor of one prominent media figure or of two junior congressmen, it wouldn't even have to think about the decision. The pundit is obviously more valuable.

If a reporter is sued for libel by a prominent but unelected personality, such as David Letterman or Donald Trump, he or she says that the offended party is a "public figure"—about whom nearly anything can be written in the press. Public figures, according to the rulings that shape today's libel law, can win a libel suit only if they can prove that a reporter knew that what he or she was writing was false, or had "reckless disregard" for its truth, and went ahead and published it anyway. Public figures, according to the law, pay a price for being well known. And who are these people? The category is not limited to those who hold public office but includes all who "thrust themselves into the public eye." Most journalists would eloquently argue the logic of this broad definition of public figures—until the same standard was applied to them.

In 1993 Sam Donaldson, of ABC, described himself in an interview as being in touch with the concerns of the average American. "I'm trying to get a little ranching business started in New Mexico," he said. "I've got five people on the payroll.

I'm making out those government forms." Thus he understood the travails of the small businessman and the annoy-
ances of government regulation. Donaldson, whose base pay
from ABC is reported to be some $2 million a year, did not
point out that his several ranches in New Mexico together
covered some 20,000 acres. When doing a segment attacking
farm subsidies on *Prime Time Live* in 1993 he did not point
out that "those government forms" allowed him to claim
nearly $97,000 in sheep and mohair subsidies over two
years. William Neuman, a reporter for the *New York Post*,
said that when his photographer tried to take pictures of
Donaldson's ranch house, Donaldson had him thrown off his
property. ("In the West trespassing is a serious offense,"
Donaldson explained.)

Had Donaldson as a journalist been pursuing a politician or
even a corporate executive, he would have felt justified in
using the most aggressive reportorial techniques. When
these techniques were turned on him, he complained that
the reporters were going too far. The analysts who are so
clear-eyed about the conflict of interest in Newt Gingrich's
book deal claim that they see no reason, none at all, why
their own finances might be of public interest.

Last May one of Donaldson's colleagues on *This Week with
David Brinkley*, George Will, wrote a column and delivered
on-air comments ridiculing the Clinton Administration's plan
to impose tariffs on Japanese luxury cars, notably the Lexus.
On the Brinkley show Will said that the tariffs would be "illegal" and would merely amount to "a subsidy for Mercedes
dealerships."

Neither in his column nor on the show did Will disclose
that his wife, Mari Maseng Will, ran a firm that had been
paid some $200,000 as a registered foreign agent for the
Japan Automobile Manufacturers Association, and that one
of the duties for which she was hired was to get American
commentators to criticize the tariff plan. When Will was
asked why he had never mentioned this, he replied that it
was "just too silly" to think that his views might have been
affected by his wife's contract.

Will had, in fact, espoused such views for years, since long
before his wife worked for the JAMA and even before he had
married her. Few of his readers would leap to the conclusion
that Will was serving as a mouthpiece for his wife's employers. But surely most would have preferred to learn that information from Will himself.

A third member of the regular Brinkley panel, Cokie Roberts, is, along with Will and Donaldson, a frequent and
highly paid speaker before corporate audiences. She has
made a point of not disclosing which interest groups she
speaks to or how much money she is paid. She has criticized
the Clinton Administration for its secretive handling of the
controversy surrounding Hillary Clinton's lucrative cat-

tle-future trades and of the Whitewater affair, yet like the other pundits, she refuses to acknowledge that secrecy about financial interests undermines journalism's credibility too.

Out of Touch with America

In the week leading up to a State of the Union address White House aides always leak word to reporters that this year the speech will be "different." No more laundry list of all the government's activities, no more boring survey of every potential trouble spot in the world. This time, for a change, the speech is going to be short, punchy, and thematic. When the actual speech occurs, it is never short, punchy, or thematic. It is long and detailed, like all its predecessors, because as the deadline nears, every part of the government scrambles desperately to have a mention of its activities crammed into the speech somewhere.

The comments were virtually all about the tactics of the speech, and they were almost all thumbs down.

In the days before Bill Clinton's address a year ago aides said that no matter what had happened to all those other Presidents, this time the speech really would be short, punchy, and thematic. The President understood the situation, he recognized his altered role, and he saw this as an opportunity to set a new theme for his third and fourth years in office.

That evening the promises once again proved false. Bill Clinton gave a speech that was enormously long even by the standards of previous State of the Union addresses. The speech had three or four apparent endings, it had ad-libbed inserts, and it covered both the details of policy and the President's theories about what had gone wrong with America. An hour and 21 minutes after he took the podium, the President stepped down.

Less than a minute later the mockery from commentators began. For instant analysis NBC went to Peggy Noonan, who had been a speechwriter for Presidents Ronald Reagan and George Bush. She grimaced and barely tried to conceal her disdain for such an ungainly, sprawling speech. Other commentators soon mentioned that congressmen had been slipping out of the Capitol building before the end of the speech, that Clinton had once more failed to stick to an agenda, that the speech probably would not give the President the new start he sought. The comments were virtually all about the tactics of the speech, and they were almost all thumbs down.

A day and a half later the first newspaper columns showed up. They were even more critical. On January 26 the *Washington Post*'s op-ed page consisted mainly of stories about the speech, all of which were withering. "All Mush and No Message" was the headline on a column by Richard Cohen. "An Opportunity Missed" was the more statesmanlike judgment from David Broder. Cohen wrote: "Pardon me if I thought of an awful metaphor: Clinton at a buffet table, eating everything in sight."

What a big fat jerk that Clinton was! How little he understood the obligations of leadership! Yet the news section of the same day's *Post* had a long article based on discussions with a focus group of ordinary citizens in Chicago who had watched the President's speech. "For these voters, the State of the Union speech was an antidote to weeks of unrelenting criticism of Clinton's presidency," the article said.

> "Tonight reminded us of what has been accomplished," said Maureen Prince, who works as the office manager in her husband's business and has raised five children. "We are so busy hearing the negatives all the time, from the time you wake up on your clock radio in the morning. . . ."
>
> The group's immediate impressions mirrored the results of several polls conducted immediately after the president's speech.
>
> ABC News found that eight out of 10 approved of the president's speech. CBS News said that 74 percent of those surveyed said they had a "clear idea" of what Clinton stands for, compared with just 41 percent before the speech. A Gallup Poll for *USA Today* and Cable News Network found that eight in 10 said Clinton is leading the country in the right direction.

Nielsen ratings reported in the same day's paper showed that the longer the speech went on, the larger the number of people who tuned in to watch.

The point is not that the pundits are necessarily wrong and the public necessarily right. The point is the gulf between the two groups' reactions. The very aspects of the speech that had seemed so ridiculous to the professional commentators—its detail, its inclusiveness, the hyperearnestness of Clinton's conclusion about the "common good"—seemed attractive and worthwhile to most viewers.

"I'm wondering what so much of the public heard that our highly trained expert analysts completely missed," Carol Cantor, a software consultant from California, wrote in a discussion on the WELL, a popular online forum, three days after the speech. What they heard was, in fact, the speech, which allowed them to draw their own conclusions rather than being forced to accept an expert "analysis" of how the President "handled" the speech. In most cases the analysis goes unchallenged, because the public has no chance to see whatever event the pundits are describing. In this instance viewers had exactly the same evidence about Clinton's performance that the "experts" did, and from it they drew radically different conclusions.

In 1992 political professionals had laughed at Ross Perot's "boring" and "complex" charts about the federal budget deficit—until it became obvious that viewers loved them. And

The point is not that the pundits are necessarily wrong and the public necessarily right.

for a week or two after this State of the Union speech there were little jokes on the weekend talk shows about how out of step the pundit reaction had been with opinion "out there." But after a polite chuckle the talk shifted to how the President and the speaker and Senator Dole were handling their jobs.

Term Limits

As soon as the Democrats were routed in the 1994 elections, commentators and TV analysts said it was obvious that the American people were tired of seeing the same old faces in Washington. The argument went that those who lived inside the Beltway had forgotten what it was like in the rest of the country. They didn't get it. They were out of touch. The only way to jerk the congressional system back to reality was to bring in new blood.

A few days after the new Congress was sworn in, CNN began running an updated series of promotional ads for its program *Crossfire*. (Previous ads had featured shots of locomotives colliding head-on and rams locking horns, to symbolize the meeting of minds on the show.) Everything has been shaken up in the capital, one of the ads began. New faces. New names. New people in charge of all the committees.

"In fact," the announcer said, in a tone meant to indicate whimsy, "only one committee hasn't changed. The *welcoming* committee."

The camera pulled back to reveal the three hosts of *Crossfire*—Pat Buchanan, John Sununu, and Michael Kinsley—standing with arms crossed on the steps of the Capitol building, blocking the path of the new arrivals trying to make their way in. "Watch your step," one of the hosts said.

Talk about not getting it! The people who put together this ad must have imagined that the popular irritation with inside-the-Beltway culture was confined to members of Congress—and didn't extend to members of the punditocracy, many of whom had held their positions much longer than the typical congressman had. The difference between the "welcoming committee" and the congressional committees headed by fallen Democratic titans like Tom Foley and Jack Brooks was that the congressmen can be booted out.

"Polls show that both Republicans and Democrats felt better about the Congress just after the 1994 elections," a Clinton Administration official said last year. "They had 'made the monkey jump'—they were able to discipline an institution they didn't like. They could register the fact that they were unhappy. There doesn't seem to be any way to do that with the press, except to stop watching and reading, which more and more people have done."

Lost Credibility

There is an astonishing gulf between the way journalists—
especially the most prominent ones—think about their
impact and the way the public does. In movies of the 1930s
reporters were gritty characters who instinctively sided with
the common man. In the 1970s Robert Redford and Dustin
Hoffman, starring as Bob Woodward and Carl Bernstein in
All the President's Men, were better-paid but still gritty
reporters unafraid to challenge big power. Even the
local-TV-news crew featured on *The Mary Tyler Moore Show*
had a certain down-to-earth pluck. Ted Knight, as the
pea-brained news anchor Ted Baxter, was a ridiculously
pompous figure but not an arrogant one.

Since the early 1980s the journalists who have shown up in
movies have often been portrayed as more loathsome than
the lawyers, politicians, and business moguls who are the
traditional bad guys in films about the white-collar world. In
Absence of Malice, made in 1981, an ambitious newspaper
reporter (Sally Field) ruins the reputation of a businessman
(Paul Newman) by rashly publishing articles accusing him of
murder. In *Broadcast News*, released in 1987, the anchorman
(William Hurt) is still an airhead, like Ted Baxter, but unlike
Ted, he works in a business that is systematically hostile to
anything except profit and bland good looks. The only sympathetic characters in the movie, an overeducated reporter
(Albert Brooks) and a hyperactive and hyperidealistic producer (Holly Hunter), would have triumphed as heroes in a
newspaper movie of the 1930s. In this one they are ground
down by the philistines at their network.

In the *Die Hard* series, which started in 1988, a TV journalist (William Atherton) is an unctuous creep who will lie and
push helpless people around in order to get on the air. In *The
Bonfire of the Vanities* (1990) the tabloid writer Peter Fallow
(Bruce Willis) is a disheveled British sot who will do anything for a free drink. In *Rising Sun* (1993) a newspaper
reporter known as "Weasel" (Steve Buscemi) is an
out-and-out criminal, accepting bribes to influence his coverage. As Antonia Zerbisias pointed out in the *Toronto Star* in
1993, movies and TV shows offer almost no illustrations of
journalists who are not full of themselves, shallow, and indif-
ferent to the harm they do. During Operation Desert Storm,
Saturday Night Live ridiculed American reporters who asked
military spokesmen questions like "Can you tell us exactly
when and where you are going to launch your attack?" "The
journalists were portrayed as ignorant, arrogant and point-
lessly adversarial," Jay Rosen, of New York University, wrote
about the episode. "By gently rebuffing their ludicrous questions, the Pentagon briefer [on *SNL*] came off as a model of
sanity."

There is an astonishing gulf between the way journalists—especially the most prominent ones—think about their impact and the way the public does.

Even real-life members of the Washington pundit corps have made their way into movies—Eleanor Clift, Morton Kondracke, hosts from *Crossfire*—in 1990s releases such as *Dave* and *Rising Sun*. Significantly, their role in the narrative is as buffoons. The joke in these movies is how rapidly the pundits leap to conclusions, how predictable their reactions are, how automatically they polarize the debate without any clear idea of what has really occurred. That real-life journalists are willing to keep appearing in such movies, knowing how they will be cast, says something about the source of self-respect in today's media: celebrity, on whatever basis, matters more than being taken seriously.

Movies do not necessarily capture reality, but they suggest a public mood—in this case, a contrast between the apparent self-satisfaction of the media celebrities and the contempt in which they are held by the public. "The news media has a generally positive view of itself in the watchdog role," wrote the authors of an exhaustive survey of public attitudes and the attitudes of journalists themselves toward the press. (The survey was conducted by the Times Mirror Center for the People and the Press, and was released last May.) But "the outside world strongly faults the news media for its negativism. . . . The public goes so far as to say that the press gets in the way of society solving its problems. . . ." According to the survey, "two out of three members of the public had nothing or nothing good to say about the media."

The media establishment is beginning to get at least an inkling of this message. Through the past decade discussions among newspaper editors and publishers have been a litany of woes: fewer readers; lower "penetration" rates, as a decreasing share of the public pays attention to news; a more and more desperate search for ways to attract the public's interest. In the short run these challenges to credibility are a problem for journalists and journalism. In the longer run they are a problem for democracy.

Turning a Calling into a Sideshow

Even if practiced perfectly, journalism will leave some resentment and bruised feelings in its wake. The justification that journalists can offer for the harm they inevitably inflict is to show, through their actions, their understanding that what they do matters and that it should be done with care.

This is why the most depressing aspect of the new talking-pundit industry may be the argument made by many practitioners: the whole thing is just a game, which no one should take too seriously. Michael Kinsley, a highly respected and indisputably talented policy journalist, has written that his paid speaking engagements are usually mock debates, in which he takes the liberal side.

Since the audiences are generally composed of affluent businessmen, my role is like that of the team that gets to lose to the Harlem Globetrotters. But I do it because it pays well, because it's fun to fly around the country and stay in hotels, and because even a politically unsympathetic audience can provide a cheap ego boost.

Last year Morton Kondracke, of *The McLaughlin Group*, told Mark Jurkowitz, of the *Boston Globe*, "This is not writing, this is not thought." He was describing the talk-show activity to which he has devoted a major part of his time for 15 years. "You should not take it 100 percent seriously. Anybody who does is a fool." Fred Barnes wrote that he was happy to appear in a mock *McLaughlin* segment on *Murphy Brown*, because "the line between news and fun barely exists anymore."

The McLaughlin Group often takes its act on the road, gimmicks and all, for fees reported to be about $20,000 per appearance. *Crossfire* goes for paid jaunts on the road. So do panelists from *The Capital Gang*. Contracts for such appearances contain a routine clause specifying that the performance may not be taped or broadcast. This provision allows speakers to recycle their material, especially those who stitch together anecdotes about "the mood in Washington today." It also reassures the speakers that the sessions aren't really serious. They won't be held to account for what they say, so the normal standards don't apply.

Yet the fact that no one takes the shows seriously is precisely what's wrong with them, because they jeopardize the credibility of everything that journalists do. "I think one of the really destructive developments in Washington in the last fifteen years has been the rise in these reporter talk shows," Tom Brokaw has said. "Reporters used to cover policy—not spend all of their time yelling at each other and making philistine judgments about what happened the week before. It's not enlightening. It makes me cringe."

When talk shows go on the road for performances in which hostility and disagreement are staged for entertainment value; when reporters pick up thousands of dollars appearing before interest groups and sharing tidbits of what they have heard; when all the participants then dash off for the next plane, caring about none of it except the money—when these things happen, they send a message. The message is: We don't respect what we're doing. Why should anyone else?

> *The message is: We don't respect what we're doing. Why should anyone else?*

Does Big Mean Bad?[2]

As the Century Winds Down, Media Power Continues to Concentrate. Here Are Some Tools for Thinking About That.

The journalist's fear of the concentrated power of the big media companies is almost instinctual. Yet what do we fear exactly? Is it the potential for misuse of journalistic properties to benefit other arms of a corporation? Is it the undercurrent of corporate values that we think we sense flowing through and shaping some news? Or do we fear mere phantoms, the anti-monopoly sentiments of a century that is passing into history?

By way of addressing such questions, *CJR* has done two things. First we have put on our Web site—www.cjr.org.—a new resource guide, titled "Who Owns What." It is a detailed road map for journalists, researchers, and others to find which corporations are financially connected with which products and media outlets. We begin with 15 of the largest and most influential companies, from Advance Publications, Bertelsmann, Cablevision, and Disney to Sony, Time Warner, and Viacom. This fall we will add seven others. "Who Owns What" will be expanded and updated regularly by its creator, Aaron Moore (amoore00@.nimbus.temple.edu). It includes a search engine. CJR also asked Tom Goldstein, dean of Columbia's Graduate School of Journalism, to explain why this kind of information is important and to examine the evolving debates about the continuing concentration of media ownership. Here is his essay:

In my last incarnation, as dean of the Graduate School of Journalism at the University of California at Berkeley, I once lobbied a top recruiter for a major newspaper chain to hire students from the school. The recruiter then explained why her company had not interviewed anyone from Berkeley for many years. The reason was simple: "Bagdikian."

I protested. Ben Bagdikian, the media critic and my predecessor there as dean, is a self-effacing giant in the field. I was missing the point, the recruiter told me. She was convinced that we drilled our students with Ben's anti-chain views, that

2. Article by Tom Goldstein. Reprinted from *Columbia Journalism Review* (on-line) Sep./Oct. 1998. © 1998 by *Columbia Journalism Review*. Goldstein is the dean of the Columbia University Graduate School of Journalism. This essay is a companion piece to *CJR*'s guide to media ownership. Kimberly Brown, class of 1998, helped with research on this article.

like some kind of witch doctor he was initiating students into the dark arts of skepticism toward media power. (In fact, in no course did we assign Ben's influential book, *The Media Monopoly*. Shame on us.) Ultimately, the recruiter shed her remarkably thin skin and began hiring Berkeley students.

In the honorable ideological tradition of Will Irwin, Upton Sinclair, George Seldes, and I. F. Stone, Bagdikian contends that no commercial power should dominate the news—just as no state power should. The media giants make up, in the haunting phrase he coined, a "private ministry of information."

In the first edition of *Media Monopoly*, in 1984, Bagdikian bemoaned that just 50 corporations controlled more than half of the media outlets in this country. He was writing when CNN was in its infancy, when most journalists still used typewriters, and long before the Internet. By 1997, in the book's fifth edition, Bagdikian pegged the "number of media corporations with dominant power in society" at closer to 10. The "new communications cartel," he wrote, has the power to "surround almost every man, woman, and child in the country with controlled images and words." With that power comes the "ability to exert influence that in many ways is greater than that of schools, religion, parents and even government itself."

Bagdikian's role as a media gadfly is gradually being taken over by a new generation, including Mark Crispin Miller, a forceful and original thinker now teaching at New York University. At a DuPont-Columbia University Forum called "Is This News?" earlier this year, Miller pointed to "increasing evidence of direct and conscious manipulation of the news process by higher corporate powers and by advertisers generally." Worse, said Miller, is "a system in which the mere fact of ratings anxiety and declining news budgets and the scramble for promotions, simple careerism inside the news business—all these things combine to help produce a kind of seamless trivial spectacle that really doesn't tell us anything."

Miller's words are potent, but they are not the last on the subject of the effects of media concentration. Nor are Bagdikian's.

The financial markets have certainly spoken. They have richly rewarded some media-company mergers and made stockholders—including journalists—happy folks. Walk into the lobby of a big newspaper these days and you might be confronted with the latest stock price of the paper's parent company.

While few have written compellingly in favor of media giants gobbling up other media giants, some thoughtful observers have made arguments that question the validity of the traditional way of looking at media concentration. In a recent issue of *Newsweek*, columnist Robert Samuelson mulled a survey by the Pew Research Center for the People & the Press documenting the shrinking audience for the television networks' nightly news programs. That survey, combined with the success that his brother, an innkeeper, reaped from advertising on his own Web site, led Samuelson to rethink some basic assumptions.

"The notion of a media elite, if ever valid, requires that people get news and entertainment from a few sources dominated by a handful of executives, editors, anchors, reporters, and columnists." Samuelson wrote. "As media multiply, the elite becomes less exclusive. Smaller audiences give them less prominence and market power (i.e. salaries)."

Writing two years ago in the extraordinary issue of the *Nation* that contained a spider-like chart illustrating the holdings of the four dominant members of "the national entertainment state," Michael Arlen, an uncommonly astute commentator, argued that the specter of a vast, monolithic, all-pervading media has been wildly overdrawn. George Orwell's vision of Big Brother in *1984* was a resoundingly false prophecy. "How disappointing it would have been to Orwell to observe the actual play-out of this romantic drama," Arlen wrote. As proof, he pointed to "the emergence over the past several decades of a startling cacophony of market-crazed citizens all over the world, with their insistence on two-way communication and their appetite for fragmentation of broadcast authority."

These competing views of media power (and there are many, many more) do not cancel each other out. They just underscore that we have no unitary explanation of the extent and impact of media concentration. If journalism is just another business, then the primary scorecard of success is justifiably the verdict of the financial markets.

Because of the First Amendment protection it enjoys, journalism is more than another business. Still, we need to know more about what differentiates media concentration from consolidation in other commercial enterprises. We see consolidation among the airlines, military suppliers, banks, brokerage firms, and telephone companies. Look at accounting firms. For years there was the Big Eight. Then, the Big Six. And now, the Big Four.

Why do efficiencies of scale work for some businesses and not, say, for journalistic enterprises? With big media ownership in fewer hands, what barriers to entry actually have been erected? (It has been quite a while since anyone tried to start a major metropolitan newspaper. Many have tried recently to start new television networks, but these latter-day broadcasting pioneers are among the very behemoths that so trouble Bagdikian and Miller.) Why is the much-touted buzzword of the early 1990s—synergy—now viewed with such distrust by journalists? Having moved from an age of

If journalism is just another business, then the primary scorecard of success is justifiably the verdict of the financial markets. . . . [But] journalism is more than another business.

media scarcity to one of media babble, what new ways do we need to analyze media concentration?

For all the Matt Drudges churning away in small rooms, there are signs that the Internet may come to be dominated by big media. In June, Disney agreed to buy a large portion of the search engine company Infoseek. NBC purchased a share of CNET and its online search engine, Snap! These new investments, wrote Matt Welch in the *Online Journalism Review* (www.ojr.org), "further confused the already byzantine web of ownership, business alliances, and competition among the parent companies of the biz/tech sites."

In the Internet Age, media concentration bears even closer watching. Ownership needs to be demystified. Customers are entitled to know what corporate entity is responsible for bringing them their news. And this is now getting harder to know, with the emergence of a crop of big media companies not normally associated with journalism. In the next century, will Softbank dominate? Or Vulcan? Or Zapata? Or Intel?

Too often, commentary on media concentration has been fragmentary or anecdotal. We need to recast the debate, which shows signs of stagnating. We need to add new perspectives. That is why we should welcome fresh efforts at understanding media concentration. Two recent efforts are noteworthy. One is Mark Crispin Miller's Project on Media Ownership, now affiliated with New York University, which will detail interlocking ownership. And "Who Owns What" (described above) will appear on the CJR Web site, at www.cjr.org. With hard data and hard analysis will come answers to the vital questions that need to be asked about media concentration.

Money Lust: How Pressure for Profit Is Perverting Journalism[3]

Some random testimony from the far-flung precincts of journalism:

- "If a story needs a real investment of time and money, we don't do it anymore." The speaker is a 40-something reporter on a mid-sized Illinois daily. "In assignment meetings, we dream up 'talker' stories, stuff that will attract attention and get us talked about, tidbits for busy folks who clip items from the paper and stick them on the fridge." He adds ruefully: "Who the hell cares about corruption in city government, anyway, much less dying Bosnians?"

- A prominent network television newsman complains: "Instead of racing out of the newsroom with a camera crew when an important story breaks, we're more likely now to stay at our desks and work the phones, rewrite the wire copy, hire a local crew and a free-lance producer to get pictures at the scene, then dig out some file footage, maps, or still photos for the anchor to talk in front of, or maybe buy some coverage from a video news service like Reuters, AP, or World Television News. If we had our own correspondent and camera covering the story, we'd damned sure get something nobody else had, and be proud of it. But everything now is dollars and cents. When you're worried about how much it's going to cost, and you have to justify your decisions to your bosses, people are less willing to take risks. The journalism that gets on our air just isn't good enough, and it's a damned shame."

- A radio news director laments that his big-city station is cutting its news staff to the bone, virtually eliminating local news, and grabbing national news from a satellite-delivered network feed. "That immediately shows a big gain in cash flow, so the owner can sell the station for a huge profit to one of the big chains, whose owners care nothing about public service to this community. One more journalistic voice is being killed off in the pursuit of profits. It's very sad."

- The editor of a profitable national magazine who's been ordered to reduce his budget 10 percent a year says: "OK, the first year I'll cut stuff I probably should have cut earlier anyway. Next year I'll have to reduce the number of editorial pages in every issue. In the third year, for damned sure, it's got to be people that will have to go:

---

3. Article by Neil Hickey. Reprinted from *Columbia Journalism Review* p28 + July/Aug. 1998. © 1998 *Columbia Journalism Review*.

editors, writers, fact-checkers, art department staff. Then I'll hit a wall. Sooner or later I will have so cheapened the product that it will just go out of business. That's simple arithmetic."

A new era has dawned in American journalism. A *New York Times* editor describes its hallmark: "A massively increased sensitivity to all things financial." As competition grows ever more ferocious; as the audience continues to drift away from traditional news sources, both print and television; as the public's confidence in news organizations and news people continues to decline; as mainstream print and TV news outlets purvey more "life-style" stories, trivia, scandal, celebrity gossip, sensational crime, sex in high places, and tabloidism at the expense of serious news in a cynical effort to maximize readership and viewership; as editors collude ever more willingly with marketers, promotion "experts," and advertisers, thus ceding a portion of their sacred editorial trust; as editors shrink from tough coverage of major advertisers lest they jeopardize ad revenue; as news holes grow smaller in column inches to cosmeticize the bottom line; as news executives cut muscle and sinew from budgets to satisfy their corporate overseers' demands for higher profit margins each year; as top managers fail to reinvest profits in staff training, investigative reports, salaries, plant, and equipment—then the broadly felt consequence of those factors and many others, collectively, is a diminished and deracinated journalism of a sort that hasn't been seen in this country until now and which, if it persists, will be a fatal erosion of the ancient bond between journalists and the public.

"It's the biggest story in American journalism," says Ray Cave, former managing editor of *Time*. Regrettably, it's also the least reported story in American journalism.

Sandra Mims Rowe, editor of the *Oregonian* of Portland and former president of the American Society of Newspaper Editors, told the ASNE convention in April that reporters "wonder whether their editors have sold out journalistic values for business ones. They long for the inspiration provided by leaders with abiding passion for the gritty world of journalism." She added that in some companies, "the talk has shifted to financial and marketing imperatives to such an extent that journalists have concluded their owners are blindly driven by Wall Street, and unconcerned about the quality of journalism."

In March, *Los Angeles Times* media reporter David Shaw wrote that while newspaper readership has been on the skids for more than thirty years and competition from cable TV news, the Internet, and magazines is on the rise, "stockholders and stock analysts have been demanding newspaper profit margins equal to—and in some cases greater than—those generated in earlier, less turbulent times."

A new era has dawned in American journalism. A New York Times editor describes its hallmark: "A massively increased sensitivity to all things financial."

Television's corporate chieftains, says Walter Cronkite, show little understanding of "the responsibilities of being news disseminators." They expect the news departments to generate the same sort of profits that entertainment programs do—an impossible task. The newspaper business isn't much different, he says. "Stockholders in publicly held newspaper chains are expecting returns similar to those they'd get by investing in industrial enterprises."

The "tabloidization" of TV newsmagazines is strictly geared to ratings and profits. "A major tragedy of the moment," Cronkite maintains, is the use TV newsmagazines are making of the valuable prime time they occupy. "Instead of offering tough documentaries and background on the issues that so deeply affect all of us, they're turning those programs into television copies of *Photoplay* magazine." News executives know better, Cronkite says, and are "uncomfortable" with what they're doing. "But they are helpless when top management demands an increase in ratings to protect profits."

News chiefs themselves perceive that the press is perilously compromising quality in pursuit of gain. Nearly half the nation's editorial and business-side executives surveyed in a January *Editor & Publisher* poll think press coverage in general is shallow and inadequate, and fully two-thirds say newspapers concentrate more on personalities than important issues. J. Stewart Bryan III, C.E.O. of Media General, Inc., and publisher of the *Richmond Times-Dispatch*, told *E&P* that serious news is being sacrificed to profits as papers reduce news holes and produce softer stories. Said he: "I don't think we can put the bottom line ahead of our commitment to quality."

Journalistic values haven't completely disappeared, says Kurt Andersen, columnist for the *New Yorker* and former editor of *New York* magazine. "But they've been significantly subordinated to the general ascendancy of market factors, especially the maximizing of short-term profit." Magazine editors, he points out, "are much more explicitly responsible for business success than in the past. I'm not saying it's black and white; some of that has always been there. It was light gray, now it's dark gray."

Even Brenda Starr, the comic strip reporter, has gotten into the act. She lamented: "Sometimes I think newspapers care more about profits than they do about people."

After scores of wide-ranging interviews conducted over several months with editors, reporters, publishers, media analysts, academics, and labor officials, *CJR* concludes that—more so than at any other moment in journalism's history—the news product that lands on newsstands, doorsteps, and television screens is indeed hurt by a heightened, unseemly lust at many companies for ever greater profits. in the service of that ambition, many editors are surrendering part of their birthright to marketers and advertising directors, and making news judgments based on criteria that would have been anathema only a few years ago.

But haven't media barons always wanted to prosper, like any other businessmen? Winston Churchill, an unrepentant Tory, once said: "It is a socialist idea that making profits is a vice; I consider the real vice is making losses." Journalism isn't philanthropy—no profits, no press. Some recent tendencies, however, alter the landscape:

- More Americans than ever are shareholders in public companies of all kinds and corporate executives, including those at media corporations, are sensitive to the vastly expanded interests of those investors.

- Top managers in media own ever larger piles of stock options—often a heftier source of income than their salaries—and thus have a direct, personal interest in their companies' profit picture. Higher profits mean a higher stock price and a bigger payoff when they cash in their holdings. Says a TV producer "The more they can squeeze out of their people, the richer they'll be in the end."

- In an age of rampant consolidations and mergers, clamping down on operating costs and budgets—no matter the effect on news coverage—can fatten the bottom line and make a *company* a more attractive takeover target, with the consequent heavy windfall to major shareholders.

- Bonuses tied to profits tempt both editorial and business-like executives to trim costs, often to the detriment of news processing.

At the University of Iowa, three professors—John Soloski, Gil Cranberg, and Randy Bezanson—are embarked on an 18-month project (funded by philanthropist George Soros's Open Society Institute) studying how ownership structures of newspapers are affecting journalistic function; and examining journalists' complaints that their interests and readers' interests are being sacrificed for the interests of shareholders. "Publicly traded media companies are in a vicious circle they can't break out of," says Soloski, director of the university's journalism school. A huge percentage of their stock is owned by institutions—mutual funds, retirement funds, insurance companies—which care little about the quality of the journalism of the companies they invest in. "Those financial institutions are graded weekly, monthly, quarterly on their own performance. So they pass that pressure along—and it's a lot—to those media companies." They in turn pressure their editors and publishers to raise their stock price by whatever means necessary. The land rush to go public in the 1980s and 1990s has had its residual effect: investors and analysts demand the kind of profits that often can be attained by mid-level papers, but are tougher for big-city dailies.

Journalism isn't philanthropy— no profits, no press.

In l990, when Geneva Overholser, editor of the *Des Moines Register*, was named Gannett's "editor of the year," she offered these thoughts in her acceptance speech:

> . . . As we sweat out the end of the ever increasing quarterly earnings, as we necessarily attend to the needs and wishes of our shareholders and our advertisers, are we worrying enough about . . . our employees, our readers, and our communities?
>
> I'll answer that: no way. . . . We fret over declining readership and then cut our news holes. . . . We fret over a decline in service to our customers. and then pay reporters . . . wages that school districts would be ashamed of. . . . Our communities are crying out for solutions, and newspapers can help—newspapers that are adequately staffed, with adequate news holes. But not newspapers where underpaid people work too hard, and ad stacks squeeze out editorial copy. . . .
>
> Too often by far, being an editor in America today feels like holding up an avalanche of pressure to do away with this piece of excellence, that piece of quality, so as to squeeze out just a little bit more money.

Other signs of the profit-pressure syndrome were apparent three years ago when a dramatic series of shutdowns, layoffs, strikes, and the emotional departures of top editors afflicted the newspaper industry. The Times Mirror Company killed the *Baltimore Evening Sun* and *New York Newsday*. Knight Ridder Inc. slashed 300 full-time jobs at the *Miami Herald* and won major labor concessions in return for keeping the *Philadelphia Daily News* going.

Some of the biggest editors in the business have quit rather than make budget cuts that they felt would devastate editorial. As editor-in-chief of *Reader's Digest*, Ken Tomlinson grew weary of repeated demands to chop editorial costs up to 10 percent annually, year after year. In late 1995, management ordered a company-wide reduction of roughly 25 percent, largely by inducing many edit people to retire. Tomlinson didn't want to be remembered as the editor who carried out this action. So he told C.E.O. Jim Schadt, "I've found a way for you to take a giant step toward your goal. Eliminate my salary." And so Tomlinson retired at 52. (He now raises racehorses in rural Virginia; Schadt's strategy failed to ease the *Digest*'s continuing problems and he later resigned under pressure.)

That same year, James M. Naughton resigned as executive editor of the *Philadelphia Inquirer*. Among his reasons: "unrelenting pressures" on the newsroom. (And talk about pressure: half the respondents in an AP managing editors poll call their jobs "highly stressful." Their median workweek: 52 hours.) Last year, Maxwell King said upon resigning as the *Inquirer*'s editor, "When I look at big newspaper companies across the board, the question that occurs to me is, 'Are they all too intent on taking profit now and not intent enough on investing in content for the future?" The paper was under orders from Knight Ridder to ratchet up its profit margin from 8 percent in 1995 to 15 percent last year.

The *L.A. Times*'s David Shaw put the problem succinctly:

Today, many newspaper owners insist on high quarterly dividends . . . thus depriving the papers of money that could be invested in improving quality; there is little question that the shift from individual and family ownership to public ownership has increased the demand for higher short-term profits. In order to make their stock attractive to investors, newspaper companies promise higher profits every year (if not every quarter). That sets up unrealistic expectations. . . . When revenues inevitably decline, even temporarily—because of recession, higher newsprint costs or other factors—most publicly held newspapers feel they must still increase profits. So they cut costs—and, ultimately, quality.

Money is one big reason that newsrooms at America's papers have an older and less satisfied workforce than ever before—more graying heads and reading glasses than fresh faces. Forty-four percent are 40 or over, says an ASNE survey. Between 1988 and 1996, the percentage of journalists 30 and under dipped from 29 percent to 20 percent. More journalists than ever are planning to quit the business before retirement age. The most oft-cited reason: money. (Average base pay at papers having 30,000–75,000 circulation: $23,000). But "working conditions" and "stress" are now a close second and third. The number of journalists rating their papers as "excellent" has dropped dramatically, and most think that newspapers will be "a less important part of American life" in 10 years' time. Over half of ASNE's sample said their newsroom budget had declined in the previous five years, and 71 percent called it inadequate.

The number of journalists rating their papers as "excellent" has dropped dramatically.

Meanwhile, the revolutionary Telecommunications Act of 1996 set the stage for huge, disruptive changes in broadcasting. Its deregulatory effects and the resultant seismic shift to corporate gigantism has been at the public's expense, especially in the way the nation's information needs are met.

One example: the act removed all limitations on the number of radio stations any one company can own nationally and greatly increased the number a single entity can operate in any single city. That triggered an unprecedented wave of buyouts and consolidations in the radio industry (with 16,000 stations nationwide), which have left listeners with a less-than-nourishing news diet in many places. (CBS, the biggest owner of radio stations, has 155 in its stable.) At many stations, including CBS's flagship in New York, all-news WCBS-AM, anchorpersons and sports reporters routinely read commercials as part of their duties, an activity that seriously blurs the line between journalist and huckster. But it saves stations the cost of hiring an announcer to intone that advertising copy. And with fewer street reporters, writers, and editors than in past years, many stations are reduced to parroting news from the morning's papers.

Local radio and TV news in many cities have indeed suffered "crippling cutbacks as group owners trim staffs to enhance their bottom lines." says Louis C. Adler, former WCBS news chief, now a professor at Connecticut's Quinnipiac College. The agglomerating of radio stations in pursuit of economies of scale by rich corporations has left listeners in many communities with diminished service. In Connecticut, for example, three New Haven stations—WELI, WAVZ, and WKCI—now belong to Texas-based Clear Channels Communications. A second Texas company, SFX Broadcasting, is grabbing WPLR, WTNH-TV, and control of WYBC and WBNE-TV. In the 1970s, at least four locally owned radio stations in New Haven County had street reporters scouring the area for news. Now there's one, WQUN. Thus, says Adler, deregulation in broadcasting benefits "corporations whose allegiance is not to listeners or viewers but to stockholders who demand an ever-increasing return on their investment, a demand satisfied by cutting costs, reducing jobs, and generally sacrificing public service on the altar of greed."

At the major print newsmagazines, *Time* and *Newsweek*, the trend over 10 years, 1987–1997, shows a distinct tilt toward more crowd-pleasing cover subjects and away from straight domestic and foreign news—in the effort to snare the interest of impulse buyers at the newsstand and thus boost revenue. (Reporting foreign news is expensive: a U.S. correspondent stationed in pricey posts such as Hong Kong, Paris, or Moscow can easily cost $500,000 a year in pay, perks, and expenses.)

In 1987, *Time* published 11 covers relating to foreign news—and only one in 1997. Its domestic hard-news covers dwindled from 12 to nine. Thus, the over-all total for straight news covers dipped from about 45 percent of the total 10 years ago to only 20 percent last year. Studying the list of *Time*'s 1997 cover choices, one sees stories on Ellen DeGeneres, Steven Spielberg, Generation X, the pop singer Jewel, Brad Pitt in a movie about Buddhism, Bill Cosby and the death of his son, plus "What's Cool This Summer," "Turning Fifty" (with a cover photo of Hillary Clinton), "How Mood Drugs Work . . . and Fail" and "The Most Fascinating People in America." *Newsweek* pitched in with 1997 covers on TV cartoon shows, JonBenet Ramsey, Bob Dylan, Deepak Chopra, plus "The Young Kennedys: A Dynasty in Decline," "Does It Matter What You Weigh? The Surprising New Facts About Fat," "The Scary Spread of Asthma and How to Protect Your Kids," "Behind the Mask: The Dark World of

Andrew Cunanan . . . Versace's Life, Death and Legacy," "Buy? Sell? How to Invest Now," and a "Special Edition" on "Your Child from Birth to Three." Both *Time* and *Newsweek* ran covers on Princess Diana two weeks in a row, giving them the biggest newsstand sales in their histories.

How come all this emphasis on soft news and life-style issues? There are at least two reasons, says Norman Pearlstine, editor-in-chief of Time Inc., the nation's most successful magazine publishing company.

First: The economy is thriving, "so there's probably less concern with what has traditionally been the hard news story."

Second: With the collapse of communism and the end of the Cold War, "it's not surprising that the country has turned more inward. There's always been a balance between educating your reader and serving your reader, but we're not getting a lot of demand for international coverage these days in broad consumer publications." Addressing a readership the size of *Time*'s (domestic circulation: 4 million) "you obviously balance telling them what you think they ought to read with giving them what they want to read, and that balance has clearly shifted away from international news in the last decade."

Pearlstine recalls that in 1995, his first year at Time Inc., among the magazine's five worst-selling covers were: two on Bosnia, two on Senator Bob Dole, and one on Social Security. (Among the best sellers: "How Did the Universe Begin?", "Is the Bible Fact or Fiction?", and "Mysteries of the Deep.")

For the recent May 18 issues of *Time* and *Newsweek*, two stories competed for the cover: India's detonation of a nuclear device, and the death of Frank Sinatra. Sinatra won both covers. Ten years ago, says Pearlstine, the decision probably would have gone the other way.

"The great threat today to intelligent coverage of foreign news," Seymour Topping, former managing editor of the *New York Times*, told *CJR* "is not so much a lack of the public's interest as it is a concentration of ownership that is profit-driven and a lack of inclination to meet responsibilities, except that of the bottom line." In newspapers, foreign news has declined drastically as a percentage of the news hole. In the newsweeklies, *Hall's Magazine Editorial Reports* found that from 1985 to 1995, space devoted to international news slipped from 24 percent to 14 percent in *Time*, from 22 percent to 12 percent in *Newsweek*, and 20 percent to 14 percent in *U.S. News & World Report*. The evening TV news programs, according to the Shorenstein Center at Harvard, gave 45 percent of their time to foreign affairs in the 1970s and a mere 13.5 percent in 1995. Result: the public is being drastically shortchanged in its capacity to learn what's going on in the world outside the U.S.'s borders.

The temptation is great in every news medium to sweeten the product for easier consumption.

Many news executives tiresomely argue that, in the late 1990s, all the research indicates that the public doesn't want to know about the rest of the world; that it's narcissistically fixated on life at home in the U.S.—its economy, celebrities, scandals, fads, and folkways. Media companies aim to feed that appetite.

But, says Ray Cave: It's no good to say that people now are not interested in consequential news. "The general public has never been truly interested in it. But we delivered it, like it or not. By so doing, we piqued public interest in the very matters that must, to some degree, interest the citizens of a democracy."

In network television, the audience for evening news broadcasts continues to dwindle. Competition grows fiercer for larger slices of a smaller pizza, and the quality of those broadcasts has suffered as they, too, offer more life-style stories and soft news in search of bigger audiences. In 1980, 37.3 percent of tuned-in homes viewed the three-network news programs every night; that slid to 24.3 percent in 1996–97.

The NBC Nightly News with Tom Brokaw has been the dominant newscast for almost two years. Staffers at CBS News and ABC News say that's because it has lowered its aim, too often substituting life style and soft features for hard news in a transparent tactic to increase audience, raise advertising rates, and meet the profit expectations of its powerful parent, GE, the nation's most successful conglomerate. NBC News denies the charge.

But the temptation is great in every news medium to sweeten the product for easier consumption. A survey by the Project for Excellence in Journalism of some 4,000 stories on the three network news programs, on newsmagazine covers, and on the front pages of major papers from 1977 to 1997 concludes that celebrity, scandal, gossip, and other "human interest" stories increased from 15 percent to an astonishing 43 percent of the total.

Indeed, an irreversible rot in the hulls of all three of the old-line networks (in entertainment as well as news) has TV executives scurrying for new ways to build viewership and counter the threat of cable, the Internet, pay-per-view, and home satellite services. The ABC and CBS networks are operating in the red, and ratings-leader NBC's profit is melting from $500 million last year to about $100 million. "It's a time of total transition," CBS boss Leslie Moonves told the *New York Times* in May. "It's all ugly."

Ironically, all three networks are looking expectantly to their news divisions to help slow the decay. How? The major networks this fall will air TV newsmagazines six nights a week—up from two in 1983. Why? They're much cheaper than most entertainment shows to put on the air; the networks own them outright, unlike sitcoms and dramas, which they lease from outside producers; and those programs get respectable ratings. NBC's *Dateline* is expanding to five nights a week. ABC is using *20/20* and *Prime Time Live* into a three-times-a-week event. CBS hankers to make *60 Minutes*—its all-time most-successful series—a twice-weekly program.

Those unprecedented schedule shifts will bring more news-and-feature programming to network audiences than ever before, but there's a flaw in the strategy. The soup will be thinner than ever. Reporters, producers, editors, and crews will be stretched over more working hours a week. The pool of story ideas inevitably will become more polluted and noxious for series that already have gone down the low road in search of ratings: e.g., Diane Sawyer's interview with Michael Jackson and former wife Lisa Marie Presley; *Dateline NBC*'s piece on *Baywatch* babe Pamela Anderson; *Prime Time Live*'s chat with sometime O. J. Simpson girlfriend Paula Barbieri. *60 Minutes*'s executive producer Don Hewitt opposes expanding his series to other nights, convinced that the program's quality can't possibly be maintained if diluted. But in CBS's no-holds-barred effort to squeeze more juice out of its prize property he'll almost surely be overruled.

Hewitt is fond of saying that *60 Minutes* ruined it for everybody in news, proving as it did that a news program could be a colossal money machine, and perking managers' hopes that comparable riches could be extracted from all news broadcasts. CNN, as well, takes the rap for the broadcast networks' scorched earth news budget cuts: Ted Turner established his all-news cable channel in a right-to-work state (Georgia), hired all nonunion journalists and staff, paid them far less than the going rates at ABC, CBS, and NBC, and built a hugely successful worldwide news organization. Corporate bosses at the broadcast networks mused: "Why can't we be as lean, mean, and successful as CNN?" They've been trying.

Ever since Mel Karmazin took over as CBS president (and heir apparent to chairman Michael Jordan), drastic fiscal strategies have been bruited in the corridors of the erstwhile Tiffany network, none of them favorable for the news division. The most attention-grabbing: CBS Corp. would sell off its money-losing CBS Television Network—which, essentially, is merely a program supplier to local stations—while retaining its very profitable station division. It consists of 18 valuable owned-and-operated outlets.

The fate of CBS News in such a deal is shrouded in uncertainty. Traditionally in the television industry, separating a network from its owned stations is a heretical, risky notion. But as Merrill Lynch analyst Jessica Reif Cohen points out, such ancient, entrenched theorems may be ready for the dustbin of history: "New CBS management is very aggressive," she writes, "toppling a variety of broadcast traditions in order to build shareholder value and willing to explore a large number of strategic options."

Indeed, Karmazin, who has no background in news, is the broadcast industry's model hero for cost-cutting schemes. When he arrived at CBS, *60 Minutes* humorist Andy Rooney told the *Minneapolis Star-Tribune*: "Nothing good has happened around here for so long I can't imagine [Karmazin's accession] is going to be good. . . . The emphasis is so much more on money than content in every decision that's made that it's discouraging to be here."

Time was when the evening news programs assigned crews to cover (as one veteran puts it) "everything that moved"— every viable news story every day all over the world. The end began with the buyouts and downsizing of the mid-1980s. More and more coverage came from local stations and independent newsfilm services, and at far less expense. That shift allowed the networks to close many bureaus at home and abroad. Frequently sacrificed, though, was the incisive, polished authority that the best TV news correspondents had brought to the reporting of important news.

Obsession with ratings is at an all-time high in television news.

Even as TV news operations cut budgets and spread their staffs thinner and thinner to the detriment of news coverage, they continue to pay "star" performers princely sums in the conviction that those engaging faces and voices are their last bulwark against even further audience defection. Thus, Rather, Brokaw, Jennings, Sawyer, and Walters each receive compensation in the $7 million a year range for their putative appeal in attracting viewers—a talent that transcends the quality of the programs they inhabit. CNN's Larry King, host of cable's top-rated, celebrity-infested interview program, is also a $7 million-a-year property. "With everything that's included in the deal, I'll be in the same ballpark as the network guys," King said proudly when the contract was signed in May. Said CNN president Tom Johnson: "Larry's ratings were up sharply last year, and he's had a great first quarter. . . ."

That was good news for King, all right, but simultaneously CNN parent Time Warner cut almost a fourth of the staff—70 jobs out of 300—at its Headline News cable channel, thus saving about $2 million but leaving cable news viewers the poorer for it. A few weeks earlier, TW chairman Gerald Levin predicted the company would increase its cash flow by 16 to 18 percent annually for the next few years. The Time Inc. magazines, collectively, are expected to raise their profits by 15 percent a year.

Obsession with ratings is at an all-time high in television news. One former high-level news producer recalls: "When I first joined the network, you'd probably be fired if you talked about ratings in the newsroom. The newspapers didn't even publish ratings at that time. Nobody ever suggested we do a story because it would get ratings. If somebody from the entertainment side or the promotion department came to us and suggested we do a piece about a lesbian coming out in a prime time sitcom, we would have yelled 'Forget about it!' It's unbelievable how much of that junk gets on the air."

The question (more relevant than ever) for journalists: Is news what the public is interested in or what's in the public interest? Says Reuven Frank, former president of NBC News: 'This business of giving people what they want is a dope pusher's argument. News is something people don't know they're interested in until they hear about it. The job of a journalist is to take what's important and make it interesting."

Closing news bureaus at home and abroad has been one of the more conspicuous effects of cost-cutting ever since ABC, CBS, and NBC changed ownership in the mid-1980s. No broadcast network now has a full-fledged bureau (with correspondent, camera crews, and office staff) anywhere in Africa or Latin America; Europe is covered mostly from London, Moscow, and Tel Aviv. (CNN, on the other hand, maintains 23 bureaus outside the U.S.)

"Roving bands of free-lance camera men," says veteran TV news producer Av Westin, "shoot coverage at every crisis spot at home and abroad and sell it to networks and local stations. He calls them "the video equivalent of paparazzi." ABC News closed its San Francisco bureau in April, around the time the news division reportedly was figuring out how to comply with a ukase from parent Disney to cut between $25 million and $50 million from its $625 million budget

Hour-long, single-subject documentaries on key issues virtually disappeared from broadcast networks years ago—illustrious series such as *CBS Reports*, *NBC White Paper*, and *ABC Close-up*. Those programs had been the news divisions' crown jewels. (But occasionally TV news surprises, with a spurt of its old energy. ABC News, for example, is embarked on the most ambitious documentary ever: *The Century*, a $20 million, 27-hour series to begin next March, a colossal survey of the last hundred years. And CNN in September will launch *Cold War*, a massively researched, 24-segment history. But even series on so grand a scale are expected to pay their own way or even make a profit.)

In the newspaper industry, last year was a watershed for two big reasons: trafficking in papers was at an all-time high; and profits boomed, even as circulation continued to slide. It was dubbed the Year of the Deal: 162 dailies out of 1,509 changed hands, up 37 percent from the year before. Mega-deals abounded: Knight Ridder bought the *Kansas City Star*, the *Fort Worth Star-Telegram*, and two other papers from Walt Disney Company for $1.65 billion; McClatchy Newspapers snared Cowles Media for $1.4 billion. Transactions for the year hit a record $6.23 billion. As of February 1, 81 percent of those 1,509 dailies were members of a chain or group. Gene Roberts, former managing editor of the *New York Times* and now a journalism professor at the University of Maryland, told a press group in California:

> News coverage is being shaped by corporate executives at headquarters far from the local scene. [The shaping] is seldom done by corporate directive or fiat. It rarely involves killing or slanting stories Usually it is by the appointment of a pliable editor here, a corporate graphics conference there, that results in a more uniform look, a more cookie-cutter approach among the chain's newspapers, or the corporate research director's interpretation of reader surveys that see common denominator solutions to complex coverage problem. . . . As papers become increasingly shallow and niggardly, they lose their essentiality to their readers and their communities. And this is ultimately suicidal.

Alarmingly, only 55 American cities now have more than one paper.

Alarmingly, only 55 American cities now have more than one paper. The sharp decline in the numbers of dailies competing vigorously against each other has damaged the quality and squeezed the amount of reporting in American papers. Studies show that in cities where competition is hot, the news holes tend to be larger and there are more reporters to fill them. "The absence of competition tends to affect the financial commitment of publishers to the news-editorial department," says a forthcoming survey by the Columbia Institute for Tele-Information.

What kind of returns do chains demand to justify high purchase prices? Steven S. Ross, a Columbia Journalism School associate professor, explains: "This is what is historically new. Today, if a paper underperforms, its stock price is threatened and it's vulnerable to takeover. A 25 percent return on gross revenues sounds pretty good to a paper's staff. But the new owner's board says, 'We paid $500 million for that company. How dare they earn only 25 percent?'"

Complaints abound from editors of large chain papers that the investment they require to produce a superior paper is being drained away to meet owners' profit demands. That shows up in large ways and small: when Gannett took over the *Asbury Park Press* in New Jersey, it cut the staff from 225 to 180, and told the theater critic there was no money for him to cover Broadway plays.

A particularly instructive case history is that of the *Patriot-Ledger* of Quincy, Massachusetts. It's a 161-year-old daily that was sold in February to Newspaper Media LLC for about $95 million by the Low family, which had owned it for four generations. The paper actually was worth $70–$75 million, according to analysts. In need of larger operating margins to service their heavy debt, the new owners decreed that the editorial budget be slashed from $7 million to $5.5 million; 17 to 18 percent of the paper's costs had been devoted to news and editorial, but that was reduced to 10–12 percent. The *Patriot-Ledger* serves 26 communities near Boston, and had at least one full-time reporter in all of them—several in larger suburbs like Weymouth, Braintree, and Plymouth. Too expensive, said the paper's new publisher, James Plugh. Also, 12 vacancies existed in the newsroom at the time of the ownership change, but Newspaper Media declined to let them be filled. The paper's value to its readers has been grievously undermined as a result of such economies.

Unwilling to function in that new environment, the *Patriot-Ledger*'s editor of 20 years (and former president of ASNE), William Ketter, resigned on May 29. Speaking generically of the nationwide profits-versus-quality controversy, Ketter says: "I'm concerned about the prices being paid for newspapers and the need for greater profit margins to meet those financial obligations. The squeezing of editorial budgets is a shortsighted way of dealing with that need. When you start diminishing and degrading the nature of newspapers' content, you run the risk of those papers being less valuable in the marketplace."

Says the *Oregonian*'s Sandra Mims Rowe: "Newspapers don't invest nearly enough in their employees, especially in training and teaching. There are journalists in the streets of every town who cannot report, write, or edit with authority, cannot provide the rich, full, detailed, accurate story the reader wants."

Evidence mounts that the blurring of editorial-advertising distinctions—as the latest technique in profit-building—is compromising news judgments and decisions, resulting not so much in fawning pieces about major advertisers but rather in self-censorship, a reluctance by some editors to take the heat for doing stories critical of space buyers.

Witness the highly publicized move by *Los Angeles Times* publisher Mark Willes to involve marketing/advertising executives in the paper's day-to-day editorial decisions, a tactic that continues to draw fire from journalists around the country. The big fear is that if journalists have to worry about advertising and profits, they may self-censor and shrink from producing tough coverage of stories inimical to advertisers' interests. But what Willes has done is being copied at many other papers in this new era of profit-worship.

In a self-justifying speech to ASNE in April, Willes pointed out that more than 200 papers have closed in the last 25 years; that overall newspaper circulation has declined 10 percent in the last dozen years (while the population has grown 12 percent); that newspapers now attract less than 22 percent of all advertising, down from 27 percent in 1980; that only 58 percent of adults read a daily newspaper, down from 81 percent in 1964; that barely a third of the population cites newspapers as their main source for national news; and that in a recent Gallup poll, Americans ranked the honesty and integrity of newspaper reporters behind police officers and TV reporters, and only slightly ahead of lawyers and building contractors. If those trends continue, Willes warned, "newspapers will be increasingly marginalized, less important and, therefore, less relevant." For such reasons, he argues, it behooves editors and business-side managers to work together, more closely than in the past, to help assure the good health of newspapers. Willes's diagnosis of newspapers' illness is impressive. But his ideas for the cure alarm many journalists.

The subject of compensation and incentive pay troubles the University of Iowa's Soloski. There are major implications when the bonuses of media executives depend solely on the economic—and not the journalistic—performance of their publications. With a direct interest in his paper's profits, can the editor truly exercise uncontaminated judgment in covering controversial subjects or advertisers that might take offense and defect? The answer is yes, of course, the honest editor can—but she or he must always be aware of the potential for conflict.

Many publishers are increasingly pressing for special sections of their papers as a magnet for advertisers and readers, even though the content of those (continuing or occasional) sections is often frivolous, and creating them places added stress on news staffs. The *Wall Street Journal* has its new Friday section called Weekend Journal, filled with entertainment and life-style advice and related advertising. In mid-May, the *New York Times* published a massive 64-page special section on the charms of eastern Long Island, mostly the fashionable Hamptons, with articles on sailing, kayaking, land development, dining, sport fishing, and (of course) the famous show biz and media folk who summer there—along with a tonnage of advertising from real estate agents, restaurants, clothing boutiques, liquor stores, nurseries, and country inns. (A study sponsored last year by ASNE and the Newspaper Association of America discovered that newspaper advertisements better meet readers' expectations than does the quality of news coverage.)

The questions: Are such sections an editor's vision of a value-added supplement that fills an important editorial need, or mainly a publisher's gambit for a quick-hit spike in revenue? And can those sections be executed without draining resources from the paper's main service?

Such one-time and continuing special sections are a greater strain on papers that don't have the legendary resources of the *Wall Street Journal* or the *New York Times*. But the criterion for success is usually the same: economic, not journalistic. At the *Los Angeles Times*, for example, where the editor of a daily section is yoked uncomfortably with a counterpart from the ad department, a section's survival chances depend heavily on its capacity to generate revenue, not on its journalistic excellence.

A comparable syndrome exists in the magazine industry: special issues, which exploit the value of a title in the effort to squeeze additional income from its brand-name identity. It's an old tactic that's employed with ever greater frequency these days to prettify the bottom line, even as editorial staffs have been pruned and there are often fewer people to take on the task. Can a magazine editor, who presumably occupies a full-time job, effectively oversee these special issues—on the passing of Frank Sinatra, Princess Diana, the Seinfeld sitcom—and still do his main job? "When the driving force is economic and not journalistic," says a senior editor of a national magazine, "the push is coming from the wrong direction. I would rather use that energy and that talent to improve my main product than to create a one-time offshoot. It's all very well to say I can do both, but I'm not sure anybody can, without weakening the core magazine."

The underlying debate continues. Profits. Return on investment. The public's right to know. Shareholder value. Journalistic responsibility. Are the terms incompatible? Not necessarily. Early in this century, the great labor leader Samuel Gompers said: "The worst crime against working people is a company which fails to operate at a profit."

But should news organizations reasonably expect the same profit levels as software companies, pharmaceutical firms, and computer makers? Or should stockholders and owners understand, when they wed their fortunes to those of working journalists, that news is a venture like no other? It's the only business protected by the Constitution of the United States, a status that brings obligations for both the shareholder and the journalist. "I wish investors and owners of media companies could be made to understand the incredible responsibility they've assumed," says Walter Cronkite, "and accept a reasonable return instead of the excessive profits that can be garnered elsewhere."

If that's too much to expect in this era of mega-media conglomerations, a surging economy, a galloping Wall Street, and chronic public dismay about the press, then the mission of journalism in America may be perilously debilitated. The big question: What doth it profit a media company to demand, unremittingly, steadily higher profit margins year after year and, in that very pursuit, lose its professional soul?

The mission of journalism in America may be perilously debilitated.

News Lite[4]

Welcome to the tabloid world of network television news, 1997. It is often a world of UFOs, psychics, daydreams, miracle cures, cuddly animals, O. J. Simpson, JonBenet Ramsey and, from time to time—for at least a few minutes—real news. But real news in 1997 usually comes by the spoonful.

It's a world that CBS anchor Dan Rather has called "news lite" and CBS veteran Marvin Kalb, now director of Harvard's Joan Shorenstein Center on the Press, Politics and Public Policy, has compared to the American tabloid newspapers of 150 years ago. It is a trend that has been underway for several years, but that has escalated sharply in the last 12 months. All three of the major networks are guilty, though all deny it.

Some of the most respected names in television have expressed deep concern. The revered Walter Cronkite has said in dismay that "the networks now do news as entertainment." And Robert MacNeil, former coanchor at PBS, has lamented: "All the trends in television journalism are toward the sensational, the hype, the hyperactive, the tabloid values to drive out the serious."

"I would say that the networks have cheapened the news," says Newton Minow, once chairman of the Federal Communications Commission and on the board of directors at CBS. "It's pretty close to tabloid." It was Minow, as FCC chairman during the Kennedy administration, who gained fame by describing the world of television entertainment programming as a "vast wasteland." Now he sees that wasteland moving into news.

Tune in to any one of the major network news shows virtually any weeknight for a sampling.

- March 14, Tom Brokaw, on *NBC Nightly News*: Another episode in a regular feature called "The American Dream"—about a woman who runs a rescue service for pets, with plenty of pictures of animals.
- March 19, ABC's *World News Tonight*: "Sex on the Internet," with graphic pictures to demonstrate just how shocking cyberspace can be.
- April 3, Dan Rather, *CBS Evening News*: A visit with UFO fanatics, some of whom claim to have visited other planets.

So went seven or eight high-priced minutes of prime time television news. You will have no trouble finding similar samples. Of course the networks do serious stories too, some very well, but the trend toward tabloid is unmistakable, con-

4. Article by James McCartney from *American Journalism Review* p18–25 June 1997. Copyright © 1997 *American Journalism Review*. Reprinted with permission.

firmed and documented by the *Tyndall Report*, a newsletter that meticulously monitors the shows. Andrew Tyndall, who runs the newsletter, says that the percentage of time devoted to hard news by the networks, as compared to features, has decreased sharply in the last decade, by at least 7 or 8 percent. But this decrease in percentage, he says, is probably not the most significant factor in what the public sees. The networks have also cut the time devoted to overall editorial matter on the shows, while increasing the time for advertising. Together, these two factors mean substantially less news.

These trends in television network news have touched off a great debate in the television industry and among those who follow television news closely. The underlying question is blunt: Are the major network news shows abandoning an unstated, yet implicit, responsibility to provide a reasonably accurate picture of the nation and the world in the service of democracy?

The networks defend their coverage saying that competition from increasing media rivals—cable news, Fox and now the Internet—are forcing them to find new formulas to attract and keep viewers. And network executives are quick to point out that just because they are focusing more on feature and lifestyle news doesn't mean the issues being covered are not important, or "news lite."

In addition, network news executives point out that, with so many news outlets, the nightly newscast does not play the central role in disseminating national news stories that it did in the days of Cronkite. Some even say the news itself has changed: With no world wars or Watergate, civil rights movements or Cold War, the news itself is not as compelling as it was in past decades. Given all these changes, the networks are reacting the same way many newspapers have: by "dumbing down" the product.

Many critics, however, believe the stakes for a civilized, self-governing society are enormous. Although the collective audience for the three network shows has dropped precipitously in recent years, with growing competition from cable and from their own technologically improved local affiliates, the Big Three together—with typical nightly audiences of more than 30 million—continue to be the nation's main source of news. More significant, they are the main source of perceptions about what is important—what matters. In years past these shows have played major roles in defining the national agenda, particularly in times of crisis. Today they appear to be abandoning that role, and there appears to be no substitute.

The leader in this feature-laden, magazine-style television trend has unquestionably been NBC, which two years ago launched a deliberate effort to redefine network television news. And it has set a pattern for the other two networks. While disturbing to many television veterans, the NBC for-

With no world wars or Watergate, civil rights movements or Cold War, the news itself is not as compelling as it was in past decades.

mula has vaulted Tom Brokaw's show to the top of the ratings in recent months, ousting Peter Jennings' *ABC World News Tonight*. NBC won the ratings battle in the first quarter this year for the first time since 1989.

In recent weeks NBC has devoted time to such subjects as baldness remedies, daydreams and telephone psychics. It has also taken an "In Depth" look at President Clinton's knee and suggested strongly in a series called "The Fleecing of America" that there is fraud in the nation's food stamp program—something the Agriculture Department has acknowledged for years. In a special investigation, labeled "The Family," NBC News discovered that some companies are less helpful than others to women trying to balance careers and motherhood.

ABC and Peter Jennings are trying hard not to be outdone, though apparently with some misgivings on Jennings' part. And although Dan Rather insists that "news lite is not our game," his show today bears little resemblance to the "that's-the-way-it-is" formula Cronkite exemplified in the golden days of CBS News. The networks insist that they are in a battle for their lives in a new and rapidly changing news world with new pressures and new competition from CNN and cable in general, from their own more sophisticated affiliates, from an inattentive younger generation and from the Internet.

The networks insist that they are in a battle for their lives in a new and rapidly changing news world.

A typical NBC newscast today leads with five or six traditional hard news items occupying the first half of the show, then turns to magazine-style features for most of the last half—some on serious subjects, some "lite." That compares to 20 or 21 hard news items on a typical show during the Huntley-Brinkley or Cronkite heydays. ABC and CBS have not gone that far, but are clearly headed in the same direction. On some nights the pattern on the three networks is quite similar. NBC has such regular features as "In Depth," "The Fleecing of America" and "The American Dream"; ABC has "Your Health," "Solutions" and "It's Your Money"; CBS has "Eye on America" and many so-called "special" reports or investigations. All three network news shows have cut back on foreign news coverage, especially NBC, and all have cut back their foreign staffs.

The increase in time devoted to advertising has also robbed the viewer of information. In the old days, by rigid formula, there were 21 minutes of editorial matter, eight minutes of ads. Now, says Andrew Tyndall, the shows have only about 19-and-a-half minutes of editorial content. In Tyndall's mind "the most notable change has been from news to advertising."

Yet this debate is not necessarily simple and certainly not black and white. On one hand are critics who charge that the network news shows are destroying themselves by pursuing cheap tabloid values, abandoning near-sacred responsibilities. On the other are defenders who argue that they are desperately trying to save the nightly newscasts by searching for new and imaginative formulas for presenting the news, battling to stay in business.

Says David Doss, executive producer of Brokaw's *NBC Nightly News*: "Because a piece is interesting, there is an assumption that it is lite. That is an asinine assumption. . . . We believe we are doing the news in a far more imaginative way than our competitors. That does not equal going lite."

Says Peter Jennings: "The difference between the old days is enormous" because the public has many more choices on where to get news. "I think we have come, some time ago, to the recognition that our role has to be a complementary one"—complementary to other sources of news.

Criticism from both Cronkite and MacNeil has been particularly bitter. Cronkite, now long retired from CBS, has said that the Big Three newscasts "frequently go too soft. Their features aren't interpretive to the day's events, and the time could be better used. . . . We've always known you can gain circulation or viewers by cheapening the product, and now you're finding the bad driving out the good." He believes the networks are forsaking an important role in democracy.

Essentially, critics believe the networks are wasting valuable network time on trivia. In doing so, they believe, the networks are bypassing the reporting of significant developments to viewers who play an important role in a democratic society.

"They aren't telling you what you ought to know about," says Kalb at Harvard, "they're telling you what they think you want to know about"—that is, they are seeking to entertain rather than to inform.

What's missing, according to virtually all of the critics, is an emphasis on traditional hard news—news of what is happening in the world and of governmental process, which NBC in particular has chosen to deliberately downgrade as not sufficiently entertaining for the masses. The other networks appear to be following suit. But the Constitution of the United States created a governmental process reliant on an informed citizenry. If reporting on that process is ignored, you can't have an informed citizenry.

"The greatest victim of all this is our political process, and in my view this is one of the greatest blots on the recent record of television news," Cronkite wrote in his memoirs, *A Reporter's Life*. "Those who get most of their news from television probably are not getting enough information to intelligently exercise their voting franchise in a democratic system."

In a speech at the University of South Dakota last fall, MacNeil explained why devoting so much time to the O. J. Simpson story was so significant. "On television when you go with something so excessively, you do not go with a lot of other things. . . . Everything gets squeezed to the margins. The consequence is that the institution risks losing credibility as a sound source of what is going on in the world."

And almost all of the critics are appalled by cutbacks in foreign bureaus and the absence of a commitment by any of the networks to reporting and explaining complex world problems that, whether Americans like it or not, are destined to affect them in the future.

Serious commentary by the networks has also been abandoned. CBS has found no replacement for Eric Sevareid. NBC has found no replacement for John Chancellor. ABC has found no replacement for David Brinkley. Razzle-dazzle, with animals, UFOs, medical miracles, violent crimes and sex changes, is being substituted for what is going on in Congress, the executive branch, the regulatory agencies—the very workings of the democratic system.

In his speech, MacNeil, retired as a joint anchor of the respected *MacNeil/Lehrer News Hour* on public television, outlined his fears. MacNeil foresees "the end of news, or . . . at least the end of news as we know it, because [news] as we know it is already changing so rapidly it could be said to be ending." Broadcast news, he said, has "an important role to play in the democracy," but "the networks have felt forced to make themselves more entertaining and more popular."

Many former television executives agree, including some from NBC. "I have thought a lot about this," says Edward Planer, a former vice president for news at NBC and now chairman of the journalism department at Chicago's Columbia College. "I think there is almost an abdication of responsibility. . . . Now a lot of what you see are preplanned features." Planer says he is discouraged by the trends, and "somewhat depressed. . . . Let's face it, the news cycle has been dominated by JonBenet Ramsey, O. J. Simpson, floods and bank robberies. . . . They are doing what is easy to do." Planer says, however, that not all of the programs are "lite," and that it's possible that networks are simply experimenting, with the best of motives. He was impressed, for example, with a lead item on NBC's March 24 show backgrounding a Supreme Court case testing police rights to enter homes without a warrant. The show featured interviews with citizens whose homes had been entered without warrants and nothing illegal was found.

Ed Fouhy, a former news executive for all three networks and onetime producer of *NBC Nightly News*, says that the network shows "are getting away from the core values of their craft. There is a question about whether a democratic society can operate this way, without some cohesive view of what is going on in the world from these three shows." Fouhy is convinced that one of the reasons the shows are losing viewers is because "they are going soft. . . . They are making a very narrow definition of their role. . . . In my lifetime the network news performed an essential service in times of national crisis. . . . There was a shared national news consensus." That is no longer true, he says.

"I don't think these broadcasts are worthy of watching every night anymore because they don't reflect the world that I live in," Fouhy adds. "They are not television you can't miss anymore. In the old days they didn't tell you what to think, but they told you what to think about. No more. I see this as a loss of core values. People have to have information to conduct their lives. That is what we need in a democratic society."

Bob Mulholland, a former NBC executive and once a producer of the highly respected Huntley-Brinkley newscast, says that "all three networks have clearly abandoned being programs of record. . . . What's different is that we felt that we were the program of record and we were trying to put on as much news as possible. . . . The networks now feel that, by the time they get on the air, everybody already knows the news," largely because of the widespread availability of CNN. But he points out that CNN has a relatively small audience. "I feel the networks make a mistake. I still think you've got to cover the news first."

Still another critical perspective comes from Kalb. He is concerned that the new formulas, which he describes as "tabloid," provide "an unrealistic perception of the nation and the world." By concentrating on stories they believe might be attractive to the public, rather than seeking to help the public understand the world we live in, the networks "skew reality," he says.

"It is unrealistic because what you see on TV today is politicians who resort constantly to lying, constantly deceiving the public, a society torn by one violent episode after another, you see a world that is much at war, and the world isn't at war anymore. It is an extremely skewed, and essentially distorted, prism through which the world is observed." Yet he feels that the motivation of the networks is understandable—"these people understand that they are on the edge" in a highly competitive news environment, Kalb says. "They are not certain that if it was handled in any other way they will survive."

Needless to say, current network news executives, and even some from the past, see the picture differently. They freely acknowledge that big changes have been made, but argue that modern technology and competitive pressures have determined the course they are taking. And, they point out, what's happening in television news is not much different from what has been happening in newspapers in recent years. Many newspapers, particularly since the advent of *USA Today*, have strained to make themselves more "reader-friendly," more colorful, more feature-laden. Even the *New York Times* has gone much more heavily into features. It can be argued that the nation's media overall have gone lite.

"Let's face it. One of the things that's happened is that there is very little news," says Reuven Frank, one of the more colorful and plainspoken former presidents of NBC News. "In my life we had the Great Depression, the New Deal, World War II, the Cold War, the civil rights movement, Watergate. Now we've got stories that aren't as compelling, that aren't worth much. We are no longer threatened with annihilation. There is less news of any crisis. We have more and more news outlets, and less and less news. Whether what's going on is 'dumbing down,' I don't know. It is certainly softening.

"I am not giving three cheers for what I see," he adds, "but I don't know that they have left anything out. I may be bored, but I am not disturbed." The birth pangs of the recent escalation of tabloidism in network television news were first felt at NBC about two years ago. "We began in earnest to rethink what we were doing about February of 1995," says David Doss, Tom Brokaw's executive producer. "There was nothing immediate. We didn't wake up one day and say, 'Today is different than yesterday.' It was a feeling we had all had. We brainstormed for many hours over a long period of time. We concluded that there is a better way."

The decision was to cut down on the number of stories presented and to try to focus on subjects considered of more immediate interest, closer to home for more people—fewer so-called "process" stories, fewer Washington stories, fewer foreign stories in light of the end of the Cold War. And there were clearly decisions to try to make the packaging more attractive with dramatic backdrops. Brokaw now stands and moves about instead of sitting behind a desk.

Doss insists that significant news has not been ignored. "We believe if you watch our broadcast you will still know what is going on of consequence in the world. We don't believe we have shirked that at all. . . . We are trying to do more than the snapshot approach to the news. We are trying to provide some context. We tend to do longer pieces, and we tend to do fewer of them."

He says the new formula "didn't really take off" until last summer and fall.

When Dan Rather used the phrase "news lite" in a *Philadelphia Inquirer* interview in February he was clearly taking a jab at NBC, and Tom Brokaw was angered. "What CBS is trying to suggest is that we're cheapening the news, and that we're somehow making it less important," Brokaw responded in a follow-up piece in the *Inquirer*. "We're not. What we are doing is not being the wire service of the air anymore. We're picking four or five topics and trying to deal with them in a way that people can feel connected to." He

It can be argued that the nation's media overall have gone lite.

added, however, that "it ain't the news they did 20 years ago."

Bill Wheatley, vice president for news at NBC, emphasizes that all of the network news shows today are "works in progress," that all are experimenting with new approaches and that the competition is brutal—"more competitive than it has ever been. . . .

"More and more of what we do is meant to get at the changes in modern lifestyles, the changes that are affecting people's lives," he says. ". . . It is important that we do not deal with frivolous material on the evening news program, but there have been some lapses. . . . We did a piece on day-dreams one night. That was absurd." Peter Jennings traces much of what is going on to tremors that went through the world of television news in the aftermath of the O. J. Simpson trial, which transfixed great segments of the public—and helped, he believes, to transform NBC.

"The O. J. Simpson trial was such an anomaly in our lives and had such an effect on competition. I think we have yet to recover from it and to find our own feet. . . . NBC was giving it an enormous shot, and we and CBS were giving it a diminished shot. We felt that if we gave it an enormous shot it would block out the rest of the news. But it benefited NBC in terms of audience. . . . We and CBS thought that [the public] could get it on the specialized channels."

He says the impact of the O. J. story is still reverberating. "You can see echoes of that in the way we nibble at the Jon-Benet Ramsey case. . . . Do I think the JonBenet Ramsey story is worth the coverage we give it? For the most part I don't. Do I think we should give better coverage to Zaire—which eventually may become a burden to us? Yes I do. Finding the journalistic competitive balance is an agony every day."

Jennings agrees with Reuven Frank's observation that there is little news as compelling to the public as in years past. "I think in all the news organizations at the moment there is something of a struggle to decide what we can do on an evening newscast. . . . I am totally confused a lot of the time. . . . I struggle with this every day because I don't know what to do about it."

The changes, he says, "have to do with technology and a changing world order . . . the changing TV universe." Technology has given local stations access to material that they did not have in earlier times, Jennings says. Each of the networks now provides local stations with "feeds" of national and international stories that those stations are able to get on the air before the evening news shows. Jennings does not accept the argument made by some that audiences already know of major news before the network shows air. "Do I assume that people know the headlines of the main stories? The answer is yes. Do they know the context? I doubt it."

As for the "responsibility" of the network shows, Jennings says, "Sometimes we don't do as well as we could. But I don't know any journalist who doesn't say that to himself every day." He says he does not believe that producers of any of the shows set out to present trivial material, but that everyone, even in newspapers, likes an occasional soft story.

At CBS, Dan Rather, mired in last place in the ratings, insisted in his *Philadelphia Inquirer* interview that "we [at CBS] are anti-news lite. It's what we're about. All news, all the time. Like a rock, we are hard news. I like it that the other two are going softer. We have to distinguish ourselves from them. CBS is a brand name. *CBS Evening News* is a brand name. We want that name to constantly be a beacon of real hard news. 'News lite' is not our game."

All of which brought something of a horse laugh from Brokaw, who says he thought it "inappropriate for our competitors, who have gone through their own incarnations—including moments like Connie Chung anchoring from Tonya Harding's rink—to judge us. . . . We're all covering the same stuff. We're doing it in different styles. The differences are on the margins. . . . Hard news is in the eye of the beholder. Dan's definition of hard news and mine may differ from time to time. But if you look at our lineups, day in and day out, you'll find hard news even in the so-called 'lite' material."

Brokaw had a point in observing that all three network shows are relatively similar. "Dan accused Tom of doing 'news lite,'" says Emily Rooney, a former producer for ABC's *World News Tonight*, "but they are all about the same." Reuven Frank agrees. The differences tend to be differences in the choices of "lite" features, and even those could be interchanged among the three almost any time without anyone noticing. Asked about Rather's insistence that CBS is going for "hard news," Newton Minow says that "CBS is in a state of denial." Andrew Tyndall says, "Rather has a short memory."

In one recent show (April 3) Rather presented as top news a feature about the "harvesting of human organs" from bodies of patients near death, which turned out to be a lengthy promotion for an upcoming *60 Minutes* broadcast. Later in the show there was another special feature called "Secrets of the IRS," in which Rather reported, in tones suggesting menace, that "any IRS worker can sneak a peak at your [tax] return" by obtaining unauthorized access to computer codes. In the same show a CBS reporter visited a meeting of UFO believers, some of whom said they had lived on other planets.

CBS executives, however, adamantly reject the assertion that CBS News has changed, that it is going "lite," or that it has abandoned a tradition favoring hard news. Jeff Fager, executive producer of the *CBS Evening News*, says flatly: "Hard news is what we are all about. Absolutely. We value hard news. . . . We aren't conflicted about our mission. I don't think it has changed at all. We put a high priority on covering the world. . . . We are trying to do the kind of reporting that we think sets us apart. We really have tried to maintain what I think has made CBS special, our legacy. Our job is to make what is important interesting."

Fager says that CBS values "enterprise" on the part of its reporters and is especially proud of their investigative work. "When you talk of featury material that is in the broadcast," he says, "that is a commitment to reporting.

"'Feature' is a word that you have to define. We do a lot of investigative reporting. . . . What we do more now is we [report] over several days, like a look at the militia movement. To say it is feature reporting implies that it is soft. . . . It is feature, but it is driven by hard news."

All of which suggests that Brokaw had it right when he observed that hard news is in the eye of the beholder. But what is remarkable about what is happening on network news is the degree to which the networks have redefined what they are calling news. As Brokaw said, "It ain't the news they did 20 years ago." In fact, it isn't the news they did two or three years ago. By some standards, much of it isn't even news.

Yes, it's often more tawdry. Yes, it's more featury. Yes, there are fewer stories. Yes, there is less attention to the world outside the United States. Yes, there is a tendency toward conflict and violence. Yes, a substantial share of it is tabloid. But is the republic in peril?

Bert Rockman, a political scientist at the University of Pittsburgh and director of the Center for American Politics and Society, has put his finger on the essential question. "It's true," says Rockman, "the news looks different, it's softening. But we're not sure what the real content of this softening is. . . . We need to find out, is it truly trivial, or is it another way to tune in to public affairs matters? . . . If they are presenting a substantive package that no one will listen to, then it doesn't do much good."

This much is certain. The three great networks have changed, and continue to change, the content of their nightly news shows. What they are doing is bound to have a significant impact on the perceptions of millions of Americans of what is important in the nation and the world. And that could have an important impact on the way the democratic system works.

It is also true that many longtime television news professionals—in a medium never famous for its depth—are appalled at what they see. The 1934 act that created the Federal Communications Commission, the agency responsible for monitoring the use of the public airwaves, stated that broadcast media are there to serve the "public interest, convenience and necessity."

What is remarkable about what is happening on network news is the degree to which the networks have redefined what they are calling news.

It is fair to ask whether the major network news shows are straying from even those vaguely worded responsibilities.

The Web Made Me Do It[5]

Velocity was the key word in the outraged debate over the media's coverage of the sexual allegations against President Bill Clinton. Critics complained that reporters, driven by the competitive backdraft of the new media—meaning the Internet, of course, but also the three cable-news channels—shattered the ethics barrier in their manic pursuit of the story. The press moved "too fast from the bullet to the atom bomb," said Joan Konner, publisher of the *Columbia Journalism Review*. "The digital age does not respect contemplation," said James M. Naughton, former executive editor of the *Philadelphia Inquirer*. Michael Isikoff, the *Newsweek* reporter whose scoop was pre-empted when Matt Drudge reported it on his Web site, the Drudge Report, weighed in, too, saying that Drudge "disposes of all the journalistic conventions and simply recycles the most sensational gossip that's going around."

The critics were right on some points. A journalistic echo effect did take over, as many reporters blindly reported what other reporters had dug up—never mind whether they had checked the details themselves. And the Internet and television's constant need to be fed did speed up the news cycle, with reporters churning out stories at a furious pace that created cycles within cycles. For instance, the *Dallas Morning News* published on its Web site and in its paper editions an article about the President and Monica Lewinsky that it retracted in a matter of hours. The next day, the *Morning News* republished its article—with modifications—after its source changed his statements. Several days later, the *Wall Street Journal*'s interactive edition blared the news that Bayani Nelvis, a White House steward, had told a grand jury he caught Clinton and Lewinsky alone together. As controversy erupted—Nelvis's lawyer called the report "absolutely false and irresponsible"—the paper's print edition backpedaled.

The turbulence made everyone a little woozy, but critics overstated the case when they heaped blame on the new media. After all, the biggest miscues, like the *Morning News*'s yo-yo and a similar goof by ABC News, involved 'old media' that went with a story too soon. Matt Drudge's contribution was straightforward and defensible: he reported, accurately, that *Newsweek*'s editors, worried about the explosive nature of Isikoff's original article on the sex charges, had decided to delay it.

So why was the criticism so intense? Perhaps because the new media exposed a wound. The real sin was that they laid bare, for all to see, how news is made. Like the preparation

Like the preparation of sausage and legislation, the process [of making the news] can be ugly.

5. Article by Jack Shafer, from the *New York Times Magazine*, p24 + Feb. 15, 1998. Copyright © 1998 by the New York Times Company. Reprinted by permission.

of sausage and legislation, the process can be ugly. Facts, rumors and hunches are collected and set down in the jigsaw puzzle of narrative. Editors and reporters move the pieces around to see if they form a pattern. Meanwhile, the competition is doing the same. The first organization to complete the puzzle wins the scoops and the readers.

When the deadline whistle howls, things get messy. But the critics seem to think the Internet has an especially demonic power to distort; Tom Shales of the *Washington Post* called it 'the new electronic Tower of Babel.' But technology is neutral. It makes as much sense to blame modems and the Internet for distorting the spread of news as it does to blame telephones. In reality, the Internet is a technological tool with the same good and bad aspects as any other. Among its positive uses, for reporters and readers alike, is its role as a tip sheet and rapid-transmission medium. In the hectic days after the scandal broke, reporters at every newsroom in the country surfed Web sites, as did droves of readers. Drudge himself maintains an E-mail list that allows him to zap his stories directly to subscribers, many of whom are journalists who don't always disdain what he has to say.

Among news consumers, details of the scandal spread like an algae bloom, as devotees of the story E-mailed breaking news stories to their comrades and posted their own messages on newsgroups like alt.current-events.clinton.whitewater. The MSNBC News Web site recorded a nearly 300 percent increase in daily hits. Thanks to the Web, regional papers like the *Dallas Morning News* were in a position to compete in real time with print journalism's front four: the *New York Times*, the *Washington Post*, the *Wall Street Journal* and the *Los Angeles Times*.

The forces that compel journalists to break news at hyperspeed may sound futuristic, but actually they hark back to the speediest time in American journalism: the turn of the century. In New York in 1900, there were at least 65 daily newspapers (counting the vital ethnic press), whose reporters scrambled to match and beat the competition. The new technology of the telephone, which many reporters disparaged when it was introduced (because it de-emphasized legwork), became as indispensable as the shorthand pad. Whenever the news cycle demanded it, dailies would publish 'extra' editions (similar to the instant 'extras' that some news organizations now publish on the Web). The variety offered by the newsstand in those times almost approached that of the Web today. Back then, New Yorkers could choose the demagogic fulminations of William Randolph Hearst's *New York Journal*, the prim institutional voice of Adolph Ochs's *Times* and papers representing all points in between. Determining the truth value of stories was left up to readers and editors. Somehow the Republic survived that info-glut.

The ethics of early journalists were often shaky, but the hurly-burly also brought vigor to reporting. H. L. Mencken, worshiped by many as a newspaper god, writes with glee in his memoirs of how he and a reporter for a competing Baltimore paper made up stories out of whole cloth. Their target was a reporter who covered their beat for the city's third leading daily and who refused to pool his reporting. The recalcitrant reporter finally joined the pool after his editors bawled him out for missing the malarkey that Mencken and his pal were publishing. To be sure, the old days are overromanticized in plays like *The Front Page* but damned if Matt Drudge's jumping the gun on Isikoff's scoop didn't sound like Hildy Johnson pulling a fast one on Walter Burns.

In the world of electronic commerce, you hear a lot about 'disintermediation'—the elbowing out of middlemen and distributors by the Web, which directly connects manufacturers with consumers. It is premature to herald the disintermediation of the news business by Web independents who leapfrog editors, libel attorneys and conventional journalistic standards. But the example of Drudge shows that anybody who has an Internet connection and something original to say can reach a global audience. Sensing this disintermediation in the works, the old media have expanded their profile on the Web. In addition to the *Newsweek* extra, practically every big daily, newsmagazine and TV network added a 'Clinton Crisis' page to their Web sites.

Disintermediation might sound like a prescription for an orgy of libel, but so far most of the alleged libel in the on-line world has centered on financial advice. The Web—like old media—appears to be self-policing: the very velocity that spreads untruths on the Web also brings instant accountability. As anyone who works on the Web knows, readers spank you via E-mail the moment you make an error.

The success of Matt Drudge also indicates that readers hunger for reporting that hasn't had the life pecked out of it by editors and lawyers who identify too strongly with the bow-tie-and-braces brigade that runs the Government and corporate America. As Drudge has repeatedly said, the sexcapade scandal was right under the noses of the Washington news establishment for months and months. Why was Isikoff the only reporter chasing it?

Ethical standards are important, but we should never ignore the price we pay for them. Listen to the muckraker Lincoln Steffens, who rebelled at the stylistic straitjacket that the *New York Evening Post* forced him to wear in 1892. "Reporters were to report the news . . . without prejudice, color and without style," he complained. "Humor or any sign of personality in our reports was caught, rebuked and, in time, suppressed. Instead of bemoaning the rise of cheeky Web characters, we should welcome them for what they are—new voices that enliven journalism."

No endorsement of new media should be unqualified. Drudge does play things fast and loose. He now faces a libel suit filed by the White House aide Sidney Blumenthal, stemming from Drudge's report that 'court records' said that Blumenthal beat his wife. No such court records exist. Although Drudge withdrew the column and apologized, Blumenthal is continuing the suit against Drudge and his distributor, America Online.

Already, electronic commerce mavens are talking about 'reintermediation,' in which a new breed of Web middleman will rise to make sense out of the chaos wrought by disintermediation. As the technology of the Web evolves, Internet devices will become as ubiquitous as telephones. Every newspaper will have the potential to break news as fast as a television station. Every television station will have the potential to become a newspaper.

But people will still only have 24 hours a day to consume news. After the novelty wears off, most readers of the news on the Web will depend on Web reintermediators to dispense journalism of dependable accuracy, just the way they turn to dependable newspapers and networks today for scrupulous reporting. That's not to say that reckless journalists will vanish from the Web. Just like the supermarket tabloids, they'll find their markets. But if we're half as sophisticated as were big-city newspaper readers early in this century, we'll quickly figure out the difference, velocity and all, between excess and excellence.

II. The Marriage of Celebrity and Journalism

Editors' Introduction

As the media has expanded, the nature of the "breaking" news story has evolved over the years to more frequently incorporate reports concerning celebrities. These pieces on the private lives of famous individuals often take precedence over "traditional" local and international news items, and have come to earn the moniker "celebrity journalism." Facilitated by the expanding multimedia outlets of the press, along with widespread interest in the O. J. Simpson, Princess Diana and Monica Lewinsky stories, this type of reporting has come under intense scrutiny in recent years.

The first article in this section, "Guilty: Objectivity Is Obsolete," by Jon Katz, explores the media's involvement in the O. J. Simpson trial. While many in the press called the trial itself a "media spectacle" due to the celebrity defendant and the high-profile attorneys involved, news coverage of the lengthy event was also subject to criticism. In many ways, the O. J. Simpson case, with its television appeal and round-the-clock coverage, set a precedent for the handling of celebrity news in the media. In this article, Katz examines the nature of objectivity in journalism, particularly as it pertains to the cultural, economic and social issues integral to the Simpson case. The writer assails the "ethnocentric Super Bowl" manner by which reporters covered the trial, releasing information in a "play-by-play" style that ignored the larger issues at hand. Katz also takes a look at the emerging online coverage of news events, including the Simpson trial, and the direction in which online news sources need to go in order to become a viable alternative to television and print media.

No news story in recent years has placed the subject of celebrity journalism in the spotlight of public scrutiny more than the death of Princess Diana in 1997. Killed in an auto accident as she was being chased by tabloid photographers, the extremely high-profile princess became a symbol for a perceived media obsession with stardom. In the face of mass condemnation, mainstream media sources rushed to distinguish themselves from the tabloids, while the tabloids struggled to distance their tactics from the "stalkerazzi" who hound celebrities for a peak inside their private lives. In the aftermath of the accident, a new dialogue was opened up on an international scale, and the public, alongside reporters, began to question openly the continually blurring lines between privacy and news in the face of celebrity.

In "Celebrity Journalism, the Public, and Princess Diana," by Joe Saltzman, the media's coverage of the death of Princess Diana is chastised. Saltzman berates the "hypocrisy" of a media that, while ostensibly reporting on the excess of celebrity coverage in the news, inundated readers with photos and stories concerning Princess Diana for weeks after her death, banking on the public's grief and reaping the financial benefits. In truth, the author argues, the difference between the traditional press and the tabloids is "unrecognizable" and the focus on celebrity has left the practice of journalism in a state of deterioration. Saltzman goes on to recommend that the media stop delivering all the intimate details of celebrities' lives, despite popular desire for such information, and concludes with a call for a redefinition of the term "news," urging a public demand to end the domination of celebrity journalism in the press.

Although not exactly located on the same tier of notoriety as actors and musicians, politicians, as public figures, have developed a celebrity status of their own. As a result, inquiry into the intimate details of their lives has been the fodder for inflated tabloid sales and high TV ratings in recent years. No political story exemplifies this more than the federal investigation into President Clinton's relationship with Monica Lewinsky. The merging of scandalous affair with national news brought about unprecedented media coverage, most of which treated those involved as any other celebrity, complete with news organizations all vying for that elusive interview. However, it also produced a great deal of inaccurate reporting, and with its unrelenting coverage, the media has found itself the object of a public backlash over the case.

Media critic Howard Kurtz, in his *Washington Post* article "Report Faults Lewinsky Coverage," scrutinizes the early reporting on the case by journalists from a variety of media sources. Citing a study released by the Committee of Concerned Journalists, Kurtz takes news organizations to task for releasing incorrect information, often based solely on rumor, as factual. In particular, he looks at early claims by reporters that Lewinsky stated that presidential friend Vernon Jordan had told her to lie about her relationship with Clinton. While this unsubstantiated accusation was widely reported as fact, the truth—that Lewinsky had never made such a statement—came to light months later, in the process shining an unflattering light on the media.

Finally, the allure of celebrity status often filters into the world of the newsmakers themselves. With the popularity of television journalism, more and more reporters and news anchors can be found gracing the pages of entertainment magazines and offering cameos in movies. Often, the focus is not on their reporting, but rather on their visibility and stature.

The final article in the section, "Celebrity Journalists," by Alicia J. Shepard, examines the new issues arising as a result of journalists moving into the role of celebrity. She explores the disparate paths taken by two of journalism's most famous practitioners, Bob Woodward and Carl Bernstein, and looks at how fame can affect the other side of the camera. Presented is one recent example of reporters taking on outside roles, that of the movie *Contact*, which featured 13 CNN journalists portraying themselves and recounting fictional information about a planet called Vega. The author reveals that as more and more media figures take on star status, news organizations are being questioned on the ethics involved. She concludes by asking whether this small segment of celebrity journalists stands to overshadow the quiet work of the diligent but unknown reporter.

Guilty[1]

Objectivity Is Obsolete

The most faithful among media watchers have always held that media don't lead, they follow. They function best as a mirror. If you watch long enough and closely enough, the truth will unfailingly emerge, however indirectly, and often in the most surprising ways. This is especially true in the trial of O. J. Simpson. For the first time in a generation, all our media are covering the same thing: *New York Times* reporters side by side with the *National Enquirer*'s; ABC News and America Online bumping up against *Inside Edition*.

The truth emerging from all this coverage in Los Angeles doesn't have much to do with blood droplets or police bungling. The story that flickers through millions of TV sets half the day is much bigger, more troubling even than murder. In the Simpson trial, the truth is this: Some of the country's most important institutions are mired in a mean-spirited standoff between factions whose primary characteristic is that they can't and won't give an inch. Our communal and civic open spaces—courts, workplaces, Congress, academe— are no longer places where issues are settled, but battlegrounds on which the most pressing conflicts will never be resolved. America is no longer one nation indivisible, if it ever was, but a land peopled by many bitterly divided tribes.

While we still come together under the aegis of public institutions to thrash out our shared values, laws, and understandings, the notion of an America united by common views of attainable equality, justice, and individual freedom is a myth. And the one institution most responsible for spotting and disclosing this big story, as well as providing a forum in which we can come to terms with it, has abdicated its duties. The role of modern journalism as a mechanism for meaningful cultural debate is a great hoax, exposed by Orenthal James Simpson and the spectacle he's provoked in Los Angeles.

One after another, our most central institutions have come down the scary road to Simpsonville only to be consumed, overwhelmed, or defeated. If the O. J. saga is one of our most interesting stories ever, it's also one of our most brutal. Day after day, some of our most cherished social verities are being chipped away, witness by witness. The police don't stand for justice, the lawyers don't represent the law, the jury

1. Article by Jon Katz, from *Wired* p128 + Sep. 1995. Reprinted by permission of Sterling Lord Literistic, Inc. Copyright © 1995 Jon Katz. Jon Katz, a former producer of CBS News and media critic for *Rolling Stone* and *New York* magazines, is the media critic for *Wired*.

doesn't promise unbiased judgment, and the judge doesn't ensure order.

But no institution is more revealed as utterly bankrupt than daily journalism. Technology lets newspapers, radio, and television bring us the words and pictures more quickly, clearly, and overwhelmingly than ever, but the press has lost the will to tell us what those images mean. It can't get us to talk to or comprehend one another; it allows us only to state our differences ever more stridently. Journalists are not prepared or permitted to acknowledge the way the enormous social, ethnic, and political changes transforming our culture permeate the story unfolding in front of them.

The Failed Cult of Objectivity

Many people, inside and outside journalism, believe that objectivity is an unattainable goal.

To be objective is to be uninfluenced by emotion or prejudice. On high school newspapers, in university journalism schools, among young reporters tackling their first beats, objectivity is taught as the professional standard—along with accuracy—to which journalists aspire. Most working journalists, especially older ones, accept it as bedrock: they are detached and impartial, setting aside any personal, political, or emotional beliefs.

Many people, inside and outside journalism, believe that objectivity is an unattainable goal. "Nevertheless, we can still distinguish personal attitudes, religious dogmas, and the like from facts and justified beliefs," write Georgetown professors Stephen Klaidman and Tom L. Beauchamp in *The Virtuous Journalist*. "The essence of some professional commitments is engagement, but in contrast to adherents of the so-called new journalism, we believe . . . that journalists are obligated to maintain a professional distance."

This ethic makes viewers' and readers' tasks more difficult. They know that total absence of belief isn't plausible, so editorial objectivity forces them to guess to what degree a journalist's offering flows from personal prejudice. And the public frequently assumes the worst: rather than being permitted to make arguments openly and support them, journalists are suspected of advancing secret agendas, and are rendered less, not more, credible. Commentators like Rush Limbaugh might be widely disliked, but they attract vast followings because they are unapologetically outspoken—though hardly "objective."

"To present a story objectively entails writing and organizing the material so as not to express or suggest a preference for one set of values over another," write Klaidman and Beauchamp. But anyone who writes (or reads) knows that all stories aren't covered, all questions aren't asked, all answers aren't included. Journalists present facts not laterally but in sequence of importance. This is in itself a subjective process.

The nature of modern politics has altered the meaning of detachment as well. To the gay person seeking a governmental response to AIDS or to the underclass mother whose family is engulfed by drugs and guns, a journalist's attitude of distance about such life-and-death issues constitutes a hostile act. Such audiences will soon find other media. So too the young, who have abandoned newspapers, TV, and radio in staggering numbers for other "non-journalistic" media that they perceive to be much more truthful—media that offer strong points of view, frank exchanges of ideas, graphic visual presentations, and lots of irony and self-depreciation.

Throughout the summer of 1995, we were reminded that this extraordinary dissonance between us and our media—so clear in the Simpson trial—was not an exception, but rather the new rule. In July, *Time* ran a "Cyberporn" cover featuring a discredited undergraduate study as its objective centerpiece. "A new study shows how pervasive and wild it really is," the cover line said of Net pornography. How did one of our primary institutions of information come to pervert reality in this way? In a country where thousands of children are killed or crippled each year by drugs and guns and knives, *Time* couldn't offer one child who had succumbed by going online.

At almost the same time, the man the FBI calls the Unabomber set out again on his quixotic, doomed, and murderous mission to dismantle technology and the people who create it. His image is haunting, though not the way he intends: what comes to mind is the brain-damaged Joker in the first *Batman*, who, it seems, has finally paralyzed Gotham, spreading panic, wreaking havoc with airplanes, shutting down parts of the postal service, sending the police scurrying. Two of the country's most powerful and influential media institutions—the *New York Times* and the *Washington Post*—debated whether and how to reproduce his lengthy message in its entirety after giving enormous amounts of space to its disjointed content. The lunatics had not only taken control of the asylum but were in charge of reporting the takeover as well.

Still, the idea that reporters must suppress their views and perceptions remains deeply ingrained. "I wouldn't dare write what I think," a reporter who helped cover the Simpson case for the *Los Angeles Times* recently told a graduate journalism seminar in the San Francisco Bay area. What the reporter thought was that Simpson was guilty and that the jury would never convict him, mostly for racial reasons. "I'll be frank," e-mailed a senior editor at *Time*, also afraid to be publicly identified. "We'd get massacred if we printed what our reporters think. I know it sounds weird, but it's true. We just couldn't get away with it." It is strange and true—and chilling—when an institution founded on free and fearless speech doesn't dare use either.

(Since we're on the subject, here's what I believe: In light of the evidence presented to date, O. J. Simpson is profoundly disturbed. I believe he killed Nicole Brown Simpson and Ronald Goldman. I also believe he will not be convicted of murder, primarily because of racial tensions in Los Angeles and because the legal system has no rational, modern system for selecting a jury able to cope with the social pressures and legal complexities of the trial.)

Taught that objectivity is a noble, ethical stance, journalists seem largely unaware that it is the antithesis of the moral media founded before, during, and immediately after the American Revolution. It wasn't until the 19th century—when improved printing technology made it possible to reach thousands of new customers—that greedy publishers conceived of "objectivity" to avoid offending their vast new market. Now, commercial news-broadcasting permits no commentary at all. Shows like *Crossfire* provide commentary as amusement, allowing only counterbalancing opinions within a narrow ideological range—one spokesperson on the "left," one on the "right," as if there are no other choices. Newspapers relegate opinion to op-ed pages, and even there the politics are militantly moderate. In contrast, talk radio—filled with opinions and commentary—is booming.

Decades back, when newspapers were homogeneous—published by white men for white men about white men—objectivity worked in both the marketing and the journalistic sense. Papers became so respectable and inoffensive that they were able to amass large audiences; they monopolized news and advertising from the 1850s to the 1960s.

But as the nation became more diverse, and as new technology provided fierce competition, objectivity paralyzed more than professionalized. Cable, VCRs, computers, and modems have created a vast new cultural outlet, not only for new kinds of advertising such as music videos but for the outspoken opinion, vivid writing, visual imagery, and informality the young prefer. Ascending media—Web pages, Oliver Stone films, Comedy Central programs, online discussions, MTV News—make no pretense of being "objective," comprehensive, or even substantial.

Were America's founding journalists assigned to cover O. J. Simpson—like Thomas Paine, for example—they would have had no truck with objectivity. They believed journalism was about telling the truth as they saw it, as loudly and bluntly as possible.

Proponents of objectivity argue that its loss will mean a chorus of shrill, confusing voices further obscuring the truth. Of course, it's okay to quote shrill and confusing voices all day, as long as the reporter is detached about it.

Journalism can continue to preach reverence for informed opinion—truth based on research, accuracy, and fairness—while allowing writers and reporters to tell us the truth as they see it.

But journalists are apt to be less strident and more even-handed than many of the people they quote. Journalism can continue to preach reverence for informed opinion—truth based on research, accuracy, and fairness—while allowing writers and reporters to tell us the truth as they see it.

What would subjective mainstream news media look like?

In the case of the Simpson story, journalists would report not only on the trial, but on the racial climate in Los Angeles, the economics of justice, the overwhelming impact of media, and the glaring inadequacies of the jury system. They would present the trial's daily developments, but would be free—encouraged, in fact—to state opinion as long as they were supported by facts and strong reasoning, and free to change their minds with explanation: "Today, I came to believe O. J. Simpson was innocent, and here's the evidence that made me come to this conclusion."

Courtroom Meltdown

But as things stand, life in Simpsonville (current national headquarters for fragmentation and imploding institutions) suggests that it is no longer possible to do business or arrive at a resolution in common settings like courtrooms. Our society has no mechanism to try O. J. Simpson rationally. We can't deal with the debilitating social tensions of the case. And our legal process virtually guarantees that informed, fair-minded people be barred from juries.

The Simpson trial, as it winds on, continues to cause a loss of faith in our system of justice. A spring American Bar Association poll found 45 percent of those surveyed said the trial has caused them to lose respect for the justice system. Only 28 percent of the people questioned in the previous year gave the same response.

Like journalism, the legal profession waxes effusive about love of law, constitutional prerogatives, passion for justice. This is hardly the picture that emerges from the bickering, posturing, and maneuvering in L.A. It seems clear that the justice system can be overwhelmed by large infusions of money, influenced by mass concentrations of media, and paralyzed by racial divisions.

Take the court's ambivalent attitude toward media. Cultural isolation might have been possible when news consisted of a daily paper, a weekly magazine, or a newscast. But news channels are now on 24 hours a day, and there are nearly 1,000 radio talk shows. There is no way to isolate a juror or anyone else from the pervasive media and their chorus of messages. Nor is there any reason to. Either potential jurors are forced to pretend they live in cocoons, or they really do live in cocoons that poorly prepare them for their roles of deciding enormously complex issues.

But the more you know about the law in general or about a case in particular, says author Wendy Kaminer, the less likely you are to wind up on a jury. Litigators, she points out, don't seek objective, unbiased jurors: they want biased ones—people they believe favor their cases. And concern about pretrial publicity, Kaminer says, favors uninformed over informed jurors.

As the drama of the Simpson trial already demonstrates, a jury no longer does what it was meant to do (function as the true conscience of the community) but represents those parts of the community, those tribes, to which individual jurors belong. Ex-juror Jeanette Harris made this contradiction clear, shocking many whites, when she told reporters that she believed none of the evidence presented against Simpson to be true and pointed out that jurors could hardly be expected to transcend racial issues, since whites and blacks had to go back to their communities after the trial. If she had made those views clear at the outset, she probably never would have gotten on the jury.

Whether they realize it or not, reporters covering the trial seem to have abandoned even the pretense that jurors can transcend racial issues. Jurors are identified by race, and it is virtually assumed that just as the loss of an African-American juror is a setback for the defense, the dismissal of a white or Hispanic juror is a defeat for the prosecution. If the reporters are right, then the jury system is unworkable in racially charged cases. If they're wrong, then they are advancing the worst kind of stereotypes.

In *With Justice for Some: Victims' Rights in Criminal Trials*, Columbia University Law School professor George Fletcher makes a number of specific, logical recommendations for reforming the courts. In the era of CNN and Court TV, Fletcher writes that high-profile cases cannot escape the notice of even the most remote citizens. Prospective jurors should be screened not to locate the ignorant or ill-informed, but to find those "capable of maintaining an open mind until they hear the evidence." Fletcher and other legal scholars point out that the historical motive in jury selection wasn't picking detached citizens, but peers of the accused who were part of his or her community and could act on its behalf. People locked in motels for months while being spied on by deputies seem far from that ideal.

In modern America, we might consider impaneling jurors willing to acknowledge and discuss racial perceptions and biases, instead of forcing them to pretend they have none. Fletcher calls for the establishment of an "interactive jury," an idea that looks pretty good in the Simpson case. "As they now function," he writes, "jury trials display little capacity for self-correction and avoidance of irrational tangents."

Rather than sequestering jurors, he argues, judges should encourage outside contact, inviting them to ask questions of the judge so they understand the law.

Most judges, however, seem to react the same way boomer parents do: rather than struggle with how best to use modern media and the attendant technology, they find it easier to ban them.

(At Least) Two Nations

The most jarring cultural division demonstrated by the Simpson story is racial. Sometime in the spring of 1995, according to numerous polls and surveys, it became clear to most white Americans—roughly 70 percent—that O. J. Simpson was probably guilty, that the DNA and other evidence was substantial, that the idea of a massive police conspiracy to frame him was ludicrous, and at best a desperate play by high-powered lawyers. Almost at the same time, it became equally clear to most African Americans—also about three-quarters—that Simpson was innocent, and that a police conspiracy was not only possible but likely.

It also became clear to both groups and everyone else that the Simpson jury was probably not going to convict him and would stalemate primarily as a result of racial differences. Journalists passed along the poll results, but seemed unable to react to the fact that these findings had become the big story, not an interesting sidelight. For those of us watching from a distance, this media dissonance became increasingly disturbing. We sensed we were not seeing and hearing the truth. However unintentionally, journalism's daily offerings seemed a great lie.

In racial terms, as political scientist Andrew Hacker declared in the title of his landmark work, *America Is Two Nations: Black and White, Separate, Hostile, Unequal.* That could as easily be the theme of the trial. Though many white Americans want to view racism as an ugly part of the past, African-Americans see it as part of their daily reality. "A huge racial chasm remains, and there are few signs that the coming century will see it closed," writes Hacker.

If whites are puzzled by black anger, they needn't be. There's lots of terrific reporting about it outside the mainstream media, in works like Hacker's or in Christopher Jencks's *Rethinking Social Policy: Race, Poverty, and the Underclass.*

The bleak and powerful writing of these scholars hardly makes the black-white schism surrounding the Simpson trial easier to take, but it moves the discussion past knee-jerk responses that stifle real comprehension or progress. It becomes much clearer why white and black jurors can look

Journalists lack the ability to be blunt enough, truthful enough, or analytical enough to help us understand not just what we're seeing but why.

at the same people saying the same things and reach totally different conclusions.

This is perhaps the heart not only of the Simpson story but of the media's failure to cover this trial incisively: journalists lack the ability to be blunt enough, truthful enough, or analytical enough to help us understand not just what we're seeing but why. Entrenched social problems, mobility, technology, immigration, and the breakup of empires and superpowers are knocking us off our civic pins. Historians, anthropologists, and social scientists have recorded the fragmentation of America for years.

In a stream of compelling literature, they've pointed out that politicians are locked in eternally warring camps, stalemating the political process with their refusal to compromise or reach beyond narrow constituencies, and that blacks and whites and Asians and Hispanics are hopelessly divided on a widening range of social and civic issues. Authors have described a culture of victimization, complaint, and rage permeating almost every part of American life. But because our mass media shy away from such indictments, we don't have to acknowledge their sobering truth—or do anything about them.

Before the age of print, writes Benedict Anderson in *Imagined Communities*, the Roman Empire easily won every war against heresy because it always had better lines of internal communication than its challengers. But by the early 1500s, Martin Luther had published 430 editions of his biblical translations, creating for the first time a truly mass readership. New media are creating a similar diversity. Television, telephones, modems, and fax technology not only leapfrog cities and countries, but are within almost everyone's reach. The number of television images or Internet exchanges in the course of a single day is incalculable.

Through the early 1960s, the common representation of America was an Eisenhowerish one: women stayed at home while prosperous men conducted the country's business. Minorities were largely invisible. Justice and opportunity prevailed. Mainstream journalism had no idea how many unhappy women, gays, blacks, and Hispanics there were because nobody much cared. Now that we claim to care, we have to listen to all the vitriol.

Fragmented Identities

If cultural anthropologists could write, a lot of journalists would have to find other work. And if journalists were given the time, education, and training anthropologists receive, we might better grasp some of the complicated problems we face. There are more reporters assembled at the O. J. Simpson trial, for longer periods, generating more words and videotape, than have gathered around any domestic story ever. Mostly, they present the trial as a sort of ethnocentric Super Bowl, offering a daily tip sheet and score card: when O. J. struggled to don the bloodied Isotoners, it was "good" for the defense, but the DNA evidence proved a "victory" for the prosecution. One legal strategy is checkmated by another: defense against prosecution, journalists against jurists, experts against experts, jurors against jurors, whites against blacks. The coverage provides staggering amounts of banal play-by-play. But it ignores the big story, a story anthropologists and social historians have been documenting for years.

There are, writes anthropologist Arjun Appadurai in *Recapturing Anthropology: Working in the Present*, some "brute facts" we must face. Central among them, he says, "is the changing social, territorial, and cultural reproduction of group identity. As groups migrate, regroup in new locations, reconstruct their histories, and reconfigure their ethnic 'projects' or goals ... the landscapes of group identity all over the world are changing."

Our journalists should be shaping and commenting upon the debate, not simply mirroring and exacerbating it.

Appadurai calls these new communities "ethnoscapes" and notes they are sprouting all over the U.S. and much of the world. Mobility, diversity, and media exposure alter groups' expectations, generate instability, cement differences, exacerbate conflict. Instead of assimilating, tribes retain their own values and reject many of those imposed by the cultures they find themselves in.

The polarization of American life is talked about all the time in living rooms and backyards and on talk radio; it's on display on the big boards like AOL and Prodigy and in countless newsgroups. Though we pretend that everybody is alike and equal and approaches our common civic duty with the same basic values, the images flickering across millions of TVs contradict this pretense. America is increasingly a collection of tribal enclaves, each responsive to its own interests but unable or unwilling to step beyond itself on behalf of a common good. Journalists are one tribe in L.A., whites another, African-Americans another, along with the police, defense attorneys, prosecutors, and jurors.

All over the planet, definitions of what nations are and mean are changing—a big story in anthropology, if not on our evening newscasts or front pages. "We live in a . . . world of crisscrossed economies, intersecting systems of meaning, and fragmented identities," writes Roger Rouse in *Diaspora*, a journal of transnational studies. We have moved into a new kind of social space.

You can see this space in every local paper, commercial newscast, and CNN hourly report, but it is not a pretty picture. From the Capitol to the town hall, our media depict a raucous quagmire. We seem stuck in a public tar pit over every issue that counts: the environment, education, budgets, poverty, gender, culture, and race. Within the fragmented media, one element accuses another of sensationalism and dumbing-down. This is a new politics of entrenchment, where sides dig in and fight for every bloody inch of ground, where the function of media is to transmit pictures and quotes of people shouting at one another.

Our journalists should be shaping and commenting upon the debate, not simply mirroring and exacerbating it. This is where new media's potential should be realized, where a new form of public space can develop in which we might iron out our differences and find rational solutions to fundamental problems. But so far, new media have also failed.

Is digital news any better? Not much. Although big online systems like Prodigy are as corporate and tepid as other mainstream media, they have too many live chat rooms and public topics to be as safe and noncontroversial as they'd undoubtedly like to be. Smaller BBSes, computer conferencing systems, and Web sites have no history of objectivity; public policy and politics are fiercely debated, and almost nothing is off-limits. . . .

Although individual discussion is much freer online than off, online news has yet to become influential or able to grasp and exploit its own potential. It hasn't defined its own ethic or its function in covering stories like O. J. Simpson's.

The biggest journalistic breakthrough made by online news has been reconnecting individuals to stories like this, giving them a chance to bypass journalists and ask questions, express themselves, share concerns. But with so many voices speaking at once, it's difficult for most people to find what they most want or need to hear. This is fertile ground for good, subjective journalism if there ever was one.

But instead of presenting themselves as distinct editorial entities willing to use new media in new ways, the big boards are content to rent space to mainstream, old-line media. And these traditional news media come online with their usual timidity, happy to let users mouth off in forums and via e-mail, but remaining as cautious online as they are on their editorial pages.

Yet the possibilities are enormous. America Online could easily set up black-white forums on which individuals could speak frankly about race and begin a dialog in a medium that permits users to encounter people they would otherwise never meet. Black people could message about their perceptions of racism and justice, white males could talk about their fear of displacement, scholars like Jencks or Hacker could come online to answer questions and share their research findings. People of different races, sexes, and sexual orientations could begin communicating with one another in radically different ways, instead of passively viewing or reading one culture's anger and laments about the other, or viewing media as a neutral transmitter of outrage and complaint.

Digital media could make it possible for people to inter-act—maybe even changing each other's minds in the pro-cess—something traditional media inhibit through their addiction to objectivity, spokespeople, and sensationalism. Every online user knows that this kind of communication often breaks down barriers, forcing sender and receiver to deal with each other as individuals rather than as group members.

There is already a precedent for opposing political forces to communicate directly via this technology. During the debate over gays in the military, gay soldiers spoke directly to wary veterans on CompuServe. There are more than a dozen newsgroups for African-American professionals on the Net, several for police officers who have shot people or been shot, one for black cops struggling to reconcile racial history with police work. Online news suggests a forum in which it would be easier for fragmented political or racial groups to begin what will be a tortuous process: teaching the members of all those tribes how to communicate and providing them with a simple means of doing so. Unfortunately, as the biggest story of our times unfolds across millions of screens, the new media have not yet risen to the task of either proclaiming the awful truth or fostering the dialog we so desperately need to deal with it.

Great Stories

For better or worse, great stories have always transformed the media that cover them and the institutions they cover. Walter Cronkite's coverage of the Kennedy assassination and the moon landing were broadcast journalism's twin high-water marks, legitimizing TV news as the country's most pervasive news medium. Watergate brought the press into its ongoing age of antagonism and self-righteousness, as reporters entered the personal and sexual lives of public fig-ures. The death of Elvis sparked a booming new tabloid news culture that's become a permanent part of our informa-tion structure. The Northridge, California, earthquake, reported first on Prodigy via wireless modem, made online communications a news medium in the traditional sense of the term. Four hours after the bombing in Oklahoma City, Internet Oklahoma (ionet) had created a World Wide Web site offering news, lists of survivors, and hospital telephone numbers. Inevitably, as the number of online users grow, online news will converge with a massive story, and digital news will become part of the media mainstream.

But if great stories transform media, they also systemati-cally shake our belief in institutions. Watergate and Vietnam eroded the credibility of the military and the presidency. The dramas of Anita Hill and Rodney King discredited Congress and the police. The Simpson trial has done the same for criminal justice and mass media. Story by story, our civic hearts seem broken, our faith shattered. For a generation, media mythologized our most important institutions—the FBI, the government, the judicial system. Then we learned shocking, revelatory new truths about the way our civil service machinery works, and we were totally unprepared for the idea that it doesn't always work. No wonder we puzzle over why we are so angry and disconnected. We are given so little truth most of the time, reality seems unbearable when we are finally confronted with it.

If one tenet of our age is that information wants to be free, its companion is that media want to tell the truth. Neither information nor media get what they want much of the time; this is one of the great ironies of the information revolution and the sad legacy of the O. J. Simpson trial.

Celebrity Journalism, the Public, and Princess Diana[2]

The stink of the hypocrisy surrounding Princess Diana's death was overwhelming. There were the self-serving politicians grabbing publicity by suggesting legislation they knew was unconstitutional and unnecessary. There were the self-serving actors who rushed to judgment because they have their own axes to grind when it comes to the dark side of tabloid journalism. There were the isolated supermarket managers who self-righteously removed all the tabloids from their stores saying they wanted no part of that kind of business, ignoring other products on their shelves that promise results impossible to achieve.

There were the family and friends of the Princess who denounced the media while ignoring the Princess's special history with it and how she knowingly used the news media to create herself anew in her own carefully crafted image. There were the American tabloids themselves who immediately promised that they would never buy or publish pictures of the dying Princess and then congratulated themselves on record sales of issues featuring stories chronicling every detail of her final hours.

There were the traditional news media, so quick to condemn the tabloids, and even faster when it came to plastering one photo after another of the Princess in their publications and TV programs. *Time* and *Newsweek* threw together more than 25 pages of photos and text, including a dramatic picture of the wreckage of the car. *People* gave Diana its cover for the 44th time, then produced two later covers offering "The Diana Interviews." CBS gave viewers "48 Hours" in the Princess's life, and every other TV newsmagazine and morning and evening news show treated the event as if it were the biggest news story of the century.

And of course there was the public, angrily denouncing the photographers while lapping up their products with so much zeal that paparazzi photographs of Diana repeatedly created record sales for any publication printing them.

The key question ignored was why were so many millions of people around the world so interested in Princess Diana? How did they come to know this woman so well and mourn her death so personally?

The reason is that the Princess epitomized the sad state of journalism around the world, culminating with the decade's

---

2. Article by Joe Saltzman, from *USA Today Magazine* p65 Jan. 1998. Copyright © 1998 *USA Today Magazine*. Reprinted with permission. Joe Saltzman, associate mass media editor of *USA Today*, is associate director, University of Southern California School of Journalism, Los Angeles.

preoccupation with celebrity journalism—journalism that not only creates instant celebrities, but gives them life through the constant repetition of countless personal details. Millions believed they knew the real Diana because they had been reading about every aspect of her royal and private life for years. When every minute detail of a person's life is printed in the press day after day, readers begin to feel as if they know this person intimately. When Princess Diana died, it was for many like losing a member of their family. In fact many believed they knew the Princess better than anyone else in their lives.

The difference between the tabloids and the traditional press and TV coverage is so subtle as to be unrecognizable. Some tabloids do buy pictures secretly taken of celebrities in hiding or snapped after some provocation, but these out-of-focus, blurred shots make up such a small percentage of celebrity coverage that it is almost meaningless. More people read about the Princess in *People* or *Vanity Fair* or favorable gushy tabloid stories. And when networks and national news magazines spend so much time covering the Princess's death, blaming the tabloids and the paparazzi for causing it may well be the worst hypocrisy of all.

The way to stop all this nonsense is to quit pandering to the public's desire for gossip and celebrity stories.

The way to stop all this nonsense is to quit pandering to the public's desire for gossip and celebrity stories. Quit publishing pictures of people whose only claim to fame is that they have money or good looks. Redefine news so it omits the bizarre and the unusual. Forget celebrities and freaks and report the news that truly affects us all—news about the economy, about the government, about the environment, about people and issues that affect the way we live and work.

You can find that kind of news buried in the *New York Times*, the *Wall Street Journal*, and a handful of other publications. You can see and hear it on PBS television and National Public Radio. An educated minority goes to these sources. But put a key economic issue on the cover of *Newsweek* and who will buy it when *Time* has a picture of some media-created celebrity smiling on its cover? Who will watch the [*News Hour with Jim Lehrer*] instead of a local newscast filled with the murder of the night, sports, weather, and the ever-present entertainment news?

This may be the time to simply change the definition of what is news. News should be events and circumstances that have an important effect on our lives. A discussion in Congress on taxes, any election in any city or state in the nation, attacks on the environment, the distribution of wealth and goods in the country—these are news stories that should be given the banner headlines they deserve.

We live in a society obsessed with celebrity. People care more about how much a new film costs and takes in at the box office than they do about local elections. The only way a politician can get on the evening news is to be caught on camera with a prostitute or a drug dealer. Talk about the issues and no one listens.

As long as you want to find out the latest dirt about a beleaguered princess or a second-rate actor, nothing is going to change much. Because, in the end, after the angry shouting of the mob and the stoning of the messenger, this is the way you want it. You tell the media every day what you want with your purchasing power. When you stop embracing celebrity journalism, when it is no longer profitable to publish pictures of every facet of a celebrity's daily life, then all of this will stop and the media—all the media, from the lowest tabloids to the loftiest national news magazines—will look for something else that you want. And then they'll give it to you.

To complain about the way things are is simply to add more hypocrisy to the stench all around us.

Report Faults Lewinsky Coverage[3]

From the first day of the Monica Lewinsky story, news organizations reported that Lewinsky was heard on secret tapes saying that presidential pal Vernon Jordan had told her to lie.

When the tape transcripts were released eight months later—oops—it turned out that Lewinsky had made no such comment about Jordan. This is among the case studies in a report released yesterday by the Committee of Concerned Journalists, a group holding forums around the country on media standards, that casts some of the Lewinsky coverage in a harsh light. "In some important cases, the press leaned on the suspicions of investigators that did not hold up and downplayed the denials of the accused," the report says.

The study took pains to point out that the press "usually relied on legitimate sources and often was careful about the facts." But although many allegations in the sex scandal turned out to be true, "it is an oversimplification to say the press has been vindicated."

Tom Rosenstiel, the committee's vice chairman, said some mainstream news outlets appeared to serve as a conduit for independent counsel Kenneth Starr. "Is it our job to print what an investigator suspects, or should we be publishing what we know to be true?" he asked. "There's a risk in publishing prosecutorial suspicions. The special prosecutor is not the disinterested prosecutor; he's there to make a case."

But the report did not deal with White House lies, from President Clinton on down, that were routinely carried by news outlets. Rosenstiel said that on the half-dozen subjects examined by the committee, administration officials often declined to discuss the details of the grand jury investigation.

Journalists, of course, routinely report on authorities investigating charges they ultimately can't prove. Sometimes, as in the case of falsely accused Olympic bomber Richard Jewell, they get burned.

The committee's massive Nexis search turned up some wrong-headed declarations, as when NBC's Geraldo Rivera said on July 8: "There is, ladies and gentlemen, absolutely no possibility that a so-called semen-stained dress exists."

More problematic was the spate of early reports on Jordan, the Washington lawyer who was helping Lewinsky find a corporate job—and whose actions provided the legal basis for Starr's inquiry into the Lewinsky matter.

In breaking the Lewinsky story on Jan. 21, the *Washington Post* reported what the former White House intern was said

3. Article by Howard Kurtz, from the *Washington Post* D p1 Oct. 21, 1998. Copyright © 1998 the Washington Post Writers Group. Reprinted with permission.

to have told Linda Tripp on the tapes: "Lewinsky described Clinton and Jordan directing her to testify falsely in the Paula Jones sexual harassment case against the president, according to sources."

That same morning, ABC's Jackie Judd reported on the Lewinsky-Tripp tapes on *Good Morning America*. One source, said Judd, "says Lewinsky is later heard saying Jordan instructed her to lie."

Five days later, also on *Good Morning America*, *Newsweek's* Evan Thomas said: "We understand from very reliable sources that when Monica Lewinsky was talking to Tripp . . . Lewinsky did say some very damaging stuff about Jordan; that Jordan said, 'Deny it, say it never happened,' that he had basically told her to lie. Now, that doesn't mean Jordan did do that."

That same week, *Time* magazine said: "Lewinsky reportedly told Tripp that Jordan said to her, 'They can't prove anything. . . . Your answer is, it didn't happen, it wasn't me.' If that turns out to be true, Jordan could be on the hook for suborning perjury and obstruction of justice."

Starr's report last month made no mention of alleged obstruction of justice by Jordan, and Lewinsky testified that no one had told her to lie under oath. In a taped conversation with Tripp, the strongest thing she said about Jordan is "what he has showed me is there's no way to get caught in perjury in a situation like this."

The ultimate source here appears to be Tripp, who told investigators and perhaps others, who in turn told reporters what Lewinsky had supposedly said about Jordan. According to summaries of Tripp's first interview with investigators, she said that "Vernon Jordan told Lewinsky to lie" and that when Lewinsky expressed concern about perjury, Jordan offered "words to the effect, 'It never happened.'"

Karen DeYoung, the *Post's* assistant managing editor for national news, said that "if the *Post* was misled, the independent counsel was misled" by Tripp's interview with investigators. "The basic question is whether it is legitimate for us to report lines of inquiry the prosecutor is pursuing without having access to the primary information. . . . I think it is legitimate. When we find out otherwise, we have an obligation to report that, which I believe we did."

In hindsight, said DeYoung, "it certainly would have been more accurate to have said Tripp told the FBI one of the tapes contained Lewinsky describing Jordan telling her to lie." But, she said, the paper had no way of knowing this at the time.

Robin Sproul, ABC's Washington bureau chief, said the network's sources had "mischaracterized" Lewinsky's comments. "Based on the two unrelated sources we had, we were confident we had a straight-ahead account," she said,

> *"The basic question is whether it is legitimate for us to report lines of inquiry the prosecutor is pursuing without having access to the primary information."*

adding that Jordan and his attorney had declined to comment to ABC.

Said *Newsweek's* Thomas: "We reported what we knew then and we were careful to qualify it as what we were hearing, and we've reported since then on what the Starr report did show."

The committee also examined coverage of the famous "talking points" that Lewinsky gave Tripp, urging her to deny knowledge of any extramarital affair involving Clinton. The issue first surfaced in Michael Isikoff's Jan. 22 *Newsweek* report: "Starr believes that Lewinsky did not write them herself. He is investigating whether the instructions came from Jordan or other friends of the president."

Eight months later, the Starr report did not challenge Lewinsky's testimony that she had written the talking points herself. Along the way, though, journalists said the chief suspect was White House aide Bruce Lindsey; others aimed even higher.

On Feb. 2, *Time* reported that "potentially the most damaging questions for Lindsey will concern the list of 'talking points' that Lewinsky allegedly gave Linda Tripp. . . . The origins of the talking points remain a big mystery, but Starr may have good reason to press Lindsey under oath."

On Feb. 4, NBC's Claire Shipman said: "Sources in Starr's office and close to Linda Tripp say they believe the instructions came from the White House. If true, that could help support a case of obstruction of justice."

On Feb. 23, Fox News cited sources as saying that Starr's team was "considering the possibility that President Clinton helped Monica Lewinsky write the so-called talking points memo."

On May 18, the *Washington Times* reported that "Mr. Starr, according to lawyers and others close to the grand jury probe, wants to know what White House deputy counsel Bruce R. Lindsey and senior aide Sidney Blumenthal know about the source of the summary, or talking points . . . which prosecutors are convinced was not written by Miss Lewinsky."

On June 17, CNBC's Chris Matthews said that "the person who may have given her the talking points may in fact have been the person who had the closest relationship with her, and that's the president."

Now, of course, the press has moved on.

Celebrity Journalists[4]

It's part of Watergate's legacy: a highly paid, star-studded media elite. That's good for a handful of journalists, but is it good for journalism?

Two journalists are playing golf at a country club in Maryland. One man, a *Washington Post* columnist who also has his own radio show and appears on local television, can barely tee off without someone interrupting him to pay homage. By virtue of his multimedia exposure, the *Post*'s Tony Kornheiser is a local celebrity.

"It was hilarious," recalls Kornheiser's golfing partner, *Post* editor Bob Woodward. "Everyone came up to him: 'Tony, I listen to your show.' 'I love this.' 'I love that.' 'What do you think about this?' 'What do you think about that?' No one ever came up to me."

Woodward, as some may recall, is somewhat famous in his own right. He and his reporting partner at the time, Carl Bernstein, brought down a president. While the work of other journalists contributed to President Richard M. Nixon's resignation in 1974, it was "Woodstein" who relentlessly pursued the bungled break-in at the Watergate complex in Washington, D.C., 25 years ago.

The Watergate affair changed journalism in many ways, not the least of which was by launching the era of the journalist as celebrity. Woodward and Bernstein, portrayed, respectively, by Robert Redford and Dustin Hoffman in the movie *All the President's Men*, were pioneers in the now widespread phenomenon in which a handful of wealthy, glamorous journalists are as famous, if not more famous, than the people they cover. "Celebrity journalists," a phrase coined in 1986 by James Fallows, abound these days, on television and in print. *People* magazine writes about them. *Vanity Fair* offers up flattering profiles. Their names appear in gossip columns and on society pages. When they come to small towns simply doing their jobs, their arrival can become front page news.

We know when they wed (witness the union of Garry Trudeau and Jane Pauley), when they become parents (Connie Chung and Maury Povich's struggles with infertility and eventual adoption captivated *People* magazine readers) and when they get divorced (Peter Jennings and Kati Marton).

4. Article by Alicia C. Shepard, from the *American Journalism Review* p26–31 Sep. 1997. Copyright © 1997 *American Journalism Review*. Reprinted with permission.

"A celebrity journalist is a journalist whose nose has risen above the wall for various reasons," former *Washington Post* executive editor (and celebrity journalist) Ben Bradlee said at a Freedom Forum seminar on Watergate and Celebrity Journalism in June. "Generally the story has taken him or her there. The first thing you can say about it is it exists, and to recognize that it exists is important. The second thing you can say is that, without television, we could write up a storm and sell a million papers a day on it, but that won't get you to be a celebrity journalist except on your own block. The third thing is it's not all bad. It sure as hell isn't all good, but it isn't all bad. It opens a lot of doors."

When Arthur Kent covered the Persian Gulf War for NBC, he became known as the "Scud Stud." Everyone remembers CNN war correspondent nonpareil Peter Arnett broadcasting live from Iraq with bombs bursting around him. And this summer more has been printed about CNN anchor Bernard Shaw's appearances in the movies *The Lost World* and *Contact* than about anything he's done as a journalist.

A celebrity, writes Daniel J. Boorstin, historian and former head of the Library of Congress, "is a person who is known for his 'well-knownness.'" And, he adds in an interview, "journalists are the creators of well-knownness. In the process of creating well-knownness for others, it's not surprising that some of them become celebrities too. It's inevitable."

Few journalists embrace the celebrity label. Woodward scoffs at the notion that he's one. But that's not how the public sees it. The public reads about journalists dining at the White House, inviting Colin Powell over for dinner, sending their kids to school with Chelsea Clinton, playing tennis with presidential assistants, partying with Hollywood stars at affairs like the White House Correspondents Dinner, receiving mind-boggling fees for hour-long speaking engagements and spouting off on TV and radio on subjects they know little or nothing about. And while the media elite is a tiny slice of the profession, it plays a major role in shaping the public's negative perception of the press.

> *"The public feels that journalists are too aggressive in the way they play their watchdog role, and they are doing it not because they are seeking the truth but to advance their careers."*

"The public feels that journalists are too aggressive in the way they play their watchdog role, and they are doing it not because they are seeking the truth but to advance their careers," says Andrew Kohut, director of the Pew Research Center for the People & the Press. "The notion that journalists were of the people, as was the case 30 or 40 years ago, is no longer the case because of the rise of celebrity journalism. I don't think this is the issue that most hurts journalism, but it's one of a cluster of things that has eroded the public confidence in the press."

Adds journalism reformer Fallows, now editor of *U.S. News & World Report*, "I don't think I'd put [celebrity journalism] on the top five list of major problems for journalism right now. By definition, it only affects an elite. But it is a problem because it aggravates other sources of people being mad at us—and therefore not listening to what we say or do."

Most media celebrities hail from the world of television: Peter Jennings, Ted Koppel, Sam Donaldson, Cokie Roberts, Diane Sawyer and Barbara Walters of ABC; Katie Couric (recently on the cover of the glossy *George* magazine), Tom Brokaw, Jane Pauley, Tim Russert and Stone Phillips of NBC; Dan Rather, Ed Bradley and Mike Wallace of CBS; Wolf Blitzer, Bernard Shaw and Judy Woodruff of CNN; Fox's Brit Hume and CNBC's Geraldo Rivera.

These are journalists who have paid their dues. They didn't burst out of the box as celebrities. But there's a new generation of journalists who have become overnight stars. Perhaps the best example is MTV's Tabitha Soren.

"We live in a celebrity culture," says *Newsweek* columnist Eleanor Clift, who herself joined the celebrity roster thanks to her frequent appearances on *The McLaughlin Group.* She adds, "When I received pundit status, it was after 20 years as an anonymous print journalist."

Clift recalls the moment during the Reagan era when she realized that celebrity journalism had become a reality. She and then–ABC White House correspondent Sam Donaldson had covered Jimmy Carter and Ronald Reagan together. "Jimmy Carter held regular press conferences, and there was no need for Sam to shout his questions above everybody else," she said at the Freedom Forum session. Reagan, on the other hand, was elusive, and as a television reporter, Donaldson needed footage of the president.

"And so Sam adopted this persona of yelling the question at Ronald Reagan that inevitably made the big news of the day," Clift continued. "When we would travel, I began to notice that the public was as interested in seeing Sam Donaldson as they were in seeing Ronald Reagan, and they would yell after him, and they would want his autograph. That was my first notion that reporters could rise above their peers and gain this."

Donaldson, who says he didn't try to become a celebrity, says such fame has a downside. "This affects my reporting," he says. "I'm very sensitive to the idea that I run around promoting myself as a big deal. When I go out with a camera crew, I find people in the crowd come running up to me asking me for my autograph. This doesn't do me any good. Do you think that my colleagues in the press corps think that's wonderful? I often miss what I should be hearing when I'm fending off well-meaning people."

The notoriety is such, says Donaldson, that when he tried to sneak into Biloxi, Mississippi, in 1989 to interview the mayor, who had been avoiding him, Donaldson himself became the story. "I got off the plane and started walking through the terminal," he says. "The front page of the paper said: 'Sam Donaldson is coming to town.'"

So what makes someone a celebrity journalist, and how does one obtain that lofty status?

"A celebrity journalist is someone who is famous for who they are instead of what they report," says media analyst S. Robert Lichter, director of the Center for Media and Public Affairs. "There's a spectrum going from journalists who are unknown to the pure celebrities whose journalism is irrelevant, like Geraldo Rivera. There are clearly celebrity journalists who are good reporters but whose celebrity is based upon [television exposure]. Dan Rather is both a celebrity and a good journalist."

John Carmody, who has written a TV column for the *Washington Post* for 20 years, says the key is "your willingness to become a celebrity. There's a lot of very solid journalists in television who keep their mouths shut and don't let their personal lives get into anything and don't sit still for interviews. But some of these people won't take the money and shut up. They have to appear on every panel and show up on all the talk shows."

> *"A celebrity journalist is someone who is famous for who they are instead of what they report."*

At the Freedom Forum seminar, *Baltimore Sun* columnist Jules Witcover pointed out that celebrity journalists come in two very distinct flavors: those who, like Bob Woodward, earn that status from exemplary work, and those who become famous simply because they appear on television.

Lichter cites the contrasting approaches of Woodward and Bernstein. "Bob Woodward," says Lichter, "is more of the old school, like Nelly Bly and Richard Harding Davis. They were journalists who, by virtue of breaking enormous stories, became public figures."

Bernstein, Lichter notes, became a public figure thanks to his Watergate coverage and then chose a different route. "Look at Carl Bernstein, who became one of the beautiful people. Where are the important works of journalism from Carl Bernstein in recent years? Woodward remained the traditional hard-working journalist, whereas Bernstein became part of the celebrity culture."

Woodward has tried to shun celebrityhood by not going on every talk show that invites him, speaking publicly only on subjects he's written books about or is reporting on. He's not a fan of "food fight" television. "I think it's a waste of time to sit around and talk about something you don't know anything about," he says.

Asked if he considers himself a celebrity, he responds quickly: "I sure don't." Long pause; Woodward clearly is uncomfortable. "I really love reporting. It's one of the great jobs." So he continues working as an editor at the *Post* and writing books.

Bernstein, on the other hand, never shied away from the glitz. "After Nixon's resignation and *All the President's Men*," Michael Kilian wrote in 1991, "Bernstein went on to an unsuccessful career as a TV Network bureau chief and correspondent, but a lasting one as a professional celebrity."

Bernstein's celebrity status was enhanced when he married author and screenwriter Nora Ephron, who later skewered him for his unfaithfulness in her book *Heartburn*. (Jack Nicholson played Bernstein in the movie.) Bernstein, who has written two books, said he was too busy to be interviewed for this story.

Despite the differences, the Watergate duo together played a major role in launching the current incarnation of the journalist as star. "Woodward and Bernstein seemed to start the trend where there's a lot more interest in the reporter than there ever seemed to be," says Maurine Beasley, who teaches journalism at the University of Maryland. "The publication of their book *All the President's Men* showed the public is more interested in learning about the people who get the news."

But the public has always been fascinated by people who report the news, says Mitchell Stephens, journalism professor at New York University and author of *A History of News*. In the 1930s and 1940s, Walter Winchell, father of the newspaper gossip column, not only made people celebrities but was himself an influential and well-known figure. The focus shifted, however, from print journalists to their television counterparts as America became a TV-saturated culture.

"I see no evidence that journalists are better known than they were in the past. . . ," Stephens says. "We look at the journalism stars of our own era—Peter Jennings, Geraldo, Woodward and Bernstein—and we think, 'Oh my God, there's no one who was ever that famous before.' But our historical understanding of journalism is very limited."

Until the television era, print journalists were the celebrities. Figures like Richard Harding Davis, Horace Greeley, Nelly Bly, Ida Tarbell, Dorothy Thompson, William Randolph Hearst, E.W. Scripps and Joseph Pulitzer were some of the giants in the field. "Because of their power, Hearst, Pulitzer and Scripps were major celebrities of their time," Stephens says. "One of the great ironies of American history is Hearst is better known as *Citizen Kane* than as the person who printed one out of every four Sunday newspapers Americans read."

But for a time, most journalists remained in the shadows. "We went through a period around the turn of the century to mid-century when reporters were supposed to be relatively anonymous unless they were columnists," Beasley says. "It was a period when it was a big deal for a journalist to get a byline. Bylines came into general use in the last 20 to 25 years as newspapers have tried to personalize their approach more. When I went to journalism school in the '50s, it was not an accepted practice to get a byline."

But with television, the celebrity machine began to crank up, albeit slowly: TV reporters often were treated like second-class citizens until the early to mid-1960s, according to Lichter. But then came the dramatic footage of the civil rights movement and later the war in Vietnam, and journalists began to take a more prominent role.

"In the 1970s, there was a creation of a star system in journalism the same way there became a star system in the movies at the beginning of the century," Lichter says. He adds that the era of celebrity journalism may have officially begun in 1976, "when Barbara Walters became the first million-dollar anchor on ABC. A million dollars a year was unheard of. I still personally remember the big flap because she had a hairdresser."

Television anchors may not have had million-dollar contracts and personal hairdressers in the 1970s, but it's the norm now, along with agents and chauffeur-driven cars. On July 23, the *Washington Post* reported that NBC anchor Tom Brokaw had signed a five-year contract. "Network sources said today that Brokaw is 'very happy' with the deal, which is expected to put him in the $7 million-a-year salary bracket, along with other media superstars like ABC's Peter Jennings and Diane Sawyer," wrote the *Washington Post*'s Carmody.

The phenomenon also was fueled by the advent of television newsmagazines, *60 Minutes* in particular. Journalists began appearing in mini-news dramas, not just as reporters on the sidelines, but as the good guys going after the bad guys. As the old line goes, there were few sentences in the English language more terrifying than the words, "Mike Wallace is at the door."

"One thing is clear: If you become a media celebrity, the competitors are going to start to put you under a microscope," says John Lavine, director of NMC, the newspaper management center at Northwestern University. Two recent examples underscore his point.

In this summer's sci-fi drama, *Contact*, in which actress Jodie Foster attempts to make contact with aliens from another planet, CNN plays a starring role. CNN's presence is not so surprising, given that the all-news network is owned by Time Warner, the corporate parent of the Warner Bros. studio that made the movie. In all, 13 CNN reporters and anchors appear on real CNN sets giving what seem like realistic updates on fictional contact with the planet Vega.

CNN anchor Judy Woodruff, a 26-year veteran of TV news, was not asked to appear in the movie, but says she wouldn't have anyway. "I'm bothered by the notion that journalists can be doing their job telling stories truthfully," she says, "and on the other hand be acting. But," she adds, "I respect their right to do it."

Woodruff, like many veteran reporters, says she's a purist and likes to stay out of stories. She thinks that journalism is under attack on so many fronts, and has enough problems with dwindling credibility, that reporters should stick to their basic mission, reporting on the increasingly complicated world we live in. Others have said it's confusing for the public to see well-known CNN faces on the screen making up the news. "The media's reporting on the world's reaction sounds very much like real CNN journalism," wrote movie critic Jeff Millar in the *Houston Chronicle* in July.

Says Valerie DeBenedette, a freelance health reporter based in the suburbs of New York City, "I think it does hurt all journalism if someone could flip through their cable channels and see Bernard Shaw with a CNN logo on HBO and on CNN simultaneously and not know which was the fiction, even if the confusion only lasted a few seconds. And when *Contact* hits cable, that could happen."

Tom Johnson, CNN's chairman and CEO, bowed to the criticism and quickly imposed an ethics policy in July prohibiting all CNN news staffers from appearing in movies, except for Larry King (who "has never pretended to be a journalist," says Johnson). ABC, NBC and CBS bar journalists from screen appearances.

Shortly before *Contact* debuted, CNN found itself embroiled in another contretemps when correspondent Jonathan Karl, 29, appeared in a Visa ad in June. After the network was criticized for allowing the New York–based general assignment reporter to star in the ad, Johnson moved to avoid a recurrence. He wrote in a memo, "CNN has a strict policy that its journalists are prohibited from appearing in any commercial advertisements except promotional spots on behalf of CNN itself." Karl was not punished because he had received permission from a senior executive who has not been identified.

In addition to Hollywood and Madison Avenue, magazines such as *People, Redbook, George* and *Vanity Fair* reinforce the notion that journalists are stars by frequently carrying articles about them. In recent years *Vanity Fair* has profiled CNN correspondent Christiane Amanpour, *New York Times* columnist Maureen Dowd, the *New Republic's* Leon Wieseltier and former *Washington Post* reporter and author Elsa Walsh, Bob Woodward's wife, who is described on the cover as "Bob Woodward's Other Writing Partner."

Asked why *Vanity Fair* writes about people who are supposed to be reporting the news, not making it, executive editor Elise O'Shaughnessy replies that television journalists are celebrities by virtue of their looks and the money they make, citing the interest in "anchors who [are] fabulous looking giving you the news, whether it's Peter Jennings or Diane Sawyer."

Journalism became more interesting to the readers of *Vanity Fair* when journalists started becoming part of the elite, she says. Having Redford and Hoffman play Woodward and Bernstein added a touch of glamour to the once-gray field.

"It used to be a trade, and somehow it became a profession," O'Shaughnessy says. "You had a lot of Ivy League graduates going into journalism. So the socioeconomic makeup changed, and it became an elite profession and of interest to the elite. The incredible salaries in TV news really begin to blur the line between entertainment and news. They get paid so well because people tune in to see Diane Sawyer because she's a personality in herself. So is Barbara Walters. Barbara Walters is as much news as the people she interviews."

So is the advent of the celebrity journalist a serious problem for the profession?

"What we want to make judgments about is what kind of journalists are they? How credible are they?

"I'm sure celebrity journalism contributes to the public mistrust," says Robert Giles, former publisher of the *Detroit News* who is executive director of the Freedom Forum's Media Studies Center in New York City. "I think the public sees some of these people as having large egos not unlike those in show business. So they become seen in the same context as other entertainment figures, as celebrities. And I think that's antithetical to the role of journalism. We all know who the cast of characters are who are making speeches and getting fees, and when there is an event, they are as much a part of the event as the event themselves." When they were in Hong Kong recently, he adds, "Tom Brokaw and Dan Rather were celebrities."

But can they help being celebrities? Brokaw has worked for NBC for 31 years. He may be known for his well-knownness, but he's also known as a competent, reliable journalist. It's what a journalist does with his or her celebrity that enhances or hurts the profession. CBS' Mike Wallace, for example, has chosen to use his well-knownness to try to find ways to make journalism more accountable to its audience, pushing for establishment of a national news council . . . .

"Simply the fact that someone has become well known isn't unto itself either wrong or bad," says Lavine. "What we want to make judgments about is what kind of journalists are they? How credible are they? How much energy do they put into maintaining their credibility and caring about the public's confidence?"

If you remain true to the craft and don't exploit your well-knownness, Woodward says, celebrity is unimportant. "I'm not saying celebrity journalism doesn't exist," he says. "I'm saying it shouldn't exist. It inhibits the work, and reporting takes time. And that time is not spent expounding on the theory of the Clinton presidency on television. It's finding out what they really are doing."

Celebrity status can be good for journalism, says Fallows. "The mere fact of books coming out from Tom Wolfe, David Halberstam or Bob Woodward is news because of interest in the author as much as the subject," Fallows says. "People watch or listen to radio or TV shows because they enjoy the approach—even the timbre—of certain well-known correspondents. This is actually good for journalism. The people are well-known based mainly on something in their work, and their renown gets people to pay attention to the news."

But when they use their renown simply to promote themselves, celebrity journalists can't be good for journalism. Recently, *Time* magazine asked high school students in South Lake Tahoe, California, whom they thought they could trust. The results: parents first, journalists dead last.

"Celebrity journalism has certainly contributed to the problem of trust in journalists," says Diane M. Dusick, head of the communications department at San Bernardino Valley College in California. "It's very sad," Dusick adds. "When I was growing up in the 1960s and 1970s, journalists were the be all and end all. Their job was to seek truth. Now they look for the big story that will get me attention, and the truth comes second."

The sad truth is that the elite journalists who appear in movies and high-profile magazines don't represent the profession as a whole, yet they command so much attention that it can seem that way. They overshadow people like Judy Woodruff or Bob Woodward or Jules Witcover, who are known but don't trade on their journalistic credentials to enhance themselves; and on the countless other journalists who do their jobs well on the sidelines.

Thirteen years ago Charles Bailey, then editor of *Minneapolis Star-Tribune*, presciently predicted the trouble this small segment of the media might cause. Bailey urged journalists to do something to "keep the privileged few from giving the rest of the news business a bad name." That hasn't proven to be an easy task.

III. Spotlight on Ethics

Editors' Introduction

In the face of spiraling competition throughout all facets of the media, there has been an increased pressure on news organizations to release their product in as quick and timely a manner as possible. But as newspapers, magazines, TV programs and even web sites struggle to "scoop" each other, media critics, along with the public, have begun to sharpen their focus on the quality of reporting that is being performed. Recently, there have been several instances of high-profile, investigative news stories which have proven controversial not only in their accusations, but in the tactics used to obtain the information supporting those charges. As such, a widespread re-evaluation of journalistic ethics is being undertaken with an emphasis on how stories are researched as well as how traditional reporting values are translated onto the Internet.

One of the most recent controversial episodes in newspaper reporting occurred at the *Cincinnati Enquirer*, where a story was released in May 1998 that accused the Chiquita banana company of improper business conduct. The reporter, Mike Gallagher, used, as part of his investigative material, hundreds of hours of company voice mail messages, and when the story broke, Chiquita immediately accused Gallagher of obtaining the messages through illegal means. After an investigation revealed that Gallagher had obtained the messages himself, the *Cincinnati Enquirer* quickly fired him, paid $10 million to Chiquita, and issued a public apology on the front page of its paper.

The first article in this section, "Rotten Banana," by Bruce Shapiro, is a detailed look at the accusations Gallagher fired at Chiquita in his report and the scope of their implication. However, the article stands apart from most others on the subject, in that it does not specifically and solely attack Gallagher for his investigative tactics. Instead Shapiro takes issue with the popular portrait of Gallagher as criminal, questioning whether his efforts, while misguided, actually uncovered unjust practices that deserve our acknowledgment. Shapiro argues that more public attention should be directed towards Chiquita's questionable business style rather than Gallagher's research methods, and that in journalism, with a story of this magnitude, sometimes the end does justify the means.

Another news story that garnered attention for its accusations, albeit implied in this instance, was Gary Webb's 1996 "Dark Alliance" series in the *San Jose Mercury News*. The story examined the connection between Nicaraguan contra supporters and the import of cocaine into the U.S. during the mid-1980s. According to two Nicaraguans who are heavily quoted in the articles, the imported drugs were sold to dealers in the mostly African-American South-Central section of Los Angeles who, in turn, made it into crack for re-selling. The money raised by this, according to Webb, funded the CIA-supported contras, and while Webb did not openly accuse the CIA of instigating an inevitable crack epidemic in urban black communities, it was strongly implied in his series that the CIA played a significant role in the affair. With their interest sparked by Webb's apparent unraveling of a CIA cover-up, newspapers across the nation began to pick apart the story, and ultimately found several holes.

In "The Web That Gary Spun," Alicia C. Shepard takes a look at the missing pieces in Webb's puzzle and asks the question, Did Gary Webb go too far in his reporting? Shepard examines the effect the story had on the black community, segments of which had already believed in a government conspiracy concerning the advent of crack, and were now stirred into action, demanding an investigation into the matter. In addition, the author looks at how credence in the series of articles was further buoyed when they appeared on the Internet, opening the doors to a whole new audience and offering a lasting, though still questionable, report on a governmental cover-up.

Television news reporting is also not without its share of criticism of late. One of the most hotly debated instances of questionable journalism occurred in 1992 when reporters from ABC's *Prime Time Live* posed as employees at Food Lion in order to secretly film deceptive food presentation practices. When the news program aired hidden-camera shots of Food Lion employees repackaging fish and attempting to alter the appearance of aging chicken, the supermarket's reputation and sales felt the blow. In retaliation, the company filed a hefty lawsuit against ABC and the controversial trial and subsequent outcome (Food Lion awarded $5.5. million in damages) opened the floodgates to fresh discourse on the journalistic propriety of certain TV news practices.

In "Beyond ABC v. Food Lion," by Walter Goodman, the undercover tactics used by *Prime Time Live*'s reporters are evaluated. Goodman examines the questions that emerge from the employment of surreptitious filming in television journalism, and addresses the notion that such practices reflect a desire for high ratings rather than ethical reporting. The author concludes that while the news program did "play up" the sinister nature of its findings, the reporters' accusations were well grounded and the network's methods proved professionally sound. Goodman ponders the impact the landmark case will have on journalism itself, and whether future reporters will be too intimidated to pursue investigative research, though they might be performing a valuable public service with their work.

In fact, the Internet, and the influx of information that this medium has made available, is a rising topic in media circles today. How information is presented on Web sites, and how those sites report news involving the corporate giants who play a major role on the Internet, e.g. Microsoft, are major concerns of media watchdogs.

Finally, in another exploration of the meaning of journalistic integrity in cyberspace, Scott Rosenberg offers the article "How do you retract a story online?" Here, the author explores how various newspapers, once they have issued an apology and retraction in print, handle the story's presence on the Internet. Some, such as the *Cincinnati Enquirer*, choose to simply remove all traces (except for their apology) of the Chiquita story on their web site. Others, such as *Time*, have decided to keep retracted stories available to users, but to implement a feature that gives readers their apology for the story first before they can go any further. Rosenberg takes a look at how this varied approach to online retractions creates a unique dilemma for web sites, and offers his view on what solution would work best to protect the future of online journalism.

Rotten Banana[1]

While the media race to condemn the *Cincinnati Enquirer* reporter who broke into Chiquita's voice mail, they're forgetting who the real villain is.

It seems just the latest of the season's media scandals: A *Cincinnati Enquirer* reporter allegedly broke into the Chiquita banana company's executive voice mail system. Yet amid the summer's epidemic of hand wringing over fabricated quotes and questionable stories, the fate of *Cincinnati Enquirer* reporter Mike Gallagher is the one journalistic controversy that really matters.

For one thing, there's the substance of the investigative reporting at issue. Not a single major story on Gallagher's firing has bothered to examine the paper's original allegations about Chiquita, a company whose brutal and autocratic operations once inspired the term "banana republic." Even more disturbing, a reporter may soon go to jail as a consequence of investigative stories that seem 100 percent accurate.

The background has been widely reported. On May 3, the Gannett-owned *Enquirer* published a massive package of stories on Cincinnati-based Chiquita Brands International, a firm headed by Republican mega-donor Carl Lindner. The series, by reporters Mike Gallagher and Cameron McWhirter, was based in part on hundreds of hours of corporate voice mail message tapes acquired by Gallagher. Gallagher and McWhirter are seasoned and respected investigative journalists, not *New Republic* whiz kids blowing smoke about the sexual fantasies of UPS drivers [See John Corry, "Hack Haven," pp. 115–118].

Gallagher had told his editors—and his editors said in print—that he obtained the tapes from a high-ranking Chiquita executive with supervisory access to the voice mail system. However, according to a suit filed last week by Chiquita, it was Gallagher himself, with help from still-unnamed Chiquita insiders, who broke into the company's voice mail system. And if this wasn't bad enough, Gallagher committed the unpardonable sin of stupidity: He allegedly called into Chiquita's voice mail system over and over again from his home phone, as if Caller ID hadn't been invented. Chiquita CEO Steven Warshaw called

---

1. Article by Bruce Shapiro. This article first appeared on July 8, 1998, in *Salon*, an online magazine, at *http://www.salonmagazine.com*. An online version remains in the *Salon* archives. Reprinted with permission.

it "an old-fashioned burglary, no different from breaking and entering." The corporation exercised its considerable political influence in Cincinnati to secure the appointment of a special prosecutor and grand jury for a criminal investigation. And the *Enquirer*'s editors, publisher and corporate bosses at Gannett, angry at Gallagher's deception and worried about their own legal liability, fired the reporter and paid Chiquita $10 million. For three consecutive days last week the *Enquirer* ran a stunning front-page retraction, denouncing Gallagher's "theft" of "privileged, confidential and proprietary information" and apologizing for creating a "false and misleading picture of Chiquita's business practices."

A "false and misleading picture"? The *Enquirer*'s lawyers may have found it necessary to bend over fast and far. But in fact the "Chiquita Secrets Revealed" series presents a damning, carefully documented array of charges, most of them "untainted" by those purloined executive voice mails. Gallagher's and McWhirter's allegations are largely based on old-fashioned reportorial legwork: land records in Central America, interviews with environmental scientists and trade unions, lawsuit records, leaked corporate memoranda and the reporters' own visits to workers' villages and camps.

Consider:

- In Honduras, Guatemala and Colombia, Chiquita "secretly controls dozens of supposedly independent banana companies," the articles charge, evading laws limiting foreign companies' ownership of farms by setting up local fronts for the corporation's under-the-table investments. One Honduran lawyer who works for Chiquita openly told the reporters that the corporation was trying to "hide its assets" to evade ownership restrictions, to "get rid of its Honduran labor union" and protect itself from "lawsuits and child labor law violations."

- Throughout much of Latin America, McWhirter and Gallagher charge, Chiquita subsidiaries spray plantations with highly toxic pesticides banned in the United States and Europe, in direct violation of an agreement with environmentalists. They uncovered the autopsy report of an 18-year-old agricultural worker at a Chiquita subsidiary in Costa Rica who died after working in a recently sprayed field. "He didn't have any experience in this kind of job and he wasn't using any protective gear like gloves and mask either," one of the young man's co-workers had told Costa Rican authorities. The company refuses to allow independent scientific researchers to study the impact of pesticides on its plantations; workers are exposed to pesticides without protective clothing, and runoff from Chiquita pesticides contaminates workers' drinking water.

- Chiquita security guards, according to the *Enquirer*

series, are widely accused of using "brute force to enforce their authority on plantations operated or controlled by Chiquita. In an internationally controversial case, Chiquita called in the Honduran military to enforce a court order to evict residents of a farm village; the village was bulldozed and villagers run out at gunpoint."

- McWhirter and Gallagher also detailed the precarious economic condition of workers on Chiquita plantations.

To repeat, none of these charges—none—depend on Chiquita's hacked voice mails. The series does present one allegation to which the voice mails are central: that company executives bribed Colombian officials to gain use of a government warehouse. And there, the voice mail messages Gallagher recorded, legally or not, were deeply revealing of Chiquita's mind-set. "We can only fire him with cause because of his involvement in the Colombian problem if we file a criminal charge against him with Colombian authorities," the series quoted company lawyer David Hills saying of another executive. "Clearly we would not want to do that because we would be implicating ourselves." Another message caught company vice chairman Keith Lindner suggesting the company muscle Panama's foreign minister out of a European Union trade mission deemed not in Chiquita's best interests.

Chiquita's top officials, as the reporters note over and over again, declined numerous offers to respond or to be interviewed. Since the "Secrets Revealed" packaged appeared, Chiquita CEO Warshaw has claimed "very little is accurate," but he has yet to challenge a single specific fact or quotation—including his own executives' incriminating voices.

Amid all these serious charges of lawbreaking and exploitation on a transnational scale, it is Mike Gallagher—fired, sued and awaiting a grand jury subpoena—who is being written about as a criminal. Certainly his mistake gave Chiquita all the ammunition it needed to torpedo the whole exhaustive series—and possibly to halt a Securities and Exchange Commission investigation, which the *Enquirer* reported had commenced based on the tapes.

But while it's easy to consign Gallagher to the journalistic pillory, it also might be worth asking why an experienced, idealistic investigative journalist might have illegally broken into a corporate voice mail system and then lied to his editors about it. In fact there are plausible professional explanations for both. It's possible he misled his editors about the tapes not just to hide his own hack work, but to protect his real sources at Chiquita, the individual or individuals who escorted him into the voice mail system in the first place; mistrust between editors and reporters is a common enough feature of newsroom life.

And while the electronic equivalent of pilfering incriminating documents may run afoul of the Scout's Code of Honor,

Covert leaking of proprietary information from inside corporate sources is basic to investigative reporting.

corporate criminals are not notably cooperative with above-board journalistic inquiry. Covert leaking of proprietary information from inside corporate sources is basic to investigative reporting going all the way back to Ida Tarbell's muckraking classic *History of the Standard Oil Company.* If Edward R. Murrow was unwilling to trespass on private property, his classic documentary *Factories in the Field* could not have been filmed. If a young Geraldo Rivera had been unwilling to invade the privacy of a psychiatric ward, patients at Willowbrook State Hospital in New York would still be living in filth and degradation. Mike Gallagher is hardly the first reporter to decide that the larger stakes in confirming a story—in this case a story alleging bribery of foreign officials, the poisoning and exploitation of workers and the subversion of countries' laws—dictated some comparatively modest legal transgression of his own.

There's far more at stake in Cincinnati than one reporter's lousy judgment or blitzed career. Civil liberties types and journalism advocacy organizations, not wanting to be seen as condoning voice mail hacking, have kept largely silent about Gallagher's impending criminal prosecution. Yet if Gallagher goes to jail for theft or Chiquita wins its trespass-defamation-conspiracy suit, corporations all over the country will be emboldened to use notions of intellectual property as a club against aggressive investigative reporting. What's the practical difference between one reporter's convincing an executive to provide voice mail and another to provide a ream of documents? Both involve what the *Enquirer*'s apology called "privileged, confidential and proprietary information." Both involve reporters' treading a very blurry line between leak and theft.

Sure, Mike Gallagher's tactics raise thorny ethical questions for information-age reporters. But Gallagher's crime—if a crime it was—pales by comparison with Chiquita's documented rap sheet. Meanwhile Chiquita's heavy-handed suppression of the *Enquirer* story poses a serious threat to all investigative reporting on corporations—and by extension, to the values of the First Amendment.

The Web That Gary Spun[2]

The awards dinner in San Francisco last November promised to be an awkward evening. Some worried what the reaction would be when the "Journalist of the Year" award was presented. How would the crowd of 240 behave when investigative reporter Gary Webb of the *San Jose Mercury News*, author of 1996's most controversial piece of journalism, received the crystal obelisk?

Webb's three-day series in August focused on two Nicaraguans who said they had imported and sold drugs during the 1980s to raise money for the CIA-backed contras, struggling at the time to overthrow Nicaragua's leftist Sandinista regime. The articles said that Oscar Danilo Blandon, Norwin Meneses and a Los Angeles drug dealer, "Freeway" Ricky Ross, had started the first mass market for crack in South-Central Los Angeles, ultimately triggering a nationwide crack epidemic.

The series, "Dark Alliance," also gave the impression—although it did not flatly assert—that the CIA was involved in crack cocaine's spread. "You can't read our series any other way than to suggest the CIA, at a minimum, turned a blind eye toward drug dealing in the United States," says Phil Yost, the *Mercury News*'s chief editorial writer and an outspoken critic of his paper's high-profile series.

When the 20-member board of the northern California chapter of the Society of Professional Journalists met in August, it was searching for outstanding local work by a single journalist. Webb, who had spent 15 months on his blockbuster series, was an obvious choice. But the board's unanimous vote took place before Webb's articles were subjected to withering criticism in early October.

Skeptics questioned the wisdom of giving Webb the award after the *Washington Post*, *Los Angeles Times* and *New York Times* had sharply challenged the series' findings. But the chapter decided to press ahead. The task of presenting the award fell to emcee Dave McElhatton, a well-known anchor for CBS' San Francisco affiliate KPIX, who handled it with characteristic aplomb.

"Elements of the *Mercury News* series and presentation are open to dispute, as are criticisms of Webb's stories," McElhatton told the audience of journalists on November 12. "A full airing is necessary and good for us all. But the chapter is convinced that the best journalism is that which is not afraid to venture into controversial areas of overwhelming national significance."

---

2. Article by Alicia C. Shepard, from the *American Journalism Review* p34–39 Jan./Feb. 1997. Copyright © 1997 *American Journalism Review*. Reprinted with permission.

When Webb accepted the award, he turned to his boss, executive editor Jerry Ceppos, who has borne much criticism. Webb told Ceppos of a bomber pilot who said that the flak is most intense when you are over the target.

The reporter received a standing ovation from virtually everyone in the audience, with the conspicuous exception of those at the two *San Francisco Examiner* tables. "I'm with the *Examiner*, and I did not stand because to stand would have shown my approval and respect," says managing editor/News Sharon Rosenhause. "You don't normally give an award to someone as 'Journalist of the Year' when there are all these questions and concerns."

The questions and concerns over Webb's story are myriad. Is what he wrote true? Was his reporting responsible? Did he selectively use information that backed up his thesis while ignoring evidence contradicting it? Was the series edited with enough care? Why didn't the executive editor read the entire series before it was published? Was any consideration given to the effect that the series might have on the African-American community, where many have long believed the crack plague is part of a government conspiracy?

After the *Mercury News* series ran, it was quickly spun in the retelling. Black talk-show hosts and listeners, the black media and the alternative press touted the story as proof that the CIA allowed the U.S.–backed contras to deal drugs in America and use the profits to buy weapons, blithely ignoring the damage to the black community. This particular sentence played a significant role in such interpretations: Cocaine "was virtually unobtainable in black neighborhoods before members of the CIA's army brought it into South-Central in the 1980s at bargain basement prices."

There are those—among them some journalists, CIA watchers, conspiracy theorists and black leaders—who argue that, regardless of the series' flaws, Webb has performed a public service by focusing attention on whether the CIA helped set off the crack cocaine epidemic. "Even though we can criticize the *San Jose Mercury News* story, the net effect is that it has generated major coverage of a scandal that really was never fully investigated and fully covered before," said Peter Kornbluh, a senior analyst at the private National Security Archive, in a radio interview.

While the core of Webb's stories may be true, he has been chastised for overselling the story by writing it in a way that would lead reasonable readers to conclude that the CIA was involved in the drug trafficking, referring repeatedly to the "CIA's army." And the series' major premise—that the trio highlighted in his series alone triggered the crack epidemic—has been contradicted by major newspapers.

For his part, Webb told a group of journalism students at the University of California at Berkeley in November that "anybody that read this story would be a fool if they came

away with the conclusion that we said the CIA ran this operation. We were very specific in saying who did what."

Webb stands firmly behind his story, and hints that there is
a part four in the works with "tons more information." He
says he can't control what others are reading into his work.

Webb broke new ground on the 10-year-old story of a con-
tra-cocaine connection. He was able to show how cheap
Colombian cocaine, brought in by Nicaraguans, was sold to a
specific drug dealer in South-Central Los Angeles, who
turned it into crack. "That's an advance," says *Los Angeles
Times* Washington bureau chief Doyle McManus. "I wish
we'd picked up that and pursued it."

Yet by overreaching, the well-respected *Mercury News* hurt
its hard-won credibility and shifted the focus from the
essence of its story to questions about the reporter and the
paper's editing process. Some journalists argue that it was
irresponsible to publish such an incendiary story without
making absolutely sure all claims could be fully supported.

The level of anger among African Americans, many of
whom interpreted the series as conclusive evidence that the
federal government encouraged drug trafficking in their
neighborhoods, was apparent when CIA director John M.
Deutch met with residents of South-Central Los Angeles at a
heated public forum on November 15. Few appeared to be
mollified by Deutch's assertion that the CIA had nothing to
do with drug trafficking and his promise to fully investigate
the affair.

*"If a journalist
thinks a story is
going to have a
big impact, you
better have an
absolutely unim-
peachable
report, and this
one wasn't."*

"The paper, in order to act responsibly, needed to recognize this story was going to have a huge impact, not just on
the black community, but on everyone's faith in the government," says Joann Byrd, who taught ethics at the Poynter
Institute for Media Studies before becoming the *Seattle
Post-Intelligencer*'s editorial page editor. "This was going to
be a terrifically big story. If a journalist thinks a story is
going to have a big impact, you better have an absolutely
unimpeachable report, and this one wasn't."

Some of the harshest criticism has come from *Mercury
News* staffers. "Virtually every claim in the opening para-
graphs has been shown to be, at best, a disputed assertion,"
says editorial writer Yost. "The story takes no account of
contrary evidence. The relationship between the CIA,
drug-runners and black America is a sensitive topic. We have
not served well the cause of getting at the truth; we have
served the cause of creating a sensation." Journalists from
other newspapers have also found fault with Webb's reporting and conclusions. The *Miami Herald*, which, like the *Mercury News*, is owned by Knight-Ridder, decided not to run the
San Jose paper's series because it raised too many red flags.

At the *Mercury News*, concerns about the intellectual honesty of the series and the torrent of negative publicity virtually paralyzed the paper for a brief period last fall. Reporters

who don't like Webb because of his aggressive style, and there are many, are quick to criticize his work. Those sympathetic to Webb's editors are more apt to defend it. "I've been here almost 20 years," says telecommunications reporter Mike Antonucci, "and I haven't ever seen a story touch a nerve internally as much as this one."

The series ran August 18–20. While its allegations were breathtaking, equally impressive were the paper's efforts to place the story and scores of supporting documents on its Web site. Not only could the paper's readers examine the story, hundreds of thousands more could—and did—read it online on its *Mercury Center* site. Yet initially it was largely ignored by network news and major newspapers.

Lori Leibovich, assistant editor of the online magazine *Salon*, asked Webb a month after his series ran why it wasn't picked up by the mainstream media. "By now, journalists have read the series, and they're figuring out how to tell this story in 12 inches because that's what most newspapers have the space to do these days," Webb replied. "Secondly, a lot of newspapers—and TV particularly—they're just [afraid]."

Thanks to the potent combination of talk radio and the Internet, "Dark Alliance" slowly and inexorably attracted national attention.

But while the Old Media weren't interested, the New Media were eating it up. Thanks to the potent combination of talk radio and the Internet, "Dark Alliance" slowly and inexorably attracted national attention.

Black-oriented talk shows in particular played a major part in bringing the series to the fore. "I think talk radio played a very substantial role in energizing audiences on this story," says Bob Ryan, director of Mercury Center. And cyberspace helped build the momentum. "The Internet," says Ryan, "made it easy for the talk radio shows and the alternative press to read the story, process it and pass it on—often with embellishments, interpretations and conclusions not present in the story."

And while the pieces appeared in a northern California newspaper, they resonated powerfully to the south, in South-Central Los Angeles, a prominent victim of crack's carnage. The fiery Rep. Maxine Waters, a California Democrat who represents the area, and other black leaders were outraged. They quickly secured promises of congressional hearings and a CIA investigation into the paper's charges.

Two of the nation's leading newspapers, the *Washington Post* and *Los Angeles Times*, both of which serve large black communities, were besieged with outraged calls. "Why aren't you covering this story?" demanded readers, some of whom accused the papers of being part of a cover-up.

Webb had predicted that the mainstream media would ignore his findings. In an effort to stimulate interest, the paper tried to take advantage of a news peg. It scheduled the series to begin just before drug kingpin Ricky Ross—a prom-

inent figure in the articles—was to be sentenced on cocaine charges.

"That way, the San Diego and L.A. papers can use the news angles of the sentencing as a way of getting into the story themselves—without having to give the *San Jose Mercury News* any credit," Webb wrote to Ross in prison on July 15, adding that the series had once again been postponed because top editors hadn't read it.

Ross's sentencing was delayed, but Webb still worked at drumming up publicity. For a time, the *Mercury News*'s Web site for "Dark Alliance" (http://www.sjmercury.com/drugs/) kept readers informed about Webb's media appearances. In September, people calling Webb at the paper's Sacramento bureau heard a message asking them to leave this information on the answering machine: "Your name or the name of your organization or show, channel, frequency, audience—including type and size—and the date and time of the requested interview or appearance."

But despite his efforts, by September's end the major papers and the networks still hadn't paid much attention to "Dark Alliance."

"I looked at it when it initially came out and decided this was not something we needed to follow up on quite the way [the *Mercury News*] put it," says Karen DeYoung, the *Post*'s assistant managing editor for national news. "When it became an issue proliferating in the African-American community and on talk shows, that seemed to be a different phenomenon."

The *Post* then turned to reporters Roberto Suro, Douglas Farah and Walter Pincus, who covered the Iran-contra affair, to look into the *Mercury News*'s story. Michael A. Fletcher reported on the firestorm Webb's story had created in the black community and on Capitol Hill, where legislators and prominent black leaders including Jesse Jackson and Louis Farrakhan were demanding—and getting—investigations.

"The phenomenon of the reaction was, in and of itself, a story," says DeYoung. "But to explain and address the phenomenon, we had to report the story ourselves."

The *Post* reporters reached conclusions strikingly different from Webb's. "A *Washington Post* investigation into Ross, Blandon, Meneses and the U.S. cocaine market in the 1980s found that the available information does not support the conclusion that the CIA-backed contras—or Nicaraguans in general—played a major role in the emergence of crack as a narcotic in widespread use across the United States," the paper reported on October 4.

The *Post* said the two Nicaraguans were small-time cocaine dealers with weak contra links and couldn't have started the crack epidemic by themselves. The paper said that, contrary to the *Mercury News*'s assertion that Blandon was the "Johnny Appleseed of crack in California," the two men's

drug deals were "only a small portion of the nation's cocaine trade."

The *Post* wrote that Blandon, according to his testimony in federal court, had actually stopped sending drug money to the contras before he began dealing with Ross in 1983 or 1984.

Suro and Pincus also challenged the way Webb obtained information from Blandon. Unable to reach Blandon after trying many avenues, Webb fed questions to Ricky Ross's attorney, who was cross-examining Blandon at the time. Some say Webb influenced Ross's trial by raising questions about Blandon's possible CIA connection.

Webb sees nothing wrong with this. "This was a perfect situation," Webb told journalism students at Berkeley. "You had the target of your investigation sitting up there on the witness stand under oath in federal district court. . . . How many people wouldn't do that if you couldn't interview him directly?"

As the *Post* was working on its story, the *Los Angeles Times* was agonizing over how to react to such an explosive story on its own turf—and in an area that the *Times* is often accused of ignoring. Members of the Los Angeles black community noted sarcastically that they had to rely on a northern California paper to confirm their suspicions about government involvement in drug trafficking. Editor Shelby Coffey III wanted his paper to do something more substantial than daily stories on the uproar.

In the middle of September, *Times* Washington bureau chief McManus got a phone call from an editor in Los Angeles. "What's this all about?" McManus was asked. "What do you think we should do?" The *Times* ultimately decided to throw three editors and 14 reporters at the story and do a three-part series. It ran October 20–22—two months after the *Mercury News*'s series.

The first part explored how and when crack had come to Los Angeles. "Crack was already here" before Blandon began selling cheap cocaine, the *Times* asserted. The second part looked at whether a CIA-sponsored operation funneled millions to the contras, as Webb had claimed. The third part dealt with why the story had such a powerful impact on the black community.

The *Times* could find no proof that "millions" had been funneled to the contras by Blandon and Meneses, as the *Mercury News* had reported. At most, *Times* reporters could substantiate that about $50,000 was sent to the guerrillas.

(When he asked the *Mercury News*'s Ceppos how the paper had arrived at the "millions" figure, McManus says Ceppos put him on hold and asked one of the series' editors, who told him it was an estimate based on the volume the dealers had sold and the prevailing market price. However, while the lead of the opening story said "millions," later in the piece

Webb wrote, "It was not clear how much of the money found its way back to the CIA's army. . . . ")

The *Times*, like the *Post*, also disputed the *Mercury News*'s timeline, saying Blandon had sold cocaine and sent the profits to the contras for less than a year. Webb wrote that this arrangement was in place from 1981 until 1986, when Blandon was arrested.

Webb counters that it's the big national papers, not the *Mercury News*, that got it wrong. "The problem was they got the information from government officials and didn't check what they were told," he told *AJR*. "I had five or six independent sources saying Meneses and Blandon were dealing [for the contras] all the way through until 1986." He noted he'd spent more than a year reporting the story while the others had spent weeks.

The *Times* also strongly disputed the *Mercury News*'s contention that Blandon, Ross and Meneses were the first to open the cocaine pipeline from Colombia's cartels to Los Angeles's inner city.

But the paper relied on anonymous sources to make important points that contradicted the *Mercury News*'s findings. McManus says that may be a valid criticism of his paper's work, adding, "I wish we had been able to identify them by names, of course."

The *Times* also rewrote history in its series. In a 1994 series on crack, the *Times*'s Jesse Katz described Ross as the biggest drug dealer in town. Two years later, as Ross's importance soared in the *Mercury News*, it plummeted in the *Times*. In its October series, Ross was depicted as just one of the city's major dealers. "So which one of these stories about Ross is true?" asks *Mercury News* reporter Pete Carey.

On October 21, the *New York Times* weighed in with a front page story discounting Meneses's and Blandon's contra credentials, suggesting they were more likely garden-variety drug dealers using the contra cause as a convenient cover. "What was really new was Blandon's relationship with Ricky Ross," says Tim Golden, who covered the contra saga in the mid-1980s for the *Miami Herald*. Among others, Golden, now the *New York Times*'s San Francisco bureau chief, describes the *Mercury News* as having inflated a newsworthy story by implying that the CIA was directly involved in starting the crack epidemic.

While the big three attacked Webb's premise, they did concede he had advanced the story beyond what had been reported on the subject in the mid-1980s, when the suggestion of CIA involvement in drug smuggling was a prominent issue that warranted a Senate investigation. Sen. John Kerry (D-MA), chairman of the investigating subcommittee, said in 1989 that, despite suspicions, the panel couldn't prove the agency had allowed coke smuggling to help the contras.

"Webb had a good story about two drug dealers loosely connected to the contras in the early 1980s—an item to add to the list of evidence linking contras and cocaine trafficking," wrote David Corn, the Washington editor of the *Nation*, who has written extensively about the CIA. "But the paper went too far, claiming without solid proof that 'millions' flowed from these mid-level dealers to the contras—it may have been $50,000—and in tying these traffickers to the rise of crack, a phenomenon bigger than a mere two pushers."

When the *Washington Post*'s article appeared, it played like a must-see movie at the *Mercury News*. Although quickly deemed a "knockdown" and attributed to professional jealousy by Webb's editors and supporters, it stunned the newsroom nonetheless. Here was one of the nation's elite newspapers tearing apart the foundation—not just a few facts—of the *Mercury News*'s series, a series many had thought offered the paper a good shot at its third Pulitzer Prize.

Here was one of the nation's elite newspapers tearing apart the foundation—not just a few facts—of the Mercury News's series.

Yet some inside the newsroom were pleased to see the *Post*'s story because the *Post* raised the same questions they had after reading it. "To me the biggest thing we should have done is to point out that there is contrary evidence," says *Mercury News* economics reporter Scott Thurm. "We shouldn't have ignored everything that contradicts our theory."

Surprisingly, Webb's story wasn't vetted by a platoon of high-ranking editors the way many investigative stories are at the *Mercury News* and other newspapers. City editor Dawn Garcia, Webb's editor, stayed with the project from beginning to end. Although the paper has an investigative projects editor, Jonathan Krim, he did not edit it because top management wanted to spread projects around rather than leave them in the hands of an elite team. Then-managing editor David Yarnold was also closely involved with the series from the start. While Garcia supervised Webb on a daily basis, the story was known as "Yarnold's baby."

But a month before it ran, Yarnold left the paper, accepting a job with Knight-Ridder's new media division. His oversight role was taken over by Paul Van Slambrouck, assistant managing editor for news. Van Slambrouck explained at a staff meeting when the controversy erupted that he had "amped down" Webb's initial story. Van Slambrouck and Garcia declined to comment.

Ceppos, who had been preoccupied with searching for a new managing editor, didn't read the entire series before it went into the paper. Nor was the series read by Ryan, director of the paper's Web site, who said it was not his responsibility. It was reviewed by one of the paper's lawyers.

After questions were raised about the series, the *Mercury News* created a committee to examine the way it carries out projects. It is considering, among other things, a formalized editing process that would ensure more top editors are involved, says editor Chris Schmitt, a committee member.

"Basically, the overall editing process broke down," says Schmitt, a former investigative reporter. "While it's true that specific people may have caught things if they'd been editing the project, that shouldn't have mattered. It was a system breakdown." Some found the internal criticism of the Webb story disheartening, prompting a Ceppos memo dated October 10—six days after the *Post* story appeared.

"I was spurred to do this by separate conversations with a couple of folks, one of whom hasn't been at the *Mercury News* very long, who expressed surprise and deep disappointment at what they perceived to be the almost gloating reaction in parts of the newsroom to the *Post*'s criticism of the series," wrote Ceppos, who became executive editor in 1994 after 12 years as managing editor.

"As one of them put it, if this is what happens when a reporter aspires to do really high-end work, what's the percentage in sticking one's neck out to do that kind of work in the future, when his or her colleagues will try to tear it down? I found that very troubling. This person was not reacting to reasoned evaluation of the series but to the backbiting, whispering and sometimes gleeful tone of some of those conversations."

Ceppos's memo did not curtail the dissent. Nor did his comments to the press end the debate. He has been criticized for failing to read the entire series before it appeared in print and for making statements supporting the series, then appearing to change his mind. On August 28, Ceppos sent a reprint of the series and a letter to editors throughout the nation saying, "At first I found the story too preposterous to take seriously: A drug ring virtually introduced crack cocaine in the United States and sent the profits of the drug sales to the U.S.–government supported contras in Nicaragua. All the while, our government failed to stop the drug sales."

On October 18, Ceppos described the series more modestly in a rebuttal letter to the *Washington Post*, which declined to print it. He said the paper had "established that cocaine dealers working with CIA-sponsored contras sold large amounts of cocaine powder that was turned into crack in predominately black neighborhoods of Los Angeles at the time that the crack epidemic was beginning there, and some of the drug profits were sent to the contras to buy war supplies."

Ceppos has given dozens of media interviews on the series, including one to *AJR* for a November article, but says he will no longer do so. He stands by the story and says that he has been misquoted. When asked to discuss "Dark Alliance" for this story, he declined, referring a reporter to his November 3 column in the *Mercury News*.

"Interestingly," he wrote, "all of the articles accept parts of our core finding as fact—that drug dealers associated with the contras sold some amount of drugs in Los Angeles at around the time the crack explosion happened. Most agree that some of the money went to the contras. I continue to believe that's news, by anyone's standards, despite the what's-the-big-deal tone of our critics."

Ceppos attempted to respond to the *Post*'s criticism in a two-page letter. The embattled editor found some support from *Post* ombudsman Geneva Overholser, who chided her paper for not giving Ceppos the opportunity to respond.

The *Mercury News* has also been criticized for using a logo in which a figure smoking crack was superimposed over the CIA seal with the words "The story behind the crack explosion" underneath. Although it wasn't used as the logo for the series, the version with the CIA seal appeared on the Web site, with the original series in the paper as a teaser to the site and in some reprints.

Some journalists say the paper has adopted a "blame-the-reader" approach.

After the *Post* raised questions about the logo's implications, Ceppos had it removed from the Web site and ordered hundreds of reprints destroyed. Ceppos told an *L.A. Times* reporter that editing standards at the paper's Web site are not always consistent with those of the print version of the paper. This angered *Mercury Center* staffers, and Ceppos personally apologized to them and wrote a letter to the *L.A. Times* modifying his earlier statement.

Ceppos says he wishes the paper had included a paragraph high up in the story stating it had not been able to conclusively prove CIA involvement (see "Spelling Out What You Don't Know," December). Webb, on the other hand, says he has problems with that approach and is glad the paper didn't do so. However, in the wake of the criticism, the paper routinely includes this sentence in follow-up stories: "The *Mercury News* series never reported direct CIA involvement, though many readers drew that conclusion."

Some journalists say the paper has adopted a "blame-the-reader" approach. Yet even its own editorial board drew the conclusions most of the public did. A headline over one editorial read, "Another CIA disgrace: Helping the crack flow."

Rob Elder, the paper's editorial page editor, says he stands by the editorial but that it might have been written differently had he read the *Washington Post* and *Los Angeles Times* articles first. "I wish I could have read them before," he says. "We all have different viewpoints after reading them."

Says the *L.A. Times*'s McManus, "It's been hard to figure out whether they stand by everything they wrote or whether they've had second thoughts because, at different times, they seem to express different sentiments. I still hate to say nasty things about other editors, and I hope I'm wrong. But it somehow seems disingenuous for the editor to say the paper never intended anyone to get the inference that the CIA had anything to do with the introduction of crack to L.A. The readers got that point. Their editorial board got that point." To its credit, the *Mercury News* did not try to hide the criticism. It put the *Post* story and others raising questions about the series on its Web site and it assigned one of its best reporters, Pulitzer Prize winner Pete Carey, to explore the *Post*'s analysis.

Peter Kornbluh of the National Security Archive recently asked Carey how he felt checking out Webb's story. "I said I had a bad feeling in my stomach the whole time," Carey told *AJR* as he recounted the conversation. Kornbluh asked why. Carey responded, "Have you ever been a reporter in a newsroom? This is an awful experience." Webb, too, says it was a "very awkward" situation.

Nine days after the *Post* story appeared, Carey had his own front page analysis examining the criticism but reaching no conclusions. Carey acted more like an ombudsman for the paper performing an in-house audit. He did not write a correction, Carey says, but rather took note of criticisms and tried to answer them. He quoted three experts disagreeing with some of the series' conclusions about the spread of the crack epidemic.

"The big issue," says Carey, "is did we structure and mold the information we had and present it in a manner that would lead readers and the many victims of the crack epidemic to blame the U.S. government for their pain and suffering?"

At presstime Carey was trying to put together the definitive explanation of how the crack epidemic began.

In the end, many would argue that, by leading reasonable readers to believe the CIA played a role in the origins of the crack explosion, the paper hurt its credibility, hurt journalism, caused irreparable damage in the black community and shed little light on the question of whether the CIA looked the other way while cocaine was smuggled into this country. Webb and his reporting have become as much the issue as the CIA and crack.

"If the holes in the story hadn't been there," says *Mercury News* telecommunications reporter Howard Bryant, "there wouldn't have been all this negative coverage by other newspapers. That's what, as a black person, bothers me. Those papers have twice the resources we have. Who knows what they would have uncovered had they used their resources to build on the story rather than discredit it. You read the story and there really were holes in it. I just wonder why we had to oversell it."

And the overselling had a steep price. "I believe we'll be left with no smoking gun on the CIA," says Susan Rasky, a journalism professor at the University of California at Berkeley and a former congressional reporter for the *New York Times*. "The *Mercury News*, a fine newspaper, will be left with a black eye, and the black community will be left to believe that not only is the government engaged in a conspiracy but the establishment media are as well."

On November 26, the Senate Intelligence Committee held a hearing on alleged CIA involvement in drug trafficking. Blandon had testified the day before in a closed hearing, telling committee members he had channeled $60,000 to $65,000 in drug profits to the contras, but before he had met L.A. drug dealer Ricky Ross. "In response to direct questions from the committee, Mr. Blandon stated that he had never had any contact with the CIA and that the CIA was not involved in his drug trafficking business in any way," said Sen. Arlen Specter (R-PA).

But that information may not matter to many who have read the series. When *Miami Herald* executive editor Doug Clifton was in Boston last fall, he saw fliers on telephone poles announcing a forum on how the CIA brought crack cocaine into the black community, based on the *San Jose Mercury News*'s series.

"So the genie's out of the bottle," says Clifton. "No amount of refinement or backtracking or setting the record straight will put the genie back in. This is probably as clear-cut an example as you can have of why newspapers have to be so careful about their revelations."

Beyond ABC v. Food Lion[3]

Are deceptive practices by a news organization justified if they reveal deceptive practices by others? How serious do suspected abuses have to be to warrant reporters' going undercover to expose them? Should certain kinds of journalistic deception be prohibited by law? Such are the questions that continue to roil about the case of *Food Lion v. Capital Cities/ABC* more than two months after the verdict.

In December, a North Carolina jury decided that two *Prime Time Live* producers went too far in 1992 when they lied on applications and obtained jobs in the back rooms of Food Lion supermarkets. The resulting program hurt Food Lion's bottom line, and ABC News was hit with $5.5 million in punitive damages. The consequences of the decision, which ABC is appealing, will assuredly be felt in future television exposes or the lack of them.

For the court's purposes, the case was narrowly construed. Food Lion did not sue ABC for libel, and the jury never saw the program at issue. Instead, the jurors were instructed to assume that it was accurate and to concentrate not on its substance or on the hidden cameras used to expose unsavory supermarket practices but strictly on how the reporters lied their way to where the food was prepared. As it turned out, the jury was sharply divided between those who would have awarded Food Lion little or nothing and those who wanted to give it hundreds of millions of dollars, but there was agreement that the producers had done something wrong. Diane Sawyer's words about Food Lion—"what can happen when the pressure for profits is great and you break the rules"—were turned against her own program.

As the ensuing debate has demonstrated, issues of journalistic propriety and public policy linger. If the network loses its appeal, executives and producers will be under pressure to tread more cautiously, which is bound to mean fewer, safer and probably less-needed investigations. One juror who now has misgivings about the judgment says he wishes Food Lion had filed a libel suit instead. Amen, brother.

In more than two hours devoted to the case by ABC News one night a few weeks ago, ABC personalities, including Ms. Sawyer, who introduced the original program, argued that those little cameras gave viewers an unequaled opportunity to see how their food was treated before it reached the shelves. Food Lion executives and lawyers asserted that scenes had been staged and that the reporting was faked.

Several viewings of the contested program and of a rebuttal tape of unused scenes put together by Food Lion persuaded

Should certain kinds of journalistic deception be prohibited by law?

---

3. Article by Walter Goodman from the *New York Times* II p F Mar. 9, 1997. Copyright © 1997 The New York Times Company. Reprinted with permission.

me of the credibility of the *Prime Time Live* report. Yes, the reporters were out to catch instances of unappetizing behavior and the most flagrant and unfragrant of them were played up, as is the way in exposes. But the program made a strong case that tricks like repackaging outdated fish and prettifying unsold chicken with barbecue sauce were common at two Food Lion stores at least. Employees seemed to be doing such refurbishment as a matter of course. To dismiss this evidence, as Food Lion does, you have to believe that the *Prime Time Live* team was devoid of basic professionalism as well as short on ethics.

It has been suggested that the reporting could have been done in a more aboveboard way, perhaps simply by buying the food and subjecting it to analysis. Such findings, although welcome, would have been no substitute for the on-the-spot evidence of malpractice. When employees and former employees told ABC of the goings-on in the back room, Food Lion called them mouthpieces for an antagonistic labor union. Even if the union instigated the investigation, however, the cameras confirmed the charges.

All journalism is to some degree packaged as entertainment, and news magazines are known for slipping into sheer show biz.

News magazines are hard to claim as exemplars of the higher reporting; critics who ascribe exposes to a desire for ratings have a point. The popular hidden-camera technique itself is often just tabloidization. Don Hewitt, the executive producer of *60 Minutes* and a hidden-camera pioneer, grants that "it's being used as a stunt in many, many instances." If nothing else, the shadowy quality of the photography implies something sinister is afoot.

To add to the air of phoniness, a network star, like Ms. Sawyer on the Food Lion program, usually has less to do with content and presentation than unglamorous, usually unseen producers; she is there for her appeal to fans and the sense of trust she conveys. The programs play "Gotcha!" with the company or individuals in their sights; the editing is always punched up for dramatic purposes, and there is more than a touch of sensationalism to the result. Yet, for all such succumbings to temptation, the undercover stories can deliver close-ups of wrongdoing that interviews and documents cannot match. In her program's defense, Ms. Sawyer reminded us of hidden-camera operations that revealed abuses of the mentally ill and of children at day-care centers, politicians living high on lobbyist junkets and so forth. I have seen most of those reports, and they struck me as zesty journalism and inimitable television. And truthful too.

Sure, such exposes are entertainments; all journalism is to some degree packaged as entertainment, and news magazines are known for slipping into sheer show biz. But when the issue is serious, when the suspicions are well-grounded, then the undercover approach becomes a weapon of last resort. Would Food Lion have invited the reporters in if they had identified themselves? If lying was required to enter the employees-only area, the violation of the letter of the law, which was assuredly not written with reporters in mind, was outweighed by the public service.

Insofar as television journalists are inhibited from finagling their way into forbidden precincts and using their hidden cameras to get at hidden doings, television news, so often so synthetic, will be even less likely to risk undertaking the worthwhile job that it was made to do.

How do you retract a story online?[4]

Time, the *New Republic* and the *Cincinnati Enquirer* map the high, middle and low roads for dealing with discredited articles on the Web.

When the *Cincinnati Enquirer* recently decided to disown a much ballyhooed investigative series alleging a variety of misdeeds on the part of Chiquita Brands International, it not only paid Chiquita $10 million and published an abject apology—it also wiped the stories off its Web site and removed them from its online archive, leaving its apology and retraction to hang forlornly out of context.

Meanwhile, over at *Time* magazine, editors were also retracting a much trumpeted *Time*/CNN investigative scoop that claimed the U.S. military had used nerve gas in Laos in 1970. But you can still read this discredited story on *Time*'s Web site—although not before being directed to *Time*'s abashed retraction and apology.

Back when newspapers and magazines first rushed onto the Web, editors and publishers dreamed of reaching vast new audiences and tapping rich new veins of advertising revenue. In those heady days, how many of them could foresee that their new online presences would also become major legal and ethical headaches for them?

The latest wave of media blunders has put print publications in a quandary that they never faced while they remained in a strictly paper universe. In the old days, if you published a flawed story in one day's edition, you ate crow in the next day's. You couldn't go out and destroy all the already-distributed copies of your publication that contained the offending work, nor did anyone expect you to. The historical record—including a full detailing of both the publication's original missteps and its efforts to make amends—remained intact. That meant the public could judge for itself how badly the publication had damaged its credibility, whether the amends it made were forthright or foot-dragging—and whether they were presented in a spirit of truth-seeking or performed under instructions from craven company lawyers.

---

4. Article by Scott Rosenberg. This article first appeared on July17, 1998, in *Salon,* an online magazine, at *http://www.salonmagazine.com.* An online version remains in the *Salon* archives. Reprinted with permission.

The Web raises vexatious new questions about just what constitutes a retraction—and new temptations for publications that might rather hide black marks on their records than keep dirty linen hanging in their online archives. Of course, Web sites have always faced thorny ethical and technological problems when they need to correct errors. Since a "published" article on the Web is merely a file sitting on the hard drive of a Web server, you can easily go into a Web page and fix a mistake so that there's no record of the original goof. Some sites keep track of every little fix they make, "paper-of-record" style; others just make their corrections with no notice at all. (Here at *Salon*, our policy has evolved over time: Today, we will simply fix minor errors, such as misspellings of names, soon after publication, without comment; more significant errors of substance are noted prominently on our Letters page.)

But the *Time* and *Cincinnati Enquirer* stories weren't simple corrections—they were high-profile, full-bore retractions of major features. In the *Enquirer*'s case, there are still serious questions outstanding as to whether the Chiquita stories deserved to be disowned—or the paper simply caved to pressure from a powerful local corporation. Under such circumstances, the alacrity with which the *Enquirer* scoured its archives of 30 or more Chiquita investigation stories is not only unseemly, it robs the public of the chance to judge the series for itself—alongside whatever disclaimers, retractions and apologies the newspaper has since deemed necessary.

In any case, the *Enquirer* can delete its stories from its own site, but it can't keep them off the Net. For one thing, for the moment you can still obtain them (for $1 per story) from directory services such as Northern Light. And individuals on the Net who believe that readers should have the chance to study these stories for themselves have also taken the liberty of reposting them. Once a text is distributed online, it's very difficult to efface it from the Net if someone is passionate about keeping it in circulation—and willing to take a legal risk.

Given all this, the *Enquirer*'s tactic looks like a model for how not to deal with the Web retraction problem—and *Time*'s approach, whatever its other missteps in this affair, looks like the way to go. *Time* has corrected the record by augmenting it rather than erasing it; while it's no longer possible for *Time* readers to read the original story without being aware of *Time*'s subsequent retraction, it's also not possible for *Time* to pretend that the goof never happened.

Contrast that forthrightness with the more dodgy approach taken by the *New Republic* in the Stephen Glass affair. In the wake of the initial revelation that a Glass story for the magazine about teen hackers was a fabrication, curious people online began combing the *New Republic* Web archive and finding other dubious-sounding yarns in Glass's backlist—

Some sites keep track of every little fix they make, "paper-of-record" style; others just make their corrections with no notice at all.

like those on inflatable Monica Lewinsky sex dolls and Alan Greenspan groupies—that were later shown to be fraudulent, too. At first the magazine left Glass's oeuvre in full view; later it took all the discredited stories down, explaining the move in a letter to readers: "When we post something to our archive, it is being continuously published, and that implies ongoing endorsement of its honesty and truthfulness."

That sounds good, but it gives the magazine a convenient out, a chance to bury the embarrassing incident. There's no reason the magazine couldn't "continuously publish" the stories with an explicit statement that they're not honest and truthful. *Time*'s approach is what the *New Republic* should have adopted: Leave the stories up, leave the historical record intact and append a note to readers (with appropriate links) explaining the subsequent history. With this method of dealing with errors, journalists can actually make the Web function better than print: After all, you don't find magazines going into the library stacks inserting notes of retraction into bound volumes.

Of course, each time a magazine tries to correct a problem, it opens the door to making new mistakes. If you take a look at the Web page for *Time*'s nerve-gas story, you'll notice something strange: The original story is dated June 15, yet the type directing readers to the retraction says, "Please see the editor's note appearing in the June 13, 1998, issue of *Time*." Make that "July"—and no need for an apology.

IV. When Journalism Fails

Editors' Introduction

The intense analysis the press has undergone in recent years is, in large part, a result of some highly visible journalistic blunders at the hands of well-established news organizations. These faux pas differ in magnitude and run the gamut of classic journalistic violations: plagiarism, fabricated quotes, unsupported allegations, and completely fictionalized articles. Their common link, however, is a shared sense of disappointment and embarrassment by both the reading public and journalists themselves. These media scandals, coupled with an overabundance of tabloid-style news, have left many readers and television viewers distrustful of their news sources, and in many cases, have crippled the reputation of both reporter and editor. In the aftermath, which is still unfolding, journalists take a hard look at why these mistakes were allowed to be made and what can be done to ensure that future journalists will approach their profession with the same degree of integrity and ethical proficiency that the best reporters have always exemplified with their work.

"Hack Haven," by John Corry, takes a look at the fictional accounts that *New Republic* writer Stephen Glass continually passed off as truth to his editors. Only after writing more than 20 columns filled with fabricated characters, companies and events was Glass challenged by an editor—from another publication. When a column Glass had written about young hackers proved unverifiable, the writer admitted to fictionalizing most of his work and he was promptly fired. Corry examines why Glass was allowed to slip through the editorial cracks for so long, and questions whether his contemporaries were disturbed by the revelation that a fellow journalist had rarely reported a word of truth. He also looks closely at Glass's work and points out obvious warning signals which the *New Republic*, as well as other journalists, evidently missed along the way.

The next piece, "Hanging Barnicle," by Dan Kennedy, explores the manner by which Mike Barnicle, a popular longtime columnist at the *Boston Globe*, was found to have plagiarized jokes from comedian George Carlin. Kennedy looks at the history of the case, including past occurrences when doubts about Barnicle's columns arose but were quietly dismissed. The article further examines the history of the *Globe* itself, and the precarious balance it has struggled to maintain between the city's ethnic, working-class residents and its wealthier, largely white suburbanites. In addition, Kennedy brings up the case of another *Globe* columnist, Patricia Smith, who was fired from the *Globe* just prior to the Barnicle incident for fabricating quotes and people in her work.

The section winds down with "An Ill Tailwind," by Susan Paterno, who explores the widely criticized *CNN/Time* expose that alleged that nerve gas used on American soldiers by the U.S. military during the Vietnam War. Highly touted as a sleek investigative report by both the network and the magazine, the story made a big splash at first. Soon, however, military officials, the government and other journalists questioned the veracity of the piece. After an investigation, it was determined that there was no factual basis for the report's claims and *CNN/Time* issued an apology. Paterno looks at how the story made its way to the airwaves, revealing how red flags emerged almost at the onset of the investigation, but pressure to produce caused the network to jump the gun before crucial information had been verified. She also looks at the damage that occurred as a result of the blunder, as a shadow was cast on not only the network and well-respected news magazines, but on noted news anchor Peter Arnett, who had served as a bastion of quality reporting for the network during the Persian Gulf conflict.

Hack Haven[1]

The Stephen Glass affair shakes the *New Republic*.

What did the *New Republic* know, and when did it know it? The venerable (est. 1914) magazine of commentary and opinion says it had no idea one of its writers was making things up until an alert reader proved it, but that's an excuse and not an explanation. The fact that the *New Republic* did not catch up to Stephen Glass until it did means either (a) that its editors had not read his articles, or (b) they had read them, but saw nothing wrong with them, or (c) they knew very well there was something wrong, but decided that was irrelevant. The *New Republic* itself suggests (b) as the only possibility, but a more likely explanation for what happened is some combination of (a) and (c). Beware when an opinion magazine falls in love with its own voice and high morality, and forgets about truth in reporting.

The article that finally did in Glass, "Hack Heaven," appeared in the May 18 issue, although some of his readers, at least, were suspicious of him long before that. In "Holy Trinity" (January 27, 1997), for example, he wrote about an 80-year-old widow who worshipped at the shrine of Paul Tsongas. In "Peddling Poppy" (June 9, 1997) he discovered The First Church of George Herbert Walker Christ. Its members observed Kosher dietary laws, and though they divided over pork rinds, they all eschewed broccoli. In "Plotters" (February 23, 1998) Glass wrote about the Commission to Restore the Presidency to Greatness. It was made up of middle-aged white guys, and Glass said he had attended one of its meetings. It had a "Vice President for Vince Foster's Death Affairs," and a Senior Deputy who insisted Bill Clinton was really a woman; he thought she was Hillary's lesbian lover.

And so on. Glass's 41 articles were always well written and often entertaining, but usually decorated with red flags. You had to notice one of them sooner or later. For this longtime reader and frequent admirer of the *New Republic*, that happened first with a single sentence in "Spring Breakdown" (March 31, 1997): "Her lipstick has rubbed off on her wine glass, leaving only the cherry outline." It was a small detail perfectly observed, and it made for a very nice sentence, although it was unlikely Glass had ever observed it. Ergo he was writing fiction. In the wake of the Glass debacle the *New*

Glass's 41 articles were always well written and often entertaining, but usually decorated with red flags.

---

1. Article by John Corry, from the *American Spectator* (on-line) July 1998. Copyright © 1998 by the *American Spectator*. Reprinted by permission.

Republic would say its fact-checking system had broken down, but that was a lame excuse. Many supposed facts defy checking, and must be submitted instead to a smell test. The lipstick, wine glass, and cherry outline, for example, would not have passed it. They were too perfect to be true. When a writer's observations and other embroideries consistently fail a smell test—as Glass's would have failed time and again, if some adult at the *New Republic* had bothered to run the test—it means the writer must be watched. Goodness knows what he might do next.

So back now to "Hack Heaven," the article in which everything finally unraveled. The 25-year-old Glass often wrote about young masters of the universe, and "Hack Heaven" purported to be about a teenage computer whiz who had broken into the database of a software company called Jukt Micronics. Then he supposedly posted the salaries of all its employees, along with pictures of naked women, on its Web site. Desperate Jukt executives, Glass wrote, then tried to hire him or buy him off. The kicky lead began as follows:

> Ian Restil, a 15-year-old computer hacker who looks like an even more adolescent version of Bill Gates, is throwing a tantrum. "I want more money. I want a Miata. I want a trip to Disney World. I want X-man comic (book) number one. I want a lifetime subscription to *Playboy*, and throw in *Penthouse*. Show me the money! Show me the money!" Over and over again, the boy, who is wearing a frayed Cal Ripken Jr. T-shirt, is shouting his demands.

Many readers probably stopped reading right there. (Who cares what the brat wants, and what's a Miata?) But Adam Penenberg, an editor at the online *Forbes Digital Tool*, kept going, and as he did he grew suspicious. Then, when he tried to verify the article, he found that nothing in it was real—not Ian Restil, not Jukt, nothing at all, in fact, right down to the ifs, ands, buts, and howevers. He also found that Glass had worked hard at his lying. To support his bogus article, he had created a fake Web site for Jukt and a phony voice mail on his brother's cell phone.

Penenberg told the *New Republic* about his findings, and, according to the *Washington Post*, Charles Lane, the editor of the *New Republic*, then undertook his own investigation. Shortly afterwards he fired Glass. "Asked if the magazine should have detected problems in Glass's work earlier," the *Post* reported, "Lane said: 'It's a perfectly fair question. I expect to be asked that repeatedly; I've asked it of myself.'"

But the answer to the question, of course, was yes; the magazine should have detected the problems, and fired Glass some 20 or 30 articles earlier. As a journalistic organization, however, the *New Republic* had suffered an institutional collapse. Good people may have been coming and going, but liberal dilettantism had taken over. What mattered was not what Glass said, but how he said it; also, journalists have more important things to do than to assemble dreary facts. Their worldview is what counts, and a show of sangfroid helps. On the day the *Post* broke the story about the *New Republic's* disgrace, there was a revealing exchange between Andrew Sullivan and Katha Pollitt. Sullivan, a former editor of the *New Republic*, is now a senior editor. Pollitt is a columnist for the *Nation*. They were posting chatty notes to one another in the online *Slate*'s "The Breakfast Table."

Sullivan went first that day, with a note just before noon. Word about the Glass scandal was all over Washington by then, but Sullivan was concerned with *Seinfeld*. He thought it a "brilliant exposition of how friendship really works and enriches our lives, and how it's possible to be happy, fulfilled, attractive and single." He wanted to know if Pollitt agreed, or whether her "anti-bourgeois knees go atwitch at its self-absorption."

Pollitt replied 43 minutes later. She thought *Seinfeld* fascinating. It proved there was "no popular tide of social conservatism—family values, back-to-basics, rural-nostalgia, recycle-your-virginity, all that." Then she went on to the day's "interesting news," particularly the piece in the *New York Times* about child marriages in India. When she eventually got around to Glass it was only to recall him as "a very amusing writer." She still smiled, Pollitt wrote, when she remembered "his piece about FedEx and UPS—Sad to think that maybe it isn't true that women all over America have erotic fantasies about their UPS man, and that UPS uniforms are not one of the most popular costumes at costume parties!"

When Sullivan got back to Pollitt almost four hours later he told her he agreed about "the atrocities in India," that he had contributed money to a group called Equality Now, and that "the religious Right is very uncomfortable defending women's equality for obvious reasons." Then he also got around to Glass. Sullivan said he was "in a state of shock." When Glass was his assistant he was "the sweetest, brightest guy imaginable." This is "one of those moments," Sullivan wrote, "when you question everything, especially about the value of journalism." Sullivan said he was going "through one of those Kubler-Ross passages, as is everyone else at *TNR*," but then he concluded with something cheery: "By the way, I can't imagine he made up the stuff about straight women/gay men having fantasies about UPS men. I have a friend in New York who used to send himself packages twice a day just to catch a sight of those brown shorts."

And then Pollitt, 2 hours 29 minutes later: "Well, Andrew —can it be? Two hearts that beat as one? I too contribute to Equality Now!" Then Pollitt talked about this and that, and then she got on to Glass: "The thing is, even if Stephen Glass made it all up (except about the UPS men, as you say, mine is also very cute, and a real union man too!) he's still a terrific writer." Pollitt concluded: "I wish young Stephen all the best."

So none of it really mattered, and no one was really to blame. Liberal dilettantism also means never having to say you're sorry. Sullivan, who had hired Glass in the first place, questioned not himself but the "value of journalism," while Pollitt wished the young serial liar all the best, presumably because he was a good writer. The young serial liar, however, had discredited the 84-year-old magazine even more thoroughly than had the old Lefties who once used its pages to defend Stalin's show trials. The old Lefties had principles, even if twisted, but Glass appears to have had none. On the other hand, God forbid, he seems to have been giving the *New Republic* exactly what it wanted.

Consider "Spring Breakdown," Glass's fantasy about the Conservative Political Action Conference at the Omni Shoreham in Washington. The *New Republic* people probably howled when they read it. Glass was some reporter. He is actually in the room when eight young conservatives, "in a haze of beer and pot, and in between rantings about feminists, gays and political correctness," think up a repulsive plan. Three of them will drive to a local bar, and "choose the ugliest and loneliest woman they can find," and one of them will lure her back to the hotel room. Then he will undress her, and after he does five of the young conservatives will spring out from underneath the beds, and shout and take her picture.

It all goes like clockwork. The three go to a bar, and soon spot their victim. ("Her lipstick has rubbed off on her wine glass, leaving only a cherry outline.") Shortly afterwards she is in the hotel room, and half an hour later she begins screaming. Then: "The door flies open, and she runs out. Tears, black from the mascara, stream down her face. She is holding her shoes and gripping her blouse to her chest." Meanwhile, "inside the room, Charlie gives Seth a high-five," and Seth "promises to get the photo developed and duplicated in the morning."

But the story reeks, and does not pass a smell test. Glass could not have been outside the room looking at the woman, and inside the room listening to the young men at the same time. They were imaginative creations, like the UPS man in shorts. Indeed very little in the story held up if you read it carefully, although it seemed the *New Republic* did not care. Even if Glass had made up the facts, he apparently had captured the essence. "This is the face of young conservatism in 1997," he wrote, "dejected, depressed, drunk, and dumb." "The repellent scene" in the hotel room, "was only a little beyond the norm of the conference."

Perhaps that was it all along. The liberal dilettantes wanted to have their worldview confirmed, and at the same time be amused. — Copyright © 1998 *The American Spectator*

Even if Glass had made up the facts, he apparently had captured the essence.

Hanging Barnicle[2]

Now that *Boston Globe* columnist Mike Barnicle is really
gone, it remains to be seen whether his media buddies will
rally behind him as they did two weeks ago—when his plagiarism of one-liners from George Carlin's best-seller, *Brain
Droppings*, first prompted *Globe* editor Matthew Storin to
demand Barnicle's resignation. Initially, when the *Boston
Herald* exposed Barnicle, he told his superiors that he'd gotten the jokes from a friend and that he had no idea his friend
had stolen them from Carlin—an excuse that seemed plausible enough until Barnicle's other employer, WCVB-TV,
broadcast a two-month-old segment from its program *Chronicle*, in which Barnicle was seen holding a copy *of Brain
Droppings* and promising that it contained "a yuck on every
page." Storin and *Globe* publisher Benjamin Taylor called on
Barnicle to resign—which seemed fair enough—but then the
defiant columnist launched a massive public relations offen-
sive that brought Don Imus, Larry King, Tim Russert, Richard Cohen, Marvin Kalb, and Mary McGrory to his defense.
Incredibly, Storin and Taylor backed down, reducing Barnicle's sentence to a two-month suspension that was supposed
to end, quite conveniently, just in time for the fall election
campaign.

At the time, Barnicle's defenders insisted they were standing up against the forces of political correctness. Getting rid
of Barnicle, they argued, was merely the *Globe's* way of making up for ousting Patricia Smith—the black columnist who
resigned in June after admitting she'd created fictitious characters in at least four of her columns. Of course, Barnicle had
been dogged by claims of fabrication and shoddy journalism
for years. But a review of 364 Barnicle articles going back to
January 1996, which Storin ordered in the wake of Smith's
resignation, had pronounced Barnicle pure. So, if all Barnicle
did wrong was lift a few jokes from George Carlin, well, that
was hardly reason to dismiss a columnist of such legendary
repute—or so the argument went.

The chief promoter of this theory, not surprisingly, was
Barnicle himself. And, when the *Globe* caved, his contrition
was something less than contrite. At a news conference in
the *Globe's* fortress-like offices, Barnicle duly apologized for
what he called "the intellectual laziness" and "sloppiness" of
stealing Carlin's lines. But, when a reporter from *Boston*
magazine attempted to press him about allegations of past
improprieties, Barnicle snapped that he wouldn't respond to
"a hotel guide." Shortly thereafter, a relaxed-looking Barnicle
was in front of the building, answering friendly questions

---

2. Article by Dan Kennedy from the *New Republic*, p18 + Sep. 7, 1998.
Copyright © 1998 the *New Republic*. Reprinted with permission.

from a WCVB reporter, while the *Boston* writer was reduced to watching a monitor inside the television van.

Unfortunately for Barnicle, more revelations were on the way. And, with new allegations of wrongdoing—among them the lifting of work by A. J. Liebling, which I reported in my newspaper, the *Boston Phoenix*—suddenly hanging over his head, Barnicle finally relented. On August 19 he announced he was resigning after all, although that may not quite be the end of the matter—or of Barnicle. As of press time, WCVB maintained it planned to keep Barnicle as a regular contributor.

Surely, at least some people will continue to see the Barnicle controversy as some kind of parable about political correctness. But, in a sense, this debate about whether Barnicle was sacrificed in the name of racial symbolism—or whether his backroom connections allowed him to cheat the executioner for as long as he did—misses the real lesson here. Like so many other major newspapers, the *Globe*—by far New England's largest and most influential news organization— has been trying for the last three decades to overcome its well-earned reputation for having an elitist, out-of-touch orientation toward the city and region it serves. Barnicle, a tough-talking Irish-American with working-class roots, and Smith, an African American with a poet's voice and a controversialist's heart, were grafted onto this culture in an attempt to broaden the *Globe's* base—to reach out to the disparate and distrusting ethnic clans that Boston comprises. Call it tokenism as journalism, or call it a quota system run amok. Either way, it was a substitute for what the *Globe* really needed—that is, a staff of city reporters more in tune with the city—and it didn't work very well.

Historically, the *Globe*, founded in 1872, was the voice not of Boston's Brahmin classes but rather of the city's dominant Irish community. But, by the mid-1960s, with most of the city's other papers having vanished, the genially complacent *Globe* had won the upscale readership by default. The paper was owned by Yankees—the Taylor family—and edited by a Yankee—Tom Winship, son of the previous editor, who set about the difficult task of turning the *Globe* into one of the best regional papers in the country. Winship imported talent from Harvard and from Boston College, the Irish-Catholic Harvard. And he largely succeeded. Under Winship, the *Globe* won a slew of Pulitzers. The paper offered superb investigative reporting, outstanding coverage of national and state politics, and more and better foreign-news coverage than readers of a regional newspaper had a right to expect. Not to mention a world-class sports section.

But, when it came to covering the city whose name adorned its masthead, the *Globe* was curiously lackluster. The *Globe*, then and now, is a paper whose publisher and editor live in the affluent, overwhelmingly white suburbs—

along with much of the reporting staff—where they are primarily exposed to well-educated, well-meaning folks like themselves. Which explains why they were so shocked when white working-class neighborhoods such as South Boston and Charlestown exploded in fury at the *Globe* in the school desegregation crisis of the mid-1970s. As vividly recounted in the late J. Anthony Lukas's 1985 book *Common Ground,* the *Globe* was literally under siege, in danger of being attacked by white mobs and/or terrorists who were enraged by the *Globe's* pro-busing stance.

Enter Barnicle, a working-class kid from nearby Fitchburg who had managed to talk his way into a prominent position on Robert Kennedy's 1968 presidential campaign, and who had later befriended Robert Redford and helped write the screenplay for *The Candidate.* Barnicle, who'd joined the *Globe* as a columnist in 1973, was invaluable during the busing crisis. Not only was he one of the few members of the *Globe's* staff who had any street savvy, but he was the only voice in the paper with the sense and the guts to criticize white suburban liberals for imposing unworkable social-engineering schemes on the urban poor of all races.

But, from the outset, Barnicle was just as contemptuous of journalistic professionalism as he was of the *Globe's* upper-middle-class sensibility. One of his very first columns quoted the white owner of a gas station in predominantly black Mattapan calling his neighbors "niggers." The gas-station owner denied using the epithet, sued Barnicle, and won a $40,000 judgment. It was just the first in what has been a 25-year career of staggering from one professional misadventure to another. He's been accused of lifting material by the late Chicago columnist Mike Royko. In 1990, he wrote that Harvard Law School professor Alan Dershowitz had once told him he loved Asian women because "they're so submissive." Dershowitz objected, and the *Globe* ultimately paid a $75,000 settlement, a fact revealed just recently by the *New York Times* and *Brill's Content.* In 1991, *Boston* magazine, in a series of solid, well-researched articles, strongly suggested that Barnicle had made up characters and quotes, the very offense that cost Patricia Smith her job. Barnicle denied it but never publicly offered any proof to the contrary.

It's because of those problems, not because of the George Carlin column, that Barnicle's critics originally charged that the *Globe* was guilty of a double standard in forcing out Smith but keeping Barnicle. And, taken as a whole, Barnicle's transgressions would indeed appear to equal Smith's. The critical difference was in how the two could defend themselves. Smith's support mainly came from a few black leaders and the city's not-terribly-influential poetry community; Barnicle could call in 25 years' worth of chits from his influential friends in the worlds of politics, media, and business. He had powerful allies within the *Globe*—like political columnist David Nyhan, who shared pallbearing duties with Barnicle at Tip O'Neill's funeral several years ago—and among key *Globe* advertisers as well. When Storin first asked Barnicle to resign, Thomas Stemberg, the chief executive of Staples office supply stores, sent the *Globe* a letter fretting about what Barnicle's dismissal would do to circulation.

Connoisseurs of hypocrisy took vicious delight as they watched the *Globe*, a leading exporter of boutique liberalism and diversity-babble, prostrate itself before the old-boy network. Within the *Globe*, many writers and editors made the same observation—if rarely with the same bemusement. More than 50 reporters and editors, a number of them white, signed a letter protesting the unequal treatment given to Barnicle and Smith. More ominously, *New York Times* editorial page editor Howell Raines wrote a blistering commentary in which he charged that "a white guy with the right connections got pardoned for offenses that would have taken down a minority or female journalist." (Since the New York Times Company owns the *Globe*, many wondered if Raines's column was simply his opinion or a message from the management.)

The real question, though, is not why Barnicle and Smith got unequal treatment—but why both didn't get fired long ago.

The real question, though, is not why Barnicle and Smith got unequal treatment—but why both didn't get fired long ago. And the blame for this belongs with *Globe* management—specifically, with the Taylor family and with Storin's predecessors, for slapping Barnicle lightly on the wrist time and again, and with Storin, for promoting Smith to a columnist's slot in 1994 despite past questions about her ethics and for meting out nothing more serious than a warning after some of her early columns came under suspicion. Indeed, the *Globe* recently announced that as many as 52 of her columns may have been faked. In ethnically divided Boston, there are good reasons to have highly visible African American and Irish-American columnists. But, by deliberately filling two of its most prominent columnists' slots with writers who were ethnic warriors first and journalists second, the *Globe* invited the disaster that has befallen it.

As the *Globe* seeks to regain the trust of its readers, it ought to consider the lesson of one of Storin's smartest moves: his naming of Eileen McNamara to a columnist's slot in 1995. McNamara, a first-rate reporter who'd come up through the ranks, had quit the paper in a huff several years earlier. Storin, despite a strained relationship with her, worked assiduously to bring her back. As a stylist, McNamara is no Patricia Smith or Mike Barnicle. Yet her carefully reported columns, engaged and passionate and filled with righteous indignation, won a Pulitzer Prize in 1997.

McNamara, in other words, is the real thing. Barnicle and Smith were gaudy wallpaper, hung to cover over the structural flaws that lay underneath. The talk of Boston now is whether those flaws can be patched over again—or if new

leadership will be brought in to undertake some major reno-
vations.

An Ill Tailwind[3]

A behind-the-scenes look at how CNN, despite red flags, aired—and was forced to retract—an explosive report on the military's alleged use of poison gas.

CNN had become far more renowned for its saturation coverage of breaking news than its blockbuster investigations.

Richard Kaplan remembers vividly his reaction to the script for "Valley of Death," the story scheduled to launch Cable News Network's new magazine show *NewsStand: CNN & Time*. The president of CNN/U.S. had just returned to CNN's headquarters in Atlanta from New York, and he was swamped.

It was less than a week before *NewsStand*'s June 7 debut, and he was focused on getting it off the ground. Back in his office, Kaplan picked up the script. "I read it, and I go, it's like, 'Hell-o Jesus!'" he recalls. In six days, CNN would make a stunning revelation: After an eight-month investigation, it was reporting "that the U.S. military used lethal nerve gas during the [Vietnam] War."

Only a few months earlier, the United States had nearly gone to war with Iraq over Saddam Hussein's stockpiling of chemical and biological weapons. Kaplan continued reading: "Peter Arnett has the story of Operation Tailwind, a raid into Laos, which, according to military officials with knowledge of the mission, held two top secrets: dropping nerve gas on a mission to kill American defectors."

It was a high-stakes, sensational expose, unusual for CNN. Since its emergence 18 years ago as the nation's first 24-hour news channel, CNN had become far more renowned for its saturation coverage of breaking news than its blockbuster investigations. It had been producing weekly newsmagazines for five years. But with audiences of under a million viewers, *Impact*, *NewsStand*'s predecessor, had never matched the huge ratings of network rivals like CBS's *60 Minutes*, ABC's *Prime Time Live* and *Dateline NBC*. "Valley of Death" might give CNN a major boost.

Instead, the broadcast turned out to be an unmitigated disaster. After it aired, so many questions arose about the story's validity that CNN hired constitutional lawyer Floyd Abrams, an advocate for press freedoms as far back as the Pentagon Papers, to reinvestigate. Abrams was assisted by CNN general counsel David Kohler, the lawyer who had

3. Article by Susan Paterno for the *American Journalism Review* p22–31 Sep. 1998. Copyright © 1998 *American Journalism Review*. Reprinted with permission.

scrutinized the piece before it aired and had raised no substantive objections.

Less than two weeks later, Abrams released his findings:
"CNN's conclusion that United States troops used nerve
gas during the Vietnamese conflict on a mission in Laos
designed to kill American defectors is unsupportable." By
early July, CNN had retracted the story and apologized for
a broadcast that had drawn on some of the network's best
talent, including *NewsStand* co-hosts and veteran journalists Jeff Greenfield and Bernard Shaw.

The story's producer, April Oliver, her senior producer,
Jack Smith, and their unit's senior executive producer,
Pamela Hill, had lost their jobs. *Time* magazine—which
ran a print version of the story as part of Time Warner's
vaunted "synergy"—also had to apologize. And Peter
Arnett, a Pulitzer Prize–winning journalist and legendary
war correspondent, was ridiculed for insisting he was simply a mouthpiece, the on-air talent who bore no responsibility for reporting the story. CNN reprimanded him for his
role in "Valley of Death," and his public drubbing exposed
"the dirty little secret of newsmagazines," as one television
news veteran explains: Highly paid on-air correspondents
often act as front people for work done by unseen producers and reporters.

CNN was widely commended for owning up to its mistakes. But it encountered criticism from the likes of Gene
Roberts, former managing editor of the *New York Times*
and one of journalism's most respected figures, for turning
to a lawyer rather than a journalist to sort out the unhappy
affair. And the verdict, rendered swiftly, failed to explain
how two of the country's leading news organizations could
produce what Abrams characterized as a seriously flawed
piece of reporting.

Extensive interviews with those involved indicate that a
series of miscalculations converged to create the "Valley of
Death" debacle. Senior executives, blinded by loyalty and
distracted by corporate concerns, abandoned their roles as
gatekeepers, unable to see the contradictions and ambigu-
ities in the broadcast. Producers at CNN and editors at
Time failed to include their own military beat reporters in
the research, then discounted the concerns of the few journalists and experts who reviewed the script the week
before it aired.

The story, born amid the hype that has come to distinguish television newsmagazines, left behind profound feelings of sadness, anger and betrayal, breaking friendships
and damaging careers and reputations. And coming as it
did around the same time as the disclosure of two
high-profile cases of journalistic fabrication and an investigative report apparently based in part on pilfered voice

*Highly paid
on-air correspon-
dents often act
as front people
for work done by
unseen
producers and
reporters.*

mail messages, the saga was yet another body blow to the already reeling field of journalism.

Kaplan, who stood by while his friend and lifelong mentor Jack Smith was fired, says the episode has been "horrible. It's like your father betrayed you. It's equally horrible for Jack, who must feel like I betrayed him."

For Smith, the disappointment lingers. "You put on the suit, you go up to the executive suite, your priorities change. With Kaplan, they changed dramatically," Smith says. "That was a deep disappointment for me. Kaplan the reporter and producer that I knew doesn't exist anymore."

Back in September 1970, the night before Operation Tailwind, U.S. pilots dropped gas—CNN's report said it was deadly sarin nerve gas, others say it was tear gas—on a village in Laos to lay the groundwork for the next day's assault, according to the broadcast. The next morning, 16 members of a super-secret U.S. squad attacked the village, firing automatic weapons and tossing grenades.

Were Americans in the camp? While "Valley of Death" asserted there were, in fact none of the on-camera eyewitnesses who said they saw Caucasians could say for sure. To assist the soldiers on their retreat, pilots dropped nerve gas on the approaching enemy troops before airlifting the Americans to safety, the CNN report said.

The covert sortie had little documentation and took place in Laos, in a conflict the military managed to keep hidden from the American public for years. No one can say with certainty that the story is false; but even if it were accurate, as Oliver and Smith continue to insist, perceived lapses in the broadcast shifted the debate to the piece's journalistic shortcomings. Particularly problematic parts of the report included having on-camera interviews that were not nearly as definitive as the program's dramatic conclusions, said to be buttressed by supporting evidence from off-camera conversations and anonymous sources.

Even so, Oliver and Smith passionately defend their story. The program, they said in the introduction to their 81-page rebuttal to Abrams' report, "neither contained a thesis nor reached a conclusion. . . . We made clear that the story was based on statements by soldiers, airmen and military officials."

After "Valley of Death" aired, top military officials denied nerve gas was used; one of the broadcast's confidential sources challenged the report's veracity; and key witnesses disputed CNN's account, including pilots on the mission who said they had told the producers they were carrying tear gas but were ignored. CNN's follow-up on June 14 pulled back somewhat from the story's initial bold assertions. And on July 21, the Pentagon's six-week investigation into CNN's charges concluded that nerve gas was never used during the Vietnam War and the men on Operation Tailwind had never encountered defectors.

While taking responsibility for having seen the script ahead of time and still having aired "Valley of Death," both Kaplan and Tom Johnson, chairman of CNN News Group, place much of the blame for the fiasco on the way senior executive producer Hill managed the project and the newsmagazine, keeping them isolated from the rest of CNN—a view vehemently supported and angrily denied by various factions of veteran CNN producers and correspondents.

Hill's unit was considered the A-team, with the best-paid and most experienced staff members, but "she thought she was her own network," says Kaplan, who says he hadn't heard word one about "Valley of Death" until about two weeks before it aired. "That's not the way it works at a network. When you do a sensitive story, you make sure your management knows about it." Arnett agrees that Hill's unit was secretive, and as a consequence, he says, "we didn't have checks and balances in that department. It was the culture of that particular investigative unit that allowed this to happen."

But others disagree. The fallout from "Valley of Death" is not about Hill and the unit, say current and former producers. It's about CNN. Everyone who read the script—including Kaplan, Johnson and the network's attorney—approved it, basing their judgment on the trust they placed in the journalists who had produced it. But by abandoning their gatekeeping role, say critics, they left CNN open to the disaster that followed.

That "Valley of Death" could appear on CNN and in *Time* magazine despite its flaws "shouldn't be dismissed as an aberration, but seen as a biopsy from a system that suffers from a serious pathology," says Ted Gup, a former investigative reporter for *Time* who is now writing books and teaching journalism at Georgetown University.

The controversy, he says, "represents most ominously of all, with the media at large, a very disturbing trend" of senior editors becoming increasingly more gullible, and a tendency for more and more journalists to work in the realm of possibility rather than truth. "You don't print possibilities when they can destroy individual and national reputations," he says. "The stakes are too high."

April Oliver developed the Tailwind story using characteristic enterprise. In the spring of 1997, her boss, Hill, asked her to check out a book by John Plaster called *SOG: The Secret Wars of America's Commandos in Vietnam*. Oliver's reporting led to "The Secret Warriors," which kicked off the fall '97 season for CNN's newsmagazine *Impact* on September 14. It contained, according to the broadcast, "the untold stories of U.S. soldiers used intentionally as bait; chemical agents used, though banned by international protocol; and American troops possibly killed by U.S. air strikes." Oliver hoped the revelations of incapacitating agents would create a buzz in the print media. But "Secret Warriors" fell flat. "There was silence, absolute silence, in the press," Oliver recalls.

About the time Oliver was wrapping up "Secret Warriors," Rick Kaplan joined CNN as president. His appointment was widely reported as an important step for CNN, which had come into the market as an innovator in the early '80s but whose success seemed largely at the mercy of major breaking news events.

Kaplan also was perceived by some as a threat, arriving as CNN management was eliminating 230 jobs to cut costs, even as he was allowed to bring in a stable of talent from his old network, ABC. At the time, CNN was in transition, faced with sagging ratings and competition from upstart cable news channels MSNBC and the Fox News Channel. Kaplan, bringing in fresh blood and new ideas in an effort to reinvigorate the network, angered the CNN traditionalists, says retired Air Force Maj. Gen. Perry Smith, who resigned in protest from his position as the network's military analyst over the handling of the Tailwind controversy. "They think [Kaplan's] destroying the network," he says, using tabloid techniques "to get the ratings up."

As CNN's new president, Kaplan promoted synergy, the latest profit-enhancing trend in an increasingly competitive media market. Synergy meant Kaplan could cross-promote Time Warner's products by launching TV newsmagazines based on collaborative work between CNN and the company's print magazines. One newsmagazine would be *NewsStand: CNN & Time,* which would replace the existing newsmagazine, *Impact,* a show Kaplan thought "uneven."

In September 1997, as Oliver began researching the Tailwind story, Hill assigned Jim Connor to oversee the investigation. Connor, a 25-year news veteran, had worked at NBC as the network's national political producer before arriving at CNN in 1990, where he became No. 2 in the newsmagazine unit. From September to February, Connor "was actively involved" in the reporting, Oliver says. She kept him apprised of her progress as she tracked down tips about the possible use of nerve gas in Tailwind and a purported mission to hunt down and kill defectors.

In October, Oliver says she told Connor of a breakthrough: In a telephone interview, Robert Van Buskirk, a Tailwind platoon leader, said he knew lethal gas had been used on the mission. As a source, Van Buskirk had the sort of background that would lead critics to assail his credibility: He had co-written a 1983 book called *Tailwind* that failed to mention nerve gas or defectors. He had spent time in prison for allegedly running guns (all charges were eventually dropped) and had been on medication for a nervous disorder. None of that, though, invalidated his account, Oliver says.

As she reported, Oliver says, she constantly updated Arnett on her findings. And, she says, she circulated a 10-page memo outlining her evidence to Connor; Hill, the unit's chief; and Hill's former second in command, John Lane. Lane, who had retired, worked on the project as a consultant, according to Kaplan.

Lane, whose credentials include stints as vice president of NBC News and CBS News, had worked with Kaplan before. He had, in fact, been one of Kaplan's mentors and had helped put him on the road to CNN's presidency. "John Lane is an idol to me," Kaplan says.

Connor also assigned Oliver a supervisor in Washington: 62-year-old Jack Smith, a political producer for CNN, formerly CBS-TV's Washington bureau chief and another of Kaplan's trusted mentors. Smith and Lane went way back to their days as newspapermen in Chicago in the '60s, where they had met Kaplan. "Jack is one of the finest human beings I know," Kaplan says. "I have more respect for Jack Smith than for anyone I can think of. I would trust him with my life." Lane and Smith, Kaplan says, "were like family to me."

Lane and Smith also remained close friends. "I love Jack Smith," Lane says. The three linked up at CNN, where Smith hired Oliver and saw in her some of the same qualities he had seen in a young Rick Kaplan.

The team assembled, Hill and Connor laid down the ground rules, Oliver recalls. Smith, working with Oliver in Washington, would "make sure all your i's are dotted and t's are crossed," she says they told her. Connor continued to provide close supervision, Oliver and Smith say, while Hill, based in Atlanta, had more intermittent contact. Connor, who divided his time between Washington and Atlanta, "received every interview, approved every interview request, approved the budget, approved the outline, approved every version of the script," says Oliver.

Oliver, 36, ambitious and smart, had done well at CNN since she arrived in 1994, say those who worked with her. With a Princeton degree and six years of experience producing documentaries and reporting for the *MacNeil/Lehrer NewsHour*, she was not as seasoned as other investigative reporters in the CNN unit, but she was among the newsmagazine's bright, young stars.

It is generally agreed that Hill's magazine unit produced "some of the finest work at CNN," says one senior executive.

It is generally agreed that Hill's magazine unit produced "some of the finest work at CNN," says one senior executive. Hill's reputation as a workaholic is legend, as is her attention to the visual details of a story, her tendency to play favorites and surround herself with loyalists—smart, sophisticated, ambitious journalists. Some who have worked for Hill are fiercely critical, but others are equally devoted and dismiss her detractors as less successful or capable than her champions, resentful because they failed to make the A-team.

The critics, award winners among them, complain that Hill emphasizes style over substance, that she knows far more about documentary filmmaking than painstaking investigative reporting and that the team she entrusted to assemble "Valley of Death" lacked the investigative skills necessary to put together a complicated expose of a top-secret operation. "I'll stand on my record," Hill says, declining further comment.

Hill's record is impressive. She has spent more than 30 years in television, much of it producing award-winning documentaries. Under her direction, ABC's "Close-up" unit won numerous awards. During her eight years at CNN, her production and reporting teams won 13 CableAce Awards, two Overseas Press Club Awards and two Joan Shorenstein Barone Awards.

"Pam has always been committed to doing TV journalism that is serious, interesting and engaging," says Nurith Aizenman, a former CNN associate producer who is now managing editor of the *New Republic*. "I really hope that picture of her isn't lost."

Hill began sending back edits for the Tailwind project six weeks before it aired, says Oliver. Hill's "primary changes were more visual, pacing, editing, dissolves vs. no dissolves, music vs. no music, those kinds of things, as opposed to" journalistic considerations, Oliver says. For example, she says Hill never suggested there were problems with the interview with Adm. Thomas Moorer, a slip that later prompted CNN to apologize and pay the 87-year-old retired admiral an undisclosed settlement. Moorer, chairman of the Joint Chiefs of Staff at the time of Tailwind, was depicted in the broadcast as supporting its thesis, although his on-camera remarks were hardly definitive.

Why didn't senior producers ask Oliver to go back and get an on-camera interview with Moorer where he would state his confirmation unequivocally? Hill and Connor declined to discuss the broadcast.

That Hill and other senior producers accepted "Valley of Death's" off-camera confirmations instead of solid statements of fact on-air surprised a few CNN journalists. Though some in the investigative unit said off-camera confirmations weren't unusual, at least one producer always worked under the assumption that the standard was: "If they don't say it on camera, you don't use it."

To answer any questions that might arise about their reporting, Oliver says Hill asked her to write a memo outlining the evidence and background she had to substantiate the story. She says she sent a 156-page briefing book to Hill

At least one producer always worked under the assumption that the standard was: "If they don't say it on camera, you don't use it."

for distribution to Connor, Lane and Kaplan. (Kaplan says he didn't see it until weeks after the broadcast.)

Kohler, CNN's general counsel, also had a copy of the briefing book. Kohler was expected to assess the story for "libel, slander, what the story would say about individuals," says chairman Johnson. "That isn't to say if he felt he needed to challenge it he couldn't. But his job was legal counsel." Kohler approved the script.

As CNN cranked up the publicity machine to herald the premiere of *NewsStand*, Oliver wrote and submitted the print version to *Time* magazine, agreeing to add Arnett's byline to help market the *Time*–CNN synergy. Marketing was an important part of the new CNN, according to a 1996 management memo circulated in Hill's unit, which said, "We are all tired of toiling in obscurity." Important stories deserve "a full and carefully coordinated press and promotion effort, and a parallel effort to reach interested organizations and government offices. Generating that support is of crucial importance; each of you should consider coordination with our press people one of your basic duties."

Toward the end of May, Hill ran into Kaplan in Atlanta and told him: "We have a neat investigation for the first show," Kaplan recalls. Kaplan says he told Hill he was going to spend the next week in New York working on the launch of *NewsStand*'s other weekly programs, collaborations involving CNN, *Fortune* and *Entertainment Weekly*.

When Kaplan returned to Atlanta from New York on June 1, he says he read the script for the first time, then called Hill and Connor. Kaplan had some "quibbles," he says, and zeroed in on what he felt was a major hole: There was no background on the Vietnam War. He also says he told Hill to send the script to CNN's Washington bureau chief, Frank Sesno. The next day, Kaplan says Hill told him CNN's lawyers had read and approved the script, as had Moorer. (Before the piece aired, Oliver and Smith had taken the unusual step of allowing Moorer to read the script.) *Time* magazine was going to run its version. And, except for a few minor problems, which they had fixed, Sesno was happy as far as Kaplan knew.

It was only much later, say Kaplan and Johnson, that they found out Jamie McIntyre, CNN's Pentagon reporter, had raised serious concerns. McIntyre read the script the same day Kaplan did, made a few off-the-record phone calls and became convinced evidence to support the broadcast's conclusions was lacking. McIntyre wrote a two-page memo to Oliver and Smith outlining his criticism. Even if the story were true, the script as written didn't establish that. It asked the viewer to take on faith that CNN had evidence, rather than presenting it on air.

McIntyre urged Oliver and Smith to consult Perry Smith, CNN's military adviser, a West Point graduate and an Air Force pilot who flew 180 combat missions over North Vietnam and Laos. Johnson also says he told Hill and Kaplan to run the script by Perry Smith. Johnson read it the week before it aired, and he thought the charges explosive enough to require the reporting be "triple-checked."

Meanwhile, Hill had appealed to Kaplan to keep the retired general out of the loop. "You can't let us deal with Perry; it will destroy the story. We've had problems with Perry in the past," Kaplan recalls her saying. So Kaplan says he went back to Johnson, vouched for the investigation, supported his producers, and lobbied against calling Smith. In the end, Johnson says, "Gen. Smith was not brought into the process as I had directed."

Meanwhile, Smith had learned about the story from CNN's heavy promotional campaign. He had consulted on "probably 1,000 stories" for CNN since 1991, but in the last year, CNN had aired two other military exposes without consulting him, he says. One, about a super-secret Air Force base in Nevada, was "as bad a piece of journalism as I have ever seen on CNN," he wrote in a memo to Johnson. The Tailwind premise concerned him as well.

He started making inquiries, talking to people from a pre-eminent military historian to an old friend, retired general Norman Schwarzkopf. He could find no corroboration. He spent a sleepless week, he says, and a few hours before the broadcast, he called Johnson and told him it was a faulty report. Johnson told him to call Kaplan. Perry Smith says he told Kaplan: "You're making a huge mistake that's going to hurt CNN big time." Kaplan had Jack Smith and Oliver call him.

"They had answers to a lot of questions, but not to the most relevant ones," Perry Smith says. But he let it go. "There was only four hours from air. I felt like there was nothing I could do to stop it. But I should have tried."

As airtime approached, Hill also was distracted by management duties, say those close to her: overseeing a prototype and pilot for the new show, continuing to direct the weekly newsmagazine and traveling between Atlanta, Washington and New York, where her husband lives. "We were all moving too fast to get to air; everybody was moving very, very, very fast," she later explained to her staff.

Changes were made, including deleting a reference to the possibility that the "defectors" were Russians. It was taken out at the direction of Connor and Hill "because of time constraints," Oliver and Jack Smith say. Despite their protests, they say, statements by a pilot who insisted tear gas, not nerve gas was used "were taken out by executive and senior producers to preserve a paragraph Rick Kaplan insisted be inserted dealing with the domestic turmoil of 1970."

In the end, Oliver says, "I thought I had a great story, and I believed that my network backed me." When Kaplan saw the video, "my editor told me Rick was beaming from ear to ear," Oliver says. Says Kaplan: "Yes, I was happy with the show, with the piece. I thought the story was clear, the charges were clear, we were accurate. I thought we did a hell of a job."

The story aired June 7. Its publication in *Time*'s June 15 issue, available June 8, "really gave [it] legs and attention in a way that wouldn't have happened otherwise," says Oliver. The producers, including Smith and Hill, were "deliriously happy," recalls one producer. But not for long. Soon gallows humor invaded Hill's unit, and "Valley of Death" was dubbed "The ValueJet of Journalism."

The day after "Valley of Death" aired, hundreds of critical comments came pouring into CNN from military groups and the Pentagon, Johnson says. He called former secretary of state Henry Kissinger and former CIA director Richard Helms, both of whom told him they doubted the veracity of the broadcast. Former Joint Chiefs of Staff chairman Colin Powell told Johnson: "Tom, I think you have one that is likely to blow up in your face. If you have further facts, you better get them out," Johnson recalls. "I was alarmed, very concerned. I knew we had a big problem."

In the weeks following the broadcast, the Special Forces Association demanded a retraction and a veterans group talked of boycotting CNN. The *New York Times* reported: "Adm. Moorer said . . . he had no firsthand knowledge of the Laotian mission, or of the use of sarin in Vietnam." The *Washington Post* quoted Moorer: "I didn't confirm it . . . can't truthfully say I've seen proof." *Newsweek* quoted one of the story's sources, an army captain in the raid, saying: "It's all lies."

His anxiety mounting, Johnson asked CNN's counsel to outline his take on the story. Kohler wrote a 10-page memo to Johnson largely supporting the conclusions of Oliver and Smith, with a few qualifying comments on his role: "Hindsight being 20/20, it probably would have been better to have described Moorer as supporting rather than confirming the use of sarin nerve gas. . . . While I think the use of 'confirmed' was reasonable and supportable, it might have been more prudent to use a less loaded term. I also note that I cleared the use of 'confirmed.'"

Doubts about the story were growing among the rank and file at CNN. Hill organized "a formal meeting to address our questions," recalls one producer. She allayed concerns by telling the staff: "Our 'Deep Throat' is impeccable, it's golden." But the onslaught continued.

Perry Smith says he pushed Johnson hard for a retraction. In return, he says, Kaplan sent him a "very nasty" e-mail accusing Smith of having a "petulant attitude" and characterizing his criticism as "the bleating of a biased amateur." Smith resigned June 14 "on the issue of journalistic ethics," went public on the Internet with evidence contradicting the broadcast, and urged Johnson to sack Arnett and Kaplan. Meanwhile, Jack Smith and Oliver were ordered not to respond publicly until CNN had investigated.

As the charges and counter-charges swirled, Johnson decided in mid-June to hire media lawyer Abrams to investigate, selecting the person he considered the "single most-qualified in the United States to take a look at this. I needed somebody who I felt would have the respect of everyone on the outside."

Although CNN counsel Kohler had approved the script before broadcast, Johnson appointed him Abrams's lieutenant. At first, Oliver says, Abrams "was not introduced as our investigator. He was our ally." Abrams says he could understand why Oliver would consider him an ally. "We were allies in the sense that I was hopeful that I could come to the conclusions that the broadcast could be supported. I was assigned not to defend the broadcast, but to determine if the broadcast was defensible." By Friday, June 26, he says, "My doubts were growing."

Jack Smith says he made repeated calls to Kohler and Abrams insisting that he and Oliver be interviewed for a rebuttal to the report. "They kept putting us off," Smith says. Kohler refused comment, but a company official speaking on his behalf says Kohler didn't recall Smith and Oliver demanding an interview.

Oliver wrote a memo to Kaplan, saying CNN and its silence made her appear "isolated and alone." But, she reminded Kaplan, "This was not a one-reporter project. This was a *NewsStand* team project." She added, "I remain deeply grateful for the mentorship and support of Jack Smith, without whom I could not have survived the past two weeks. . . . He should not be sacrificed for corporate politics, or for the purpose of assuaging the military's wounded honor. Neither should I."

On July 1, Smith and Arnett were summoned to Atlanta to meet with Johnson, Kaplan, Hill, Connor and other senior executives to review the Abrams findings. Oliver, eight months pregnant, was unable to fly.

Abrams had rebuked "Valley of Death" and its producers for sloppiness, unfairness and deception, recommending that CNN and *Time* retract the story.

Smith refused to continue unless Oliver was included. He returned to Washington, where he met with Oliver until 1 a.m. Smith called Kohler, who, he says, agreed to let them "raise our objections and make corrections" to the report before it was released to the public. (A company official says Kohler made no promises.) After reading the report, "We were stunned," Oliver says. Jack Smith says he felt "misled and deceived."

On July 2, CNN broadcast its apology and posted the Abrams report on its Web site; on July 5, it aired a special *NewsStand* elaborating on the retraction. Johnson was determined to retract the story with "the same emphasis we gave the original report," in the belief, he says, that "the huge reservoir of respect and trust in CNN will not be erased as a result of this."

Hill resigned, commenting, "I believed the knowledge of the reporters, the oversight we had in place, and the considerable body of information submitted to support the story insured its accuracy. . . . I now believe we were wrong to air the report as we did, and I fully support CNN's retraction." Connor, who was named to succeed her on an interim basis, declined to be interviewed. He will likely be replaced soon as senior executive producer of *NewsStand*, says Kaplan.

Meanwhile, the gag and gloves had come off and the verbal brawling intensified. Oliver, Jack Smith, Kaplan, Johnson and a multitude of pundits appeared on talk shows and held forth in news articles. On CNN's *Reliable Sources*, Kaplan accused Smith and Oliver of falling "in love with their story." On ABC's *Good Morning America Sunday*, Oliver accused CNN executives in Atlanta of falling "in love with their jobs."

Hundreds of angry CNN staff members demanded to know "why the network's top managers stayed on the job," reported the *New York Times* on July 7. Johnson says he tried to resign twice, but Time Warner's corporate management turned him down. Kaplan did not quit, he says, because "the easy thing to do is walk out." He did, however, send a letter of apology to Perry Smith "saying he was wrong," Smith says.

Severing his relationship with CNN, says the general, "has caused me a considerable amount of sadness." He adds, "I had fought the good fight and had failed and failed miserably. It was clear this Greek tragedy was going to play itself out."

In the end, a system being rebuilt to meet the growing demands of competition broke down, resulting in disastrous consequences not just for CNN but for the people whose lives it changed forever.

Oliver and Jack Smith refused to resign and were fired. Oliver is convinced that at some point, "the decision was made, 'OK, we're going to kill this story, we're going to put this behind us, we're going to drive a stake through the heart of it, make it go away, and somebody's got to be responsible, so April and Jack are out the door. They're

On CNN's Reliable Sources, Kaplan accused Smith and Oliver of falling "in love with their story."

no-names. They'll never be heard from again. She's eight-and-a-half months pregnant; he's 62. He'll retire. She'll have a baby. It's the end of it.'"

Jack Smith says he blames Kaplan and Johnson for running away "from the story so quickly without giving it a thorough review. They relied on the Abrams-Kohler review. They approved the story, but when the heat rose, they bailed." Ultimately, Smith says, "The question should be: 'Where was Rick Kaplan?' If he let this major unit, with so much riding on it, not get his attention and scrutiny, if that's the case as he now claims, then he wasn't doing his job."

In the past, the system at CNN worked well for breaking news, says Kaplan, but not necessarily for investigations, which require a much higher level of scrutiny.

While accepting responsibility, Kaplan has regrets. "I will take this to my grave," he says. "I should have just said, 'We'll hold it.' I should have said, 'Never mind that Smith and Lane and Hill and Connor and legal and *Time* magazine are all happy.'" "The sadness," he says, "is horrible. Jack Smith is a great human being, a family man, mentor, teacher, example, a thoroughly moral, ethical human being. But he lost his cynicism. He wants to be there for April, a woman he has great affection and respect for, who's nine months pregnant. He's on a white horse. Jack stands by, he's very loyal. But loyalty is what got us into a lot of trouble."

For Johnson, the episode was due to a series of breakdowns: "Failure to include our Pentagon correspondent in the original research; failure to include our military affairs adviser in the analysis and reporting phase; failure to give adequate weight to those interviewed who said it simply did not happen; failure to bring to the attention of senior management—me and Kaplan—the serious questions about the sources."

But, he adds, "I hold myself responsible for this. I trusted an experienced team of journalists more than I did a military analyst. And that was a mistake. I have always believed in trusting journalists and producers. I will make certain in the future that we're much more careful."

Toward that end, CNN has instituted changes, including a Johnson decree that "we don't use correspondents as fronts as a rule," he says, and the appointment of Richard Davis as executive vice president for news standards and practices. His mandate is to ensure no inaccurate or unfair stories air.

In the past, the system at CNN worked well for breaking news, says Kaplan, but not necessarily for investigations, which require a much higher level of scrutiny. Kaplan "bears this responsibility too," says Johnson, "but I brought him in as president of CNN. I didn't bring him as a show producer. That was Pam's responsibility. He was relying rightly or wrongly on this unit. I am not placing blame on this unit alone. I shouldn't have let it on the air. Rick

shouldn't have let it on the air. How I wish I could go back
and get the information I have now."

V. Press Freedom at Home and Abroad

Editors' Introduction

Congress shall make no law respecting an establishment of religion, or prohibiting the free exercise thereof; or abridging the freedom of speech, or of the press; or the right of the people peaceably to assemble, and to petition the Government for a redress of grievances.
—The First Amendment to the U.S. Constitution

The United States differs strongly from other nations in that, throughout its history, it has established laws to protect the above-mentioned freedoms. All these freedoms are essential to the preservation of democracy and thus have a relationship to politics. This may be easy to forget in a nation where journalism is often criticized for its focus on celebrity stories and "light" news and inattention to "hard" news. But in many nations, press freedom does not exist, or is a relatively new phenomenon that must be reconciled by governments in transition. The former Yugoslavia, parts of the former Soviet Union, and Hong Kong are just a few places where press freedom must be incorporated into a new governmental system.

Yet while some nations struggle to establish a free press, other nations do not—and this means that nonsanctioned publications are outlawed or that a journalist can be jailed for reporting a controversial story. Human rights groups, many of them based in the U.S., have made an effort to track attacks on members of the press, which may include censorship, harassment, imprisonment, or expulsion from their nations. One such group is the Committee to Protect Journalists. This chapter opens with the introduction to one of their publications, *Attacks on the Press in 1997*. In this piece, William A. Orme Jr. offers an outline of the types of attacks and the impact his group has made in generating awareness of violations of press freedom internationally. He notes that in some nations, to be a journalist is to place oneself on the frontlines of national debate and struggle. He praises journalists' challenges to authority and the status quo.

In the second article, Fredrick L. McKissack Jr., writing for the *Progressive*, criticizes the Nigerian government's repression of freedom and challenges the influence it has tried to exert on African American newspaper publishers in the U.S. He explains that a group of representatives from the American black press visited Nigeria in an effort to take a stand for black solidarity and to challenge the "pessimistic" coverage that Nigeria has historically received in the mainstream American press. Eager to dispel myths of totalitarianism and dictatorship, this group began publishing what was, in McKissack's view, propaganda. He comments that shortly after the group's return to the U.S., a leading writer/activist was executed in Nigeria. He criticizes this group's continued support of the Nigerian government, and expresses disappointment in this vital community press.

The third article, "Press Freedom Under the Dragon," by A. Lin Neumann, describes the challenges writers and the government now face in Hong Kong since its turnover to mainland Chinese control in 1997. Hong Kong has traditionally been exceptionally open to freedom of expression when compared to other Asian capitals and regions; there has been no official crackdown since the turnover, but some journalists have felt the need to modify their coverage. In addition, the article outlines some links between freedom of commerce and freedom of expression in Hong Kong.

The final article in the chapter, Douglas Lee's "1998 Chips Away at Freedom of the Press," is a response to trends in the U.S. that he considers damaging to American press freedom. He lists closed courtrooms, paparazzi laws, and an overall rejection of secret sources as a few of the obstacles to a free press as provided by the First Amendment to the Constitution.

Introduction to *Attacks on the Press in 1997*[1]

For journalists, 1997 was a year of unusual scrutiny, most of it by journalists themselves. Photographers were pilloried for their purported role in Princess Diana's fatal car crash. Editors were criticized for their indefensibly (take your pick) disrespectful or hagiographic coverage of Diana's death and life. In a paroxysm of self-analysis, journalists then assiduously covered the criticism of the journalists.

In editorial meetings and academic conferences, meanwhile, American newspaper editors and media scholars earnestly debated the merits of "public" or "civic" journalism, without ever quite clarifying what this means when translated into front-page agate.

In early 1998, the all-absorbing preoccupation of the press was President Clinton's sex life and—even more—its own reporting on same. Media critics observed that the public seemed at once hostile to the relentless focus on alleged Oval Office dalliances and riveted by the salacious content of the unfolding scandal. News commentators soberly questioned their reliance on anonymous leaks, lamented the overshadowing of Pope John Paul II's Cuba visit and preparations for war with Iraq, and examined anew the ethics and logistics of public reporting on private lives.

Are these the great journalistic issues of the day?

Such concerns seem somewhat remote when viewed from the confines of a Lagos prison, where *Sunday Magazine* editor Christine Anyanwu is serving a 15-year term for publishing stories challenging the official version of an alleged coup plot, or from a Tijuana hospital, where editor-publisher Jesús Blancornelas recuperated from a machine-gunning by the drug traffickers his newsweekly *Zeta* so zealously covers.

In Kashmir, local journalists who face violent retribution from all sides in the armed conflict must decide every day if a story is worth the risk of an abduction or a terror bombing. Editors in West Africa and Eastern Europe aim thumb-in-your-eye satire at their presidents, deliberately testing the boundaries of discourse in societies where offending a head of state is an act of treason; many end up in court, bankrupted by huge fines and legal bills.

The professional dilemma for a journalist in Algiers is whether even to try to venture outside the capital to report on vicious massacres, knowing that you risk summary execution by insurgents while you are reporting, and prosecution by the military if you get back safely and publish your reporting. In Chechnya, where NTV reporter Yelena Masyuk spent 101 days as the hostage

1. Article by William A. Orme Jr., from *Attacks on the Press in 1997*. Copyright © 1998 the Committee to Protect Journalists. Reprinted with permission. William A. Orme Jr. is the executive director of the Committee to Protect Journalists.

of a rebel splinter group, the questions for Russian journalists are basic: Do they succumb to the intimidation of terrorists and the hostility of their military, and walk away from a raging civil war within the borders of their own country? And if they persist despite these pressures, who will defend them?

Hong Kong newspaper publishers must gauge Beijing's tolerance for real journalism, fearing that despite all official assurances to the contrary, overstepping certain undefined lines could jeopardize not only their own publications, but freedom of expression for the entire former colony. In countries as different as Indonesia and Cuba and Turkey, reporters seek out alternative foreign outlets for stories they fear would otherwise be suppressed—often working without pay, or bylines, simply to get information out into the world.

They are fighting openly for their rights, and sometimes for their lives.

The truly critical challenges for journalism today can be found in the scores of countries that are only now slipping free of the authoritarian shackles of the past—countries where reporters can now operate, but where the concept of an independent press is not yet enshrined in law or comprehended by political leaders. In some of these countries, making the problems much more acute, a brief flowering of press freedom in the recent past is being washed away by a new wave of repression and intolerance.

Just by doing their jobs, journalists in these societies are challenging authority and demonstrating to society at large the value—and the risks—of independent newsgathering and commentary. They are fighting openly for their rights, and sometimes for their lives.

They are also grappling daily with fundamental philosophical dilemmas: How does a newly aggressive, critical press expose the inevitable kickback scams, cronyism, and political abuses in fledgling democracies without undermining popular support for the entire fragile democratic experiment—especially since most citizens heard nothing of such seamy things when the authoritarians ruled? Is it possible for a young and sometimes irresponsible popular press to police its ethics without inviting official reprisals against colleagues whose ethics are found wanting?

Can a country torn asunder by intra-ethnic violence survive open democratic discourse without restricting "hate speech"—and can it survive as a democracy if the government dictates what can and cannot be said? In a society without a legacy of constitutional and common-law press freedom guarantees, will well-intentioned free-media statutes be used to regulate rather than protect the press? Is it responsible for editors to assign investigative reporters to stories on drug cartels and arms traffickers when the enemies of these criminal gangs are executed with apparent impunity—and, conversely, is it responsible to succumb to intimidation and leave such stories untold?

Should mainstream journalists in places where the press is under siege unite in defense of marginal muckrakers or fire-brands who face jail or censorship—and suffer the consequences of perceived association with extremist or even repugnant viewpoints?

Even when the answers appear self-evident, the cost of doing the right thing can be extraordinarily high.

In contrast to their jaded brethren in London or Washington, these editors and writers and broadcasters are quite consciously engaged in nation-building. They see themselves—correctly, though not necessarily happily—as actors, not just scribes. Some unhesitatingly cross a line their first-world colleagues perceive as dividing journalism from activism. Americans, especially, should look back at their own history before passing judgment: Dissident journalists in Zagreb or Hanoi may have less in common with the editor of the *Washington Post* than with John Peter Zenger or Tom Paine. It is not just that the news media are an integral part of the political process: In some places, they are the political process. In Central Europe or sub-Saharan Africa, where emerging anti-government forces are fractious or inexperienced, or in South America, where old political parties have been fatally weakened by corruption and compromise, the independent press becomes almost by default the de facto opposition. And those in power respond to that threat accordingly.

These are the people on the profession's front lines, uncovering news that matters, in their own countries and beyond, at great risk to their news organizations and themselves. It is not as if the rest of us don't have a stake in this. Almost invariably, it is local journalists who alert the international media to what is really going on in Russia, or Mexico, or Nigeria, or Israel, or even China. And in this age of instantaneous satellite feeds and Internet news services, local journalists increasingly provide the text and video we see from the latest global flash points.

The chief concerns confronting many of these journalists are whether it is possible to go with a story and stay in business, or stay out of jail, or simply stay alive. At least 26 journalists were murdered in 14 countries in 1997 because they were working journalists. At the end of the year at least 129 journalists were held in prison in 24 countries because of alleged offenses directly related to their journalistic work. Scores more were threatened with legal reprisals or violent retribution.

These people are the focus of [the work of the Committee to Protect Journalists (CPJ)]. We have learned that international pressure, from journalists on behalf of their fellow journalists, can be highly effective. "I look at CPJ as a kind of giant crane that suddenly appeared overhead and plucked me out of jail," Ocak Isik Yurtçu told me last year, shortly after a CPJ mission had persuaded the new Turkish govern-

Even when the answers appear self-evident, the cost of doing the right thing can be extraordinarily high.

ment to release the imprisoned newspaper editor and six colleagues. But at least 29 journalists remain in prison in
Turkey, plus 17 in Nigeria, 16 in Ethiopia, 15 in China, and
eight in Burma.

In 1997, CPJ put extra emphasis on illuminating and, ide-
ally, reversing disturbing trends in places we view as leading
indicators for press freedom worldwide: China, Mexico, Jordan, Turkey, and the Caucasus region. . . . Some of CPJ's
work, such as in Azerbaijan and Hong Kong, was largely
fact-finding: documenting the details of the life of the daily
press under difficult new circumstances. In other cases, such
as Turkey and Mexico, our emphasis was on working with
local journalists to reform repressive laws, get journalists out
of jail, or to keep journalists from being sent to jail.

But the bedrock of CPJ's work are the many specific cases
of threats and abuse we document and respond to on a daily
basis. . . . Without this detailed, painstakingly documented
case information, and our track record of rapid and effective
response to such incidents, CPJ's more analytical work
would be an essentially academic exercise.

The hundreds of cases reported in [1997] represent just a
fraction of the year's attacks on journalists and press freedom violations, but we attempt to include the most significant incidents in the more than a hundred countries we
regularly cover. In aggregate, these incidents provide a compelling picture of the challenges facing journalists in places
where journalism is constantly under siege. They also give a
sense of the magnitude of the problem: The cases that CPJ
can actively and effectively address are in themselves a small
fraction of the minority of cases that we are able to confirm
and put on the public record in the course of the year.

The often grim statistics . . . —journalists jailed, newsrooms ransacked, reporters murdered—should not be misinterpreted as a kind of inversely proportional press freedom
index. For journalists to get into trouble, there must first be
journalists: In truly totalitarian societies there are no independent editors or reporters to attack or prosecute. In Russia
today, journalists work under constant fear of legal reprisals,
political coercion, and violent attack—at least 13 reporters,
editors, and broadcasters have been murdered because of
their work in the 1990s. A decade ago, CPJ had little to report
about the former Soviet Union, save for the occasional
harassment of a foreign correspondent and the repression of
samizdat dissidents. Yet it would be absurd to conclude that
were was less press freedom in Russia in 1997 than in 1987.
In scores of other shakily emerging democracies, CPJ now
has a full logbook of press freedom violations, whereas a
decade ago we would have simply noted for the record the
continuing restrictions on press freedom and moved on.

Most of the approximately 100 countries CPJ routinely covers are neither the best nor the very worst examples of jour-

nalistic freedoms. We also focus our advocacy work on behalf of local journalists in countries where international opinion is likely to have an influence. That leads to what some governments perceive as a double standard on our part. We pay much closer attention to South Korea, now one of Asia's most democratic societies, than we do to North Korea, one of the most repressive regimes on earth. For the past year, CPJ's highest research and advocacy priority has been the imprisonment of journalists in Turkey, and even some of our colleagues in Istanbul ask why we aren't spending equivalent energy on neighboring Iraq, for example, where an independent journalist would risk not jail, but execution.

We are also often chastised for ignoring the real press freedom problems in our own country. Because CPJ was founded with the express intent of not replicating the work of well-funded and effective domestic journalism organizations, we do not cover the United States—or, for that matter, the other industrial democracies, where journalists also tend to be well organized in defense of their own interests. The exceptions we make are rare. We are vigorous in demanding investigations when journalists in the United States are murdered, an occurrence not as uncommon as is often supposed. We make our views known on U.S. actions or policies which we believe endanger journalists abroad, whether they are nationals or visiting correspondents (an example is the CIA's insistence on having the option to recruit journalists as spies and use journalism credentials as cover for its own agents in the field).

Homicide is the leading cause of job-related death among journalists worldwide.

Both are fair criticisms. We concentrate our limited resources on countries where journalists tell us that they want and need international support, and that skews both our newsgathering process and our reporting priorities. We are also sometimes accused of defending people—the imprisoned, even the dead—who are in the view of some not really journalists. This is a critique we respectfully reject.

Of the 26 cases of murdered journalists confirmed by CPJ in 1997, all but six were the victims of deliberate political assassination, and all were clearly targeted because of their work. This pattern has held true for more than a decade: Homicide is the leading cause of job-related death among journalists worldwide. Accidental deaths while on assignment, including combat casualties, are the relatively rare exceptions to this rule.

Again, it is not the number of deaths that we should emphasize. Thousands of innocent civilians lose their lives every year in civil conflicts, and journalism is by no objective statistical measure among the world's most dangerous professions. What matters is the intent of those murders, and their result. These are calculated and all too frequently effective acts of censorship. The ultimate target is not a journalist as an individual, but society at large.

Governments are rarely directly responsible for these crimes, but governments—especially in self-described democracies—are responsible for aggressively investigating and prosecuting those responsible for these crimes. Yet this rarely happens, and almost never without sustained domestic and international pressure. That is why it is always a priority for CPJ to document these cases carefully, to publicize them as widely as possible, and to hold government accountable. Still, the pattern in 1997, as always, has been one of impunity: Only 5 of the 26 cases have led to arrests, and even in those instances those believed to have ordered the killings have not been charged or even questioned. There were many other cases of journalists murdered last year where there is reason to suspect a causal relationship between the crime and the victim's work, but where governments have failed to conduct even the most basic investigations.

Some of the horrors of recent years abated in 1997, reducing the numbers of journalists killed in the line of duty. For the second straight year there were no journalists killed in any part of the former Yugoslavia, a dramatic change wholly attributable to the Dayton peace process. Algeria, which had seen 60 journalists murdered since 1993—more than any other country—was spared the tragedy of additions to this toll in 1997. Tajikistan, which had by mid-decade become one of the most dangerous places for journalists on the globe, with at least 29 documented assassinations, was also absent from 1997's list. The apparent contract murders of investigative reporters in Moscow and the kidnapping and executions of correspondents in Chechnya had combined to make Russia a nation with an alarmingly high death toll in recent years. In 1997, however, there were no instances where the evidence made clear that a reporter or broadcaster or editor had been murdered as a result of his or her professional work.

Still, the continued inability of the Yeltsin government to find and prosecute those responsible for earlier murders put a palpable chill on Russian investigative journalism in 1997. And the fact that no Algerian journalists were killed last year should not be misinterpreted as a sign of improvement in press freedom there. Algerian journalists continue to function under a virtual state of siege, suffering threats of violence from militant Islamists and threats of legal reprisals from the military government. There are fewer victims in large part because so many Algerian journalists have gone underground, fled into exile, or left the profession entirely, while those who remain on the job live and work under the most extreme security precautions. In the former Yugoslavia, where at least 47 journalists were killed in the past decade, there have been no casualties among journalists since the 1995 signing of the Dayton peace accords. The Dayton accords put at least a temporary stop to the killings. But the press in Bosnia and Croatia and Serbia is still far from independent, or free from the fear of violent reprisals.

In every reported case of a press freedom abuse, CPJ must first determine the people involved were journalists and the attack or prosecution was related in some direct way to their profession. This is necessarily a somewhat subjective process. Who is a journalist? For the purposes of our work, we define the profession as broadly as possible. Journalists who are sentenced to prison or targeted for assassination include renowned newspaper editors and struggling provincial stringers, political polemicists and by-the-book news service reporters, star television correspondents and shoestring community radio activists. In totalitarian societies, where by definition there is no independent journalism, dissident pamphleteers or pirate radio operators will be defended by CPJ if punished for what they have written or broadcast. Journalists jailed for campaigning for freedom of expression also get our support: If journalists don't stand up for other journalists who are fighting for press freedom, who will?

We will also defend as journalists those who would not define themselves primarily as journalists: That is because governments sometimes define people into our profession for us by prosecuting them for what they have published in newspapers or said on the radio. If a political leader who pens occasional opinion columns is assassinated, we would presume that the murderer was motivated by politics, not by a specific newspaper piece. Such a case would be a tragedy, but not an entry in CPJ's ledger. But if a politician were prosecuted and imprisoned on the basis of what he had written as a columnist, we would defend the politician as a journalist—because journalism would be the nature of that alleged offense.

It is a painful paradox that as press freedom increases around the world, so does the number of casualties in the press corps. But the multiplying incidents of violence and legal harassment against journalists should not obscure the real news: There is more press freedom and more independent journalists are taking advantage of that freedom than ever before in history.

That doesn't mean that press freedom progress is now a straight, unbroken line, or that it is obtained without a struggle. In part, the story of 1997 was one of worrisome backsliding in many countries where this decade had begun with unprecedented freedoms.

The 1990s have witnessed an unprecedented explosion of independent news media around the world. In scores of countries, regimes marked by authoritarianism or outright despotism were forced to cede power to new, more pluralistic

In the former Yugoslavia, where at least 47 journalists were killed in the past decade, there have been no casualties among journalists since the 1995 signing of the Dayton peace accords.

The 1990s have witnessed an unprecedented explosion of independent news media around the world.

governments which at least in principle ascribed to the notion that freedom of expression is a fundamental right. State propaganda networks were dismantled or transformed into genuine news agencies, while upstart private newspapers and broadcast outlets vied for audiences hungry for real, uncensored news and commentary.

The triggering event was the collapse of Soviet communism, the single most dramatic advance of the century for press freedom. Almost overnight, journalists in the former Warsaw Pact republics began aggressively asserting their independence, and courting an audience that was no longer a captive of state media. In Central Asia, a region that had in its history never experienced an independent press, tiny newspapers and fledgling radio outlets appeared within months of the Soviet Union's dissolution. The short-lived democracy movement in China, propelled by reverberations from Gorbachev's Moscow, revealed a generation of eager, idealistic young reporters and commentators. One of the instructive surprises of this transformation was that so many reporters and editors for Soviet-era state media—whom many Western journalists had viewed not as colleagues but as apparatchik cogs in a Communist propaganda machine— were both eager and able to act as authentic journalists, once given the political chance. This is an important, encouraging lesson for those of us dealing today with reporters for state news services in China, or Vietnam. We should give them the benefit of the doubt.

Not only the Communist world—or the ex-Communist world—was caught up in this revolution. In Africa and Latin America, military dictators and civilian autocrats who had survived by exploiting Cold War rivalries were abandoned by foreign patrons, and then by their own people. In contrast to the Soviet bloc, where independent media emerged in the aftermath of the system's collapse, the local news media in these countries were in the vanguard of change from the start. From Central America to Southern Africa, fledgling news organizations of the 1990s have their roots in democratic rebellions and popular insurgencies of the 1980s. This thawing effect seemed contagious: In the Middle East, the news media in Algeria and Jordan and Yemen became much more openly critical at the beginning of the decade, while in East Asia the best newspapers of Manila and Taipei and Seoul aggressively asserted their independence. Not all of this newfound media independence was handled responsibly: unverified rumors were often peddled as news, and hatemongers in Central Europe and Central Africa took to the airwaves to incite genocide. Much more the pattern, though, was an almost startlingly fast and lasting consolidation of a vibrant, independent, and increasingly professional news media, from Bangkok to Warsaw to Buenos Aires.

Now, however, the distressing pattern in many places is a return to repression. The Algerian military has clamped down on coverage of Islamists and counterinsurgency campaigns. In most of Central Asia the once-nascent independent press has been smothered out of existence by violence and censorship. In the Caucasus, Azeri censors and Georgian hit men keep independent reporters under control. Peruvian journalists again live in fear of military harassment. Hanoi has abruptly turned away from the path of liberalization. In Liberia and Sierra Leone, the once-independent press functions under something akin to martial law. And in nearby Lagos, once home to perhaps the most vigorous press on the continent, journalists are ruthlessly driven underground or into exile. These are the exceptions to the rule, but they are necessarily the places where CPJ must focus its efforts in the coming months and years.

This annual report can be read as a catalogue of horrors, and the physical dangers and political pressures facing journalists around the world are unquestionably acute and increasing. But beneath this press-abuse case log is a substratum of good news: Journalists around the world are defying this intimidation and creating loyal new audiences for fearless, independent newsgathering, and neither they nor their readers will easily tolerate a return to the days of state propaganda and censorship.

This [report] is a chronicle of resistance. It is a reminder that the highest standards of our profession are being upheld at great personal cost by journalists like Nigeria's Christine Anyanwu, Mexico's Jesús Blancornelas, and Turkey's Ocak Isik Yurtçu. This latest annual edition of *Attacks on the Press* is dedicated not just to the 129 journalists who were imprisoned at year's end and to the 26 journalists who lost their lives in the line of duty in 1997, but to the hundreds of bold, enterprising reporters and editors and broadcasters who insist on doing their jobs under conditions that would make most of us abandon the profession for dentistry or carpentry. They are paying a price, but they are also making history. By paying attention, by offering moral support, by reporting to the world about them and their stories, we can help them to continue to do their jobs.

[Editors' note: The Committee to Protect Journalists maintains a Web site at http://www.cpj.org.]

Black Press for Sale: The Nigerian Government Buys Cover[2]

In the early history of the black press, with magazines such as W. E. B. DuBois's *The Crisis* and Marcus Garvey's *Black World*, black Americans could expect their own papers to take a stand in solidarity wlth other oppressed people.

During the 1930s, several black newspapers brought the atrocities of the Italian invasion of Ethiopia to the homes of black Americans. During the 1980s, the black press helped step up the campaign to free Nelson Mandela and South African blacks by running stories and editorials that shed light on the ravages of apartheid.

But apparently that mission has changed, at least when it comes to Nigeria. Last September, a delegation of black newspaper publishers, led by Dorothy Leavell, president of the National Newspaper Publishers Association (NNPA) and publisher-editor of the *Chicago Crusader*, traveled to Nigeria. The publishers went, they said, to contest the mainstream media's coverage of Nigeria, which they termed "pessimistic."

The NNPA represents more than 230 black newspapers read by approximately 15 million people. Besides acting as a lobbying arm for the black press, the organization operates a wire service that distributes copy to member newspapers.

When Leavell was elected last June, she said the NNPA "will remain fully in the forefront of the continuing struggle for black rights." But when she reported her Nigeria findings at a press conference in New York after her trip to Nigeria, readers had to wonder who the NNPA was struggling for.

"There was no evidence of a dictatorship or 'thug-ocracy' in Nigeria, contrary to widespread media reports about that country," Leavell stated during the October 4 press conference. "While there was spirited debate and often disagreement, it was in the form of loyal opposition among people who want to be permitted to work out their own problems among themselves without foreign intervention. . . . As a concerned group, we wish to say that everyone in America who has an interest in Africa and Nigeria should start to look to the pages of black newspapers across the country."

Leavell's statements came one month before the Nigerian government, led by General Sani Abacha, executed writer-activist Ken Saro-Wiwa and eight others on trumped-up murder charges.

---

2. Article by Fredrick L. McKissack Jr. for the *Progressive*. Copyright © 1998 the *Progressive*. Reprinted with permission. Fredrick L. McKissack Jr. is the co-editor of the Progressive Media Project.

Saro-Wiwa was the leader of the Movement for the Survival of the Ogoni People and known for his stinging criticism of the Nigerian government and the Shell Oil Company.

But the fact that Saro-Wiwa and his codefendants were facing execution at the time of the black newspaper association's tour did not seem to bother Leavell.

"To this point, Nigeria has made three false starts at emulating democracies, we conclude that we should not . . . impose an alien democracy on that country as some in America demand to be done," Leavell said.

What Leavell's October 4 comments—and subsequent articles about Nigeria from the organization—failed to mention was who paid for the trip. According to William Reed, executive director of the NNPA in Washington, D.C., the Nigerian government covered most of the expenses.

Doesn't this pose a serious conflict of interest? "No," Reed says. "What they saw is what they saw."

As for Ken Saro-Wiwa, Reed says, "The press was trying to make this man look like St. Francis of Assisi." While Saro-Wiwa may not have pulled the trigger, "he put out the hit."

"We disagree categorically," says Adotei Akwei, the African government program officer for Amnesty International in Washington, D.C. "We considered Ken a prisoner of conscience. He never advocated violence."

Akwei says that the NNPA lost all credibility when it took the fact-finding trip to Nigeria on the government's money, then bought into Abacha's disinformation campaign concerning Saro-Wiwa.

Leavell did not return phone calls. But she remains unapologetic about taking the trip, according to an article in the April 6 edition of *Editor & Pubiisher*, a newspaper trade publication.

"If *Editor & Publisher* would like to send us on a trip, we'll be glad to accept," she told that publication.

Leavell said the U.S. government should use "even-handed tactics" in dealing with Nigeria. "You've got China, which has committed some of the worst human rights atrocities in the world, and there are no sanctions against that government," she said.

On its trip, the NNPA managed to ignore one of the principal actors in the Nigerian controversy: Shell Oil.

"I don't think anyone with the delegation dealt with Shell Oil," Reed says. "A meeting was not under consideration"

How could Shell and the environmental destruction of Ogoniland, as well as other regions, be overlooked by the delegation and its reporting on Nigeria? Reed says the "suggestion could be made" that such a meeting between the NNPA and the company take place in the future.

Reed, however, has met with Shell officials. "It's a dirty business. It doesn't enhance the environment," Reed says, but he insists that Shell has worked with local residents and the government in order to curb environmental abuses.

"Shell officials said that Ken Saro-Wiwa had 'extracted his pound of flesh,' Reed says, adding that Shell officials told him Saro-Wiwa had received consulting contracts and fees from the company.

"There is no information to that effect," Akwei says. "This is being done to discredit Ken."

The National Newspaper Publishers Association continues to front for the Nigerian government. Readers of the March 3, 1996, edition of the *Oakland Post*, for example, found a colorful eight-page insert, NIGERIA: A CLOSER LOOK. The *Post* advertisement doesn't make clear who paid for the insert, although the Nigerian national seal is prominently displayed throughout.

The coverage of Nigeria by the NNPA has brought into sharp focus the need for a coherent policy toward Africa by black leaders in this country.

Approximately 200 newspapers nationwide used the tabloid, which was distributed through Amalgamated Publishers in New York. Amalgamated is the advertising representative for many black newspapers.

The insert included a December 26, 1995, letter to President Clinton from Roy Innis, national chairman of the Congress of Racial Equality, and a letter to the editor from the Reverend Maurice A. Dawkins, a freelance writer for the NNPA. Both letters accused Saro-Wiwa and the Ogoni opposition group of being murderers and terrorists.

Dawkins's letter also accuses the United States and the British governments of being racist and neocolonial for denouncing the current Nigerian government and its leader, General Abacha.

Keith Jennings, executive director of the African American Human Rights Foundation in Washington, D.C., and the former mid-Atlantic director of Amnesty International, does not spare his feelings for the NNPA.

"Look, they are in the payment of Abacha and they are confusing people," he says "When are we going to be consistent? You can't talk about democracy here and not there. As for Ken Saro-Wiwa, they want to rewrite history. These guys, if they were honest, they'd say they were doing this for Abacha."

It irked Jennings that the same arguments used by the NNPA in its support of Abacha were used in defense of Clarence Thomas during his Senate confirmation hearings.

"We've got to get away from this give-the-brother-a-chance thing," Jennings says. "You don't need a lot of foreign-policy experience to see what's right and what's wrong. You can have legitimate debate but [the NNPA] is being dishonest. They should admit there is a material benefit. They are getting advertising dollars."

The coverage of Nigeria by the NNPA has brought into sharp focus the need for a coherent policy toward Africa by black leaders in this country. "What should our foreign policy be toward Africa?" asks Jennings, adding that simply saying Africa doesn't need to be run by white folks isn't the solution. "Transnational corporations, along with the World Bank and the International Monetary Fund and their destructive structural adjustments—there you have your neocolonial dynamic."

Where the South African conflict was black versus white—which was easy to sell to black America—the Nigerian conflict is black versus black. Nigeria is involved in class warfare, with Abacha and the Nigerian ruling class searching for and finding friends among America's black bourgeoisie. The black press is at a disadvantage when it comes to covering Africa because of limited resources. Most papers do not have an international section, much less an Africa one. But this doesn't excuse fronting for repressive regimes and the World Bank, as in the case of an April 29, 1995, story in Leavell's paper, the *Chicago Crusader*.

"With World Bank advice and financial help—interest-free (forty-year) loans to Africa totaling $10 billion over the last four years from the International Development Association, the soft-loan arm of the World Bank—many African countries have undergone remarkable changes bringing greater effciency and better use of resources," says a page-one article without a byline, entitled AFRICA: A CONTINENT OF OPPORTUNITY. "But not only is IDA good for Africa, it is good for America. Business profits from it."

A month later, the paper printed an editorial on the Ebola virus outbreak in Zaire, EBOLA—SPONTANEOUS GENERATION OR GENETIC ENGINEERING?, that crossed the line between skepticism and paranoia. The editorial writer openly wondered if the World Health Organization was purposely spreading the Ebola and AIDS viruses in Africa.

"Once again—why Africa? Some people can't help but think something is fishy and that we don't have the real story" the May 20, 1995, editorial reads. "The AIDS virus . . . has demographics in Africa that coincidentally follow the path of WHO immunization projects."

Of course, not all black newspapers have lost their way like the *Chicago Crusader*.

The *City Sun*, a Brooklyn-based weekly, is one of the few black newspapers that features an international page. The paper ran the NNPA's Nigeria insert, but also ran an opposing editorial.

"In terms of the black press in general, I think most African-American papers are just kind of focused on black people in this country and not in general," says Karen Carrillo, deputy editor of the *City Sun*. "The sad thing is that the NNPA can get away with this because most people don't know what's going on."

The mainstream media, she said, has not done a good job of covering Africa, save for spot coverage of wars and fam-

The black press is at a disadvantage when it comes to covering Africa because of limited resources.

ines, and the black press does not have the resources of the mainstream. This void allows the Nigerian government, through the NNPA, to play upon the longstanding notion that the mainstream white media are ruthlessly attacking a poor, beleaguered African nation.

"We get letters in support of Nigeria from people and they can't even spell Abacha's name right," Carrillo says. "There is just an ignorance about what is going on."

On February 7, the *Richmond Afro-American/Planet*—the oldest continuously run black newspaper, founded in 1883—went out of business. For the black press, this was an unmistakable symbol of hard times.

As with the mainstream press, circulation is falling among black newspapers. According to the NNPA, 90 percent of the black community subscribed to a black-owned newspaper in the 1950s. Readership today has fallen to less than one in three.

Meanwhile, newsprint costs have skyrocketed 83 percent since 1994 alone. This combination of falling circulation and rising costs could prove fatal for more black newspapers in the months ahead.

But if black papers continue to act as apologists for brutally repressive governments like the one in Nigeria, maybe they deserve to go out of business.

Press Freedom Under the Dragon[3]

It did not take long for the Hong Kong Journalists Association to serve notice on executive secretary Tung Chee-hwa that it would be watching his office closely. On July 10, just days after the handover of Hong Kong to China by the British, the HKJA sent Tung a letter criticizing perceived "favorable treatment" given to official Chinese state news agencies in coverage of the handover.

The group complained that China Central Television was given special access to some of Tung's early official appearances. "If Chinese official media have privileges in reporting, then news and information will very likely be held in the hands of the official media, seriously threatening press freedom," said the letter, signed by HKJA's chair, Carol Lai.

It was the kind of outspoken approach that has become the hallmark of the HKJA. Currently in its 29th year, with some 500 members, it is the largest press association in the territory and has lobbied consistently for the continuation of Hong Kong's free press under Chinese rule. The group says it will tolerate no backward movement in the battle for free expression. In their letter, the journalists urged Tung to "make efforts to preserve the existing media coverage system, which is based on fairness for all involved." In response, Tung's office called the incident a misunderstanding.

HKJA vice chairman Liu Kin-ming, a frequent and vocal critic of Beijing, said it is the association's responsibility to remain engaged with the new administration of Tung Chee-hwa and to fight any effort to curb the liberties enjoyed by Hong Kong's reporters and editors. He summed it up this way in an interview with CPJ: "To my colleagues, I ask them to please say no to the censors. To the publishers, I say, without your support we cannot win this battle. And to the outside world: Keep your eyes on Hong Kong."

What's at stake immediately in Hong Kong is the vibrancy not just of local media but of the vast network of regional and international press operations based in the territory. Hong Kong has long been East Asia's English-language news media capital and more important the principal safe haven for professional, independent Chinese-language reporting about the internal political and economic affairs of the People's Republic. Readers in the vast Chinese diaspora from Taiwan and Malaysia to British Columbia and California have depended on Hong Kong reporters and publications for

3. Article by A. Lin Neumann. Excerpted from a special report by the Committee to Protect Journalists. Copyright © 1999 the Committee to Protect Journalists. Reprinted with permission.

decades. If this dynamic journalism culture disappears or is significantly eroded, it will have profound repercussions for all of Asia.

Equally important to the region's future is the inextricable relationship between the free flow of information and the strength of financial markets. Hong Kong's robust economy flourished in a climate of free expression that allowed for the rapid exchange of information necessary for the smooth functioning of the regional economy. Investors will still need Hong Kong's free press if they are to understand the dynamics of the changes that are underway in China and the rest of Asia. Without this continual supply of accurate, uncensored economic information, it is hard to imagine Hong Kong retaining its position as the region's premier financial marketplace.

Leaders of the international financial community have begun to articulate this concern. U.S. treasury secretary Robert Rubin raised the issue of press freedom during Tung's first official visit to Washington in September.

In a private session with Tung, Rubin linked freedom of information to Hong Kong's continued financial health. "I think Hong Kong can remain and will remain a major market center, a major financial market center, as long as Hong Kong continues to have the free flow of information [and] the rule of law," Rubin told CNN following the closed-door meeting. "I think that's something that we can all be hopeful about but also have to watch very closely."

Hong Kong's new leaders contend such concerns are misplaced. And on the surface, little seems to have changed. After the smoke of fireworks and celebration cleared, Hong Kong businesses resumed their usual frenetic pace, and reporters for the former colony's 16 major daily newspapers continued to file their stories as they had before the handover. Even the most critical dailies have continued to publish without overt reprisals. "The government is functioning as normal," Tung said in early September. "The financial market is moving. Demonstrations are continuing arguments everywhere—What has changed is that Hong Kong is now a part of China. There is a sense of pride here that this has happened, and happened without a hitch."

The resumption of Chinese sovereignty in Hong Kong has enormous geopolitical significance, signaling an end to the last vestiges of the British Empire and the emergence of China as an economic and political superpower. The people of Hong Kong have been anticipating this transition for many years, and few seasoned observers predicted dramatic upheaval in the immediate aftermath of the British withdrawal. China's leaders and supporters steadfastly maintained prior to the transition that no major changes would take place. "One Country, Two Systems," the phrase coined by the late Deng Xiaoping to describe the principle that

Equally important to the region's future is the inextricable relationship between the free flow of information and the strength of financial markets.

would allow Hong Kong's quasi-democratic, free-market system to coexist with the motherland's one-party Communist rule, was supposed to work this way. The Special Administration Region (SAR), as Beijing calls Hong Kong's territory, is meant to be making money, not trouble.

Beneath the calm, however, much has changed. Hong Kong today is a different place than it was before the turnover and a much different place than it was before the reality of the return began to sink in during the last several years. The climate of free expression in Hong Kong has shifted in subtle but distinct ways: In the vibrant Hong Kong press, self-censorship has become a fact of life. Newspapers owned by powerful business leaders with wide-ranging economic interests in China have become less willing to criticize Beijing.

Given China's history of tolerating little, if any, critical reporting or commentary in its national press, Hong Kong journalists have been left to wonder what might really be in store for them. "We don't know the Chinese bottom line yet," said one veteran reporter as she discussed the handover with colleagues inside the cavernous Hong Kong Convention Center press room two days after the fact. "I think Hong Kong journalists will be learning the Chinese bottom line."

Reporter Mak Yin Ting, sitting at the same table, quickly shot back, "Sure, we have to search for a bottom line. But why should there be a bottom line? That is an infringement on freedom. Why is it you can advocate Chinese patriotism but you cannot advocate other ideas?"

What about you, a visitor asked the first journalist, will you challenge the Chinese government's press freedom bottom line once you find it?

"Unfortunately, there is a point beyond which I cannot go and I will not go. Because I do not want to be locked up," she replied.

Tung's Friends

It should come as no surprise that Tung Chee-hwa, a shipping magnate with a history of close ties to Beijing, is more interested in preserving Hong Kong's economic vibrancy than its freewheeling journalism. But Tung's open admiration for Singapore's autocratic leader Lee Kwan Yew may signal more than just disinterest in free expression, presaging harsh treatment of independent journalists. Lee, the architect of Singapore's rise to prosperity through stern governance and laissez-faire economics, is the principal proponent of the view that a free press is incompatible with "Asian values." Lee has been openly critical of Hong Kong's democrats. China is too powerful to be influenced by their calls for democracy, Lee told the Singapore newspaper *Straits Times* in June. "If you don't believe that the Hong Kong people understand that, then you don't understand Hong Kong," he said. "Let's not waste time talking about democracy . . . If I were a Hongkonger I would think twice before interfering in the political affairs of the mainland."

Under Lee, Singapore offers little space for democracy to flourish, and the notion of modeling Hong Kong on Singapore raises reporters' worst fears. In May, for example, a government critic was ordered to pay senior officials a $5.7 million libel judgment for defaming them. The critic, Tang Liang Hong, called Singapore leaders liars because they had attacked him as an ethnic Chinese chauvinist. Over the years, Singapore has been the bane of journalists. Two Hong Kong-based regional publications, the *Far Eastern Economic Review* and the *Asian Wall Street Journal* have been periodically banned, and their reporters have been sued or barred from the country in disputes with Singaporean officials. In Singapore, journalists may even be prosecuted not simply for critiques of government leaders, but for the publication of mundane, accurate trade statistics prior to their authorized release by the government.

Tung agrees with Singapore's Lee on the issue of the cultural relativism of rights, supporting Lee's view that Asian countries put a higher value on group harmony and discipline than on the individualism prized in Western cultures. "Human rights is not a monopoly of the West," Tung told reporters in August. "When you talk about this, you have to look in terms of different countries, different historical processes, different stages of development." When asked by reporters for his reaction to Malaysian prime minister Mohamad Mahathir's call for a revision of U.N. covenants on human rights to reflect Asian values, Tung said, "I'm sympathetic to this argument. I really am."

Will Tung lead Hong Kong to become a constrained city-state like Singapore, with a tame and timid press? In the rush to please both big business and Beijing, will Hong Kong come to resemble capitalist autocracies like Indonesia and Malaysia, where civil liberties often fall victim to the leaders' whims?

Already, the Beijing-appointed provisional legislature, which supplanted the elected legislature on July 1, has quietly begun to rubber-stamp important pieces of legislation in advance of legislative elections scheduled for May 1998. Hong Kong residency rights have been amended to deny residency to mainland-born children of Hong Kong Chinese residents. This ostensible technicality has great significance in Hong Kong, where mainland-born children of parents with legal Hong Kong residency have long had the right to live in the territory. In a move supported by some business leaders, the appointed legislature also suspended a number of labor laws, passed before Britain returned the colony to China, which gave workers the right to collective bargaining, protected labor activists, and allowed unions to contribute to political campaigns.

A new law governing legislative elections, which are scheduled for May 1998, will dramatically limit the extent of popular electoral participation and roll back the near-universal suffrage enacted at the end of British rule. The new proposal allows only 20 of the legislative council's 60 members to be popularly elected. Ten would be named by a Beijing-appointed electoral college. Another 30 would be picked by "functional constituencies," made up of corporate leaders, bankers, and professional groups. The changes virtually ensure that the top vote-getter under the British, the Democratic Party, will have a limited voice in the new legislature. "Tung's new election laws are nothing less than a great leap backward for democracy in Hong Kong," Democratic Party chair and ousted legislator Martin Lee wrote in the *Washington Post* during Tung's U.S. visit.

What is emerging from these changes may be a corporatist model in which an entrenched business elite, backed by a powerful overseer in China and led by Tung, is guaranteed an electoral majority. In such a model, it is not difficult to envision attacks on press freedom or civil liberty easily passing a parliament with only a nominal opposition presence.

Regardless of the promises enshrined in the agreements that govern the handover and the transition to the new Chinese Hong Kong, it seems certain that the press will become less free, more cautious. "The feeling we have is of inevitability," said Daisy Li, a former editor at the Chinese-language *Ming Pao* daily. "Freedom of the press will be cut back."

Li's career reflects many of the changes that some journalists both fear and resist. Widely respected by her colleagues, she has held a number of leadership positions in the Hong Kong Journalists Association. In 1993, worried about the impending transition to Chinese rule, Li led a campaign to reform antiquated British-era official secrecy and sedition laws that could be used to restrict press freedom if they remained on the books. She also helped lead an international campaign to free *Ming Pao* reporter Xi Yang, who was imprisoned in China in 1993 for his reporting on Chinese government gold trading. For her efforts in these campaigns, Li was awarded an International Press Freedom Award by CPJ in 1995.

But Daisy Li sees little future for the mainstream press in Hong Kong. She says her newspaper, once one of the most critical voices in Hong Kong in its coverage of China, has gone soft. Self-censorship is a fact of life in the newsroom, Li says, and she wants no part of it. In August, she left *Ming Pao*, as have three other top staffers and HKJA members in recent months, citing displeasure with editorial changes. "Publishers have ties to big business and to Beijing," she said. "That just encourages self-censorship." But instead of

Self-censorship is a fact of life in the newsroom, [Daisy] Li says, and she wants no part of it.

leaving her home in Hong Kong or her profession, Li plans to start a Hong Kong-based on-line magazine. "I'm just leaving my paper," she explained. "I'm not leaving journalism."

The frustration Daisy Li and others feel is captured in a survey of Hong Kong journalists conducted last May by Joseph Chan, a professor at the Chinese University of Hong Kong. Over a third of those surveyed practiced some form of self-censorship in criticism of China or large Hong Kong corporations. More than half of the respondents believed that their colleagues censored themselves. In another survey of journalists undertaken by Hong Kong University in 1995, 88 percent said self-censorship was well-entrenched; 84 percent in that poll expected the situation to deteriorate under China. Eighty-six percent of Hong Kong business executives polled by the *Far Eastern Economic Review* shortly before the handover predicted the press would no longer be free under China.

If the polling data on self-censorship are accurate, the shift to Chinese rule has already had a profound impact on Hong Kong's journalists. The anecdotal evidence of self-censorship is abundant; journalists frequently begin a conversation on Hong Kong's media by conceding that self-restraint now pervades the newsrooms. "It is self-censorship rather than direct intimidation that will undermine the freedom of expression in Hong Kong," said Carol Lai of the Hong Kong Journalists Association. "We are on a dangerous path that can only lead the media to accept greater restraint. So far all the signs do not seem positive but we can only hope."

One of the most respected foreign correspondents in Hong Kong, Jonathan Mirsky, the Asia editor of the *Times* of London and a long-time Hong Kong resident, eloquently described the gradual tightening of controls in a piece for the *Index on Censorship* in January: "This is the way we live now in Hong Kong. Sometimes Beijing barks angrily or just murmurs. More often its likes and hatreds are so well understood that, like the colonial cringe of yesteryear, local collaboration with the 'future sovereign' is automatic and preemptive."

Such pessimism, however, is not universal among journalists in Hong Kong. L. P. Yau, the editor in chief of the weekly *Yazhou Zhoukan* (*Asia Week*), a regional Chinese-language news magazine, is well regarded among Hong Kong journalists. He predicted before the turnover and insists now that Chinese sovereignty presents no direct threat to press freedom. "Two months after the handover, the Hong Kong press sees no problem of political interference," said Yau. "There is no commissar to tell any publications how to run the newsroom, nor do the readers feel any deprivation of information. There are still all kinds of criticisms of China in the media, as well as those magazines that are specialized in criticizing China."

Yau related an anecdote that he believed offered another positive measure of press freedom. At a recent banquet hosted by Taiwan's Central News Agency's Hong Kong bureau, the bureau's editor in chief declared that his staff has had no problem functioning in Hong Kong since the handover. In contrast, Taiwanese journalists have had a rough time on the mainland, where they are forbidden to set up bureaus and occasionally experience government harassment. So their treatment in Hong Kong is important not only as an indicator of that territory's press conditions, but for what it augurs for China's relationship with Taiwan as Beijing seeks to woo Taiwan into reunification. If "One Country, Two Systems" will work in Hong Kong, the thinking goes, then it should be applied in Taiwan.

"It seems that the SAR government and Beijing are determined to project an image that Hong Kong, unlike China, remains free in the wake of the handover," said Yau. "My personal feeling is that Hong Kong is doing a good job for the time being, yet its destiny is closely related to stability in Beijing. As long as the economy is all right, Hong Kong will relish the good taste of press freedom."

The Basic Law

If Hong Kong is to remain free, its legal lifeline is the Basic Law, the mini-constitution governing the Special Administration Region. Yet to be fully defined by the courts and open to contradictory interpretations, the Basic Law is the sole guarantor of press freedom and the rule of law for Chinese Hong Kong.

Much of what happens to Hong Kong also may be determined by the attitudes that emerged from the 15th Communist Party Congress held in Beijing in September, the occasion for President Jiang Zemin to formally solidify his hold on power. And as the Congress neared, tantalizing hints of possible political reform in China began to emerge. Early in September, Liu Ji, a senior aide to Jiang, broke with a nearly decade-long moratorium on discussion of reform and called for more political liberalization to satisfy rising popular demand. "The continued rapid development of China's economy is safeguarded by reform of the political structure," Liu Ji said in an interview with the official China news service. "Otherwise the consequences are unimaginable."

Expressing sentiments that have not been heard in official China since the People's Liberation Army violently crushed the democracy movement in June 1989, Liu, who is vice president of the Chinese Academy of Social Sciences, said, "When the people have enough food to eat and enough clothes to keep warm and as cultural standards increase, they will then want to express their opinions. The people wanting to take part in political thinking is a good thing, it is a sign of the prosperity and strength of the nation and is also a tide of the age that cannot be turned back."

Jiang himself hinted at political reform during his speech before the Congress. "As a ruling party, the Communist Party leads and supports the people in exercising the power of running the state, holding democratic elections, making policy decisions in a democratic manner," Jiang said. While hardly a manifesto for free expression, Jiang's remarks were bold by recent Chinese standards. Since 1989, Chinese officials have avoided public discussion of reform because of the assumption that official calls for easing restrictions on expression in the late 1980s contributed to the student uprising in Tiananmen Square.

Chapter Three, Article 27, of the Basic Law . . . provides for "freedom of speech, of the press and of publication."

It is too soon to assess whether such talk of reform will lead to action. And the recent rhetoric of democracy is not likely to erase the cumulative weight of Chinese officials' more typical public pronouncements about the press. For example, Lu Ping, Beijing's Director of China and Macao Affairs, evoked Hong Kong journalists' worst fears about Chinese rule last June in his warning to the press against "advocating" independence for Taiwan, Hong Kong, or Tibet. That, he said, would be a violation of national security restrictions in China. "It is all right if reporters objectively report. But if they advocate, it is action. That has nothing to do with freedom of the press."

Lu's statements reflect a view of the relationship between speech and action whose ultimate extension is the massacre of demonstrators in Tiananmen Square. It is a position incompatible with the freedoms that Hong Kong people have enjoyed under the territory's rule of law.

Yet because the Basic Law, hammered out in often-contentious negotiations between Beijing and London after the 1984 Joint Declaration agreeing to the handover, gave half a loaf to each side in the debate over press freedom, there is uncertainty about how the two views will be reconciled in the post-handover period. Chapter Three, Article 27, of the Basic Law, titled "The Fundamental Rights and Duties of the Residents," provides for "freedom of speech, of the press and of publication." The same article guarantees freedom of association, assembly, procession, demonstration, and the right to strike and form unions; there is also the right of academic freedom, and of literary and artistic creation. Framing these freedoms is Article 39, which promises to comply with the International Covenant on Civil and Political Rights. It also prohibits the introduction in Hong Kong of any restrictions incompatible with the covenant.

But Article 23 seems potentially to contradict Articles 27 and 39. It instructs Hong Kong to pass laws prohibiting "treason, secession, sedition, subversion against the Central People's Government, or theft of state secrets," and prohibits political organizations from establishing ties with foreign political organizations.

The relationship of these three potentially contradictory clauses has never been clarified. This "is the great fascination for me as a constitutional lawyer," Hong Kong legal scholar Yash Ghai said in a wide-ranging analysis published by Dateline: Hong Kong, a Web site devoted to the handover. "It is also the great challenge of the Basic Law."

The Basic Law will be adjudicated both in the Hong Kong courts and by a committee of the Chinese People's Congress, notes Ghai. "You have this one document which is subject to two different regimes of interpretation." Questions about freedom of expression in Hong Kong would ostensibly be handled by the Hong Kong courts, which are to remain independent of Beijing. But Article 23 broadly dictates that certain questions of freedom of expression fall under China's jurisdiction. So, for example, criticism of Chinese authorities might be deemed as within the purview of Article 23.

Hong Kong courts might take the line, consistent with common law, that the Basic Law is binding and creates rights and obligations. But the two bodies could have different approaches to those rights. Ghai said, "I suppose that ultimately the standing committee of the national People's Congress will prevail because it also has a general power of interpretation of all the laws passed in the People's Republic of China."

While such thorny interpretive and jurisdictional issues arising out of the Basic Law may take years to be fully adjudicated, Beijing's decision to dismiss all opposition members of the elected legislature as of July 1 and to appoint a provisional legislature seemed a clear enough sign that civil liberties would suffer. "National security can be anything [Chinese government officials] say it is," noted Robin Munro, the director of the Hong Kong office of Human Rights Watch-Asia, "and that is absolutely worrying."

Will China be able to tolerate an irreverent, independent Hong Kong press climate?

Will China Rein in Hong Kong's Press?

Will China be able to tolerate an irreverent, independent Hong Kong press climate, in which reporters, writers, commentators, and editors seek to push the boundaries?

With 16 major daily newspapers, two commercial television stations, and two commercial radio stations, in addition to the seven English and Chinese-language outlets of government-owned but independently run Radio Television Hong Kong, the territory's media have flourished under an open system. The city is home to dozens of foreign news bureaus that cover Asia out of Hong Kong because of its ease of transport and climate of freedom. The regional press is also based in Hong Kong, and news magazines such as the *Far Eastern*

Economic Review, Asia Week, and *Yazhou Zhoukancan* freely publish objective reports on virtually any topic with little fear of interference.

Hong Kong is one of the few places in Asia where journalists operate with almost no government control. Indonesia, Singapore, and Malaysia require licenses and special visas for journalists. In Hong Kong, anyone can be a journalist. There are no government-issued press cards or journalists' visas. When press rights are threatened elsewhere in the region, Hong Kong is the place of refuge, where regional activists can meet journalists with little fear of apprehension or sanction from local authorities.

Hong Kong's role as a media center and a press freedom haven has continued with little change under the new dispensation. Human rights observer Michael Davis of Chinese University of Hong Kong has said that one important measure of press freedom will be Chinese treatment of dissident publications. "Hong Kong is the one Chinese-language press that regularly confronts Beijing," Davis said. "Watch *China Rights Forum* and other such publications to see how they fare. That will be a test."

China Rights Forum, a small independent magazine published by the group Human Rights in China, has had no trouble, according to director Sophia Woodman. "As far as how things are going here, nothing seems very different," she said in late August. In addition, according to Woodman, *Beijing Spring*, a Chinese dissident magazine produced in the United States, is still on Hong Kong newsstands.

Writing in the *International Herald Tribune* in late August, Philip Bowring, the former editor of the *Far Eastern Economic Review*, said he saw Hong Kong's media little changed after the transition. "Although there was an evident increase in media self-censorship in the months leading up to the handover," Bowring wrote, "the situation has not become worse. Indeed, there are signs of greater determination now to exercise old freedoms and test the new limits. Commentators may be wary of being too rude about leaders in Beijing, but they are familiar enough with many of Mr. Tung's acolytes to feel free to display their views, and sometimes their contempt."

While Hong Kong's journalists may continue to tread lightly on stories about Beijing's power elite, they already regard Tung and the provisional legislature as fair game. Many of the legislators, and certainly Tung himself, have long been subjects of scrutiny by the local media, and they may quickly establish a rhythm in their relationship quite different from that between Beijing and the mainland press.

During the party congress, *Apple Daily* gave front-page play to the full text of a letter signed by former Communist Party leader Zhao Ziyang, who has been persona non grata in China since his ouster just before the Tiananmen Square massacre. Zhao's letter, which called on Politburo leaders to reassess the government's violent suppression of the pro-democracy demonstrators, provoked only stony silence from party officials. But Jimmy Lai's newspaper once again displayed its penchant for airing Beijing's dirty linen in public.

Still, China's record of inflexibility toward the press on the mainland raises the question of how long it will be before China acts to rein in Hong Kong's feisty journalistic culture. With Hong Kong's media often seeping into Southern China, will pledges to leave the broadcast news alone be honored in the longer term? In the event of social or political unrest in China, or other occurrences that could cast Beijing in a less than positive light, how will China's leaders react if Hong Kong reporters cover the story?

Beijing traditionally has been sensitive to the point of paranoia about the reporting of economic information. In 1994, Chinese reporter Gao Yu was sentenced to six years in prison for her reporting on China's economic reforms for the generally pro-Beijing Hong Kong magazine *Mirror Monthly*. Last May, when UNESCO honored Gao in absentia on World Press Freedom Day, Beijing called her a "criminal" and threatened to close the UNESCO office in China.

It is not hard to imagine a scenario in which powerful economic interests in Beijing bridle at critical reporting about so-called "red-chip" stocks, issued by Hong Kong-based China-owned companies. These red-chip companies, currently the darlings of the market, have defied the tumble in Hong Kong share prices that has accompanied the economic downturn in Thailand and the rest of southeast Asia. Yet some financial analysts say that many of these companies are wildly overvalued, and the lack of transparent reporting about the nature of their ownership in China make them inherently unreliable. Eventually even bullish business writers in Hong Kong could uncover potential scandals in the red-chip market. Would China regard an exposé of a scandal in a Hong Kong-traded, Beijing-owned company as a threat to "national security"?

Covering the new Tung government has caused some journalists to complain about lack of access and lapse into nostalgia for the public relations–conscious British administration. "The level of access and the culture of secrecy is already worse," said Stephen Vines, a veteran Hong Kong reporter and editor who has worked in both the local and foreign media. "Something happens when you phone Tung's office and you get no answer. [Former Hong Kong governor] Chris Patten was very media-savvy and media-friendly. Now there is no one you can phone up for a straight answer."

Tung's inaccessibility is symptomatic of an executive-led government that tolerates the press as a necessary evil, Vines

China's record of inflexibility toward the press on the mainland raises the question of how long it will be before China acts to rein in Hong Kong's feisty journalistic culture.

said. Patten lobbied long and hard to get the Hong Kong media to believe in his efforts to democratize the territory. Tung doesn't see the press as a partner in the public discourse. "But," cautioned Vines, "it's not as bad as China. Not yet anyway."

Vines's attitude seems to prevail in Hong Kong, where journalists often take to heart the old adage: Hope for the best, prepare for the worst. It is no coincidence that Hong Kong's amazing economic growth [has made it] the world's eighth-largest trading economy, with a per-capita income that rivals many European countries has been accompanied by great freedom. It is that freedom to report and challenge and exchange information that has brought the world to Hong Kong as Asia's financial and business hub.

If China and Tung Chee-hwa confound the critics and allow the one-country, two-systems philosophy to flourish in Hong Kong, it may open the way toward greater press freedom for all of China. At the 15th Party Congress, Jiang set in motion the further privatization and modernization of the Chinese economy by calling for the sale of state-owned companies to private shareholders. As the Chinese government proceeds with privatization, the last vestiges of a socialist economy will likely whither away, further erasing the barriers between China and the rest of the world. The next aspect of the Chinese system to go should be the apparatus of one-party control over information and the press. No country has built a successful, dynamic modern economy on the scale of China without allowing its people democracy and free access to information. Hong Kong knows how to be free; it can point the way for China.

Success in Hong Kong will be measured in large part by freedom of information and the rule of law. At stake in Hong Kong is the health and vigor of one of the world's great trading economies, a vital cog in the great wheel of Asian commerce and development. In that sense, the whole world will be watching and living with the outcome of Hong Kong's drama.

1998 Chips Away at Freedom of the Press[4]

In an environment in which no news usually is good news, 1998 would appear to have been a fairly good year for the freedom of the press.

The U.S. Supreme Court didn't issue any landmark media decision. Congress didn't pass any law abridging press freedom. The president didn't conduct even his private affairs in secret.

Unfortunately, however, the media were not freer at the end of 1998 than they were at the beginning. Newsgathering in particular took several significant blows during the year, as did the overall openness of the judicial system. Subpoenas to reporters became more commonplace, as did closed courtrooms, anonymous juries and sealed depositions. The law in most cases did not change, but judges' application of it did. As a result, reporting the news today is indisputably more problematic than it was a year ago.

The media, of course, did not lose every court battle in 1998. A number of courageous judges threw out libel suits, rejected requests to close courtrooms and upheld reporters' rights to keep sources and materials confidential. Those cases, however, were the exception rather than the rule. The most significant media losses were seen in three areas—closing the judicial system, requiring the media to provide evidence and restricting newsgathering. Examples of these losses can be found throughout the country.

The media were not freer at the end of 1998 than they were at the beginning.

- **Closing the judicial system**. Almost every high-profile case found judges limiting media access to the judicial system and the participants in it. The judge in the Unabomber case refused to disclose the names of jurors. Mountains of evidence in the Paula Jones case were kept under seal, even after portions had been leaked to the media. Despite a federal law that clearly allowed the media to attend Bill Gates' deposition, access to that proceeding was denied. In a corruption trial involving a state welfare official, an Illinois federal judge sealed documents and permitted Gov. Jim Edgar's testimony to be videotaped in private. A federal appeals court upheld a Louisiana trial court order prohibiting jurors from discussing their deliberations. A judge in Los Angeles banned several reporters from covering a prosecutor's opening statement after they refused to promise not to report what they heard. A judge in Florida closed his

---

4. Article by Douglas Lee for the Freedom Forum Web site (http://www.freedomforum.org). Copyright © 1999 the Freedom Forum. Originally published on January 4, 1999, the article is available in the Freedom Forum's online archives. Reprinted with permission.

courtroom during testimony about possible prosecutorial abuse and then ordered the witnesses who testified not to reveal what they had said. Judges in several other states also issued gag orders to prevent attorneys and witnesses from speaking with the media about their cases.

- **Requiring the media to provide evidence**. Attempts by prosecutors and other lawyers to learn the identities of confidential sources and to obtain other unpublished information were once routinely rejected. Today, however, judges are granting these requests with alarming frequency. Reporters in California and North Carolina are awaiting appellate court decisions to learn whether they must disclose their confidential sources or serve jail sentences. A reporter in Georgia was ordered to testify about an interview subject's mental state. A Pennsylvania court required a reporter to surrender his notes from an interview. A New Orleans television station was one of several stations across the country ordered to provide lawyers with unaired portions of interviews. Several newspapers also were forced to turn over unpublished photographs, including the Casper, Wyo., *Star-Tribune*.

What judges perceive as media excesses also appear to make them less sympathetic to First Amendment rights.

- **Restricting newsgathering**. Two cases testing whether the media should be allowed to accompany law enforcement officials executing search warrants on private property are currently before the U.S. Supreme Court— *Hanlon v. Berger* and *Wilson v. Layne*. In October, California became the first state to adopt anti-paparazzi legislation, which allows celebrities and crime victims to recover damages from reporters, photographers and camera operators who trespass in order to obtain pictures or audiotapes of the celebrity or crime victim engaging in a personal or family activity. Similar legislation is pending in Congress. Lexington police interpreting a Kentucky law claim that they have a right to censor addresses, phone numbers and information about injuries from traffic accident reports. Despite new legislation designed to increase access to information about campus crime, university officials across the country still routinely refuse to release many crime reports and disciplinary records.

These setbacks and the trends that they exemplify are easier to document than explain. An underlying theme in many of these cases, however, is a frustration with how the media gather and report news. Knowing that they can't control how the media cover a case or report a story, many judges and legislators attempt to obtain more orderly coverage by restricting access to events, people and documents. What judges perceive as media excesses also appear to make them less sympathetic to First Amendment rights.

Unfortunately, nothing about the end of 1998 and the beginning of 1999 suggests that any of these trends will reverse, or even slow. To the contrary, the increasing role of the Internet and other technology in news reporting and the increasing competition among media entities suggests that newsgathering will be even more aggressive in 1999. If 1998 is any indication, we should expect judges and legislators to react unfavorably to that aggressive reporting and to continue chipping away at media freedoms.

Bibliography

Books and Pamphlets

An asterisk (*) preceding a reference indicates that an excerpt from the work has been reprinted in this compilation or that the work has been cited.

Anderson, Rob; Dardenne, Robert; Killenberg, George M. *The Conversation of Journalism: Communication, Community, and News.* Praeger Publications, 1994.

Applegate, Edd. *Journalistic Advocates and Muckrakers: Three Centuries of Crusading Writers.* McFarland and Co., 1997.

*Bagdikian, Ben. *The Media Monopoly.* Beacon Press, 1997.

Bird, S. Elizabeth. *For Enquiring Minds: A Cultural Study of Supermarket Tabloids.* University of Tennessee Press, 1992.

Bozell, L. Brent, III, ed; Baker, Brent H., ed. *And That's the Way It Is(n't): a Reference Guide to Media Bias.* Media Resource Center, 1990.

Chalaby, Jean K. *The Invention of Journalism.* Macmillan Press: St. Martin's Press, 1998.

Dennis, Everette E., ed; Snyder, Robert W., ed. *Media and Democracy.* Transaction Publications, 1998.

Ettema, James S; Glasser, Theodore Lewis. *Custodians of Conscience: Investigative Journalism and Public Virtue.* Columbia University Press, 1998.

*Fallows, James M. *Breaking the News: How the Media Undermine American Democracy.* Vintage Books,1997.

*Frank, Reuven. *Out of Thin Air: The Brief Wonderful Life of Network News.* Simon and Schuster, 1991.

Fuller, Jack. *News Values: Ideas for an Information Age.* University of Chicago Press, 1996.

Hachten, William A. *The Troubles of Journalism: a Critical Look at What's Right and Wrong With the Press.* Erlbaum, 1998.

Hamill, Pete. *News is a Verb: Journalism at the End of the Twentieth Century.* Ballantine Publishing Group, 1998.

Harper, Christopher. *And That's the Way It Will Be: News and Information in a Digital World.* New York University Press, 1998.

Herman, Edward S; Chomsky, Noam. *Manufacturing Consent: the Political Economy of the Mass Media.* Pantheon Books, 1988.

Kasoma, Francis Peter. *Journalism Ethics in Africa.* ACCE, 1994.

Krajicek, David J. *Scooped!: Media Miss Real Story on Crime while Chasing Sex, Sleaze, and Celebrities.* Columbia University Press, 1998.

Merritt, Davis. *Public Journalism and Public Life: Why Telling the News is Not Enough.* Erlbaum, 1998.

Mongerson, Paul. *The Power Press: Its Impact on America and What You Can Do About It.* Fulcrum, 1997.

Nerone, John C. *Violence Against the Press: Policing the Public Sphere in U.S. History.* Oxford University Press, 1994.

Schudson, Michael. *Origins of the Ideal of Objectivity in the Professions: Studies in the History of American Journalism and American Law, 1830–1940.* Garland, 1990.

Seib, Philip M. *Journalism Ethics.* Harcourt Brace College Publications, 1997.

Solomon, Norman and Cohen, Jeff. *Wizards of Media Oz: Behind the Curtain of Mainstream News.* Common Courage Press, 1997.

Additional Periodical Articles with Abstracts

Those interested in reading further on the subject of the power of the press may refer to the articles listed below. Please note however, that some of the articles listed reflect issues not addressed in this book, and are intended to provide readers with a more comprehensive look at the broader theme of contemporary journalism.

Journalism for the brave. Stacy Lu. *American Journalism Review* 18:15 Je '96

Reporters in America's ethnic press have to be careful to stay on the right side of things. Immigrants bringing their customs with them—from China or Haiti, for example—do not always go along with the American ideal of free speech. Consequently, political, social, historical, or criminal barriers often mean that immigrant journalists are unable to tell the truth. Some have been fired, blackballed, or beaten up, while others have even been killed.

A furor over the CIA and drugs. Kelly Heyboer. *American Journalism Review* 18:10-11 N '96

Rumors of federal involvement in illegal drug trafficking and in the narcotics epidemic that has ravaged black neighborhoods were brought to the surface by a three-part series in the *San Jose Mercury News*. The series, written by Gary Webb and published August 18-20, 1996, reported that CIA-backed supporters of the Nicaraguan Contras raised money to acquire weapons by importing crack cocaine and selling it to street gangs in Los Angeles. Some black activists, politicians, and conspiracy buffs seized on the story as proof of a link between the U.S. government and the ill-treatment of African-Americans. Other journalists have questioned the basis of the stories, however, and an article in the October 4 Washington Post concluded that the series had exaggerated the drug ring's significance and raised questions about Webb's reporting technique.

Is there life after Marv? Rem Rieder. *American Journalism Review* 19:6 N '97

Journalism's addiction to celebrity and tabloid stories needs to be overcome. The coverage of such stories is so pervasive that it can seem as though these stories are the only things in the world that matter. Sandy Rowe, editor of Portland's *Oregonian* and president of the American Society of Newspaper Editors (ASNE), has started an ASNE initiative, including a think tank from America's major newspapers, to help rescue journalism's credibility.

The Diana aftermath. Jacqueline Sharkey. *American Journalism Review* 19:18-25 N '97

Media excesses surrounding the death of Diana, Princess of Wales, have heightened public outrage and sparked calls for restrictions on the behavior of the media and the paparazzi. A number of journalists and analysts believe coverage of Diana's life and death mirror the way in which entertainment values have taken the place of traditional news values in numerous American newsrooms. Proposed laws in the area of media intrusion are the most recent in a series of moves by lawmakers and the courts to cite privacy as a reason for limiting the activities of journalists.

Preserving Old Ethics in a New Medium. J.D. Lasica. *American Journalism Review* 19:52 D '97

What may be called transaction journalism, the quid pro quo between a Web publication and outside concerns such as advertisers or business partners, could soon dwarf all other ethical issues in cyberspace. To the extent that it blurs the division between editorial and commercial interests, it poses a danger to the integrity of online journalism. Consequently, in the still developing conventions of this nascent medium, journalists should embrace the standards and values of traditional journalism: editorial integrity, balance, accuracy, respect for others, and fairness.

The intervention dilemma. Susan Paterno. *American Journalism Review* 20:36-43 Mr '98

The ethical quandary raised by a powerful series in the *Los Angeles Times* on the mistreatment of children by their drug-addicted parents is discussed. "Orphans of Addiction," a two-part series that ran in the paper in November, was the result of long-term observation by a photographer and a journalist. Media ethicists and legal and social welfare experts who reviewed the series argue that journalists should retain their distance from the events they witness most of the time, but not when they are seeing children suffer, especially over months. The complicated reactions the series provoked nationwide are examined.

When the Story is About the Owner. Carol Guensburg. *American Journalism Review* 20: D '98

The impact of conglomerate media ownership on journalistic integrity is examined. In October a news story criticizing Walt Disney Company was shelved by the corporation's *20/20* newsprogram, raising questions as to the accuracy of news in the age of the expanding multi-media conglomerate. The role of the corporate giant and the ethical issues involved in the newsprograms run by these companies is explored.

Mud and the mainstream. Andrea Sachs. *Columbia Journalism Review* 34:33-38 My/ Je '95 Despite the *National Enquirer's* enviable circulation, which approaches 3.5 million copies a week, the tabloid is still considered disreputable. Increasingly in recent years, however, it has won grudging respect from its mainstream rivals for the thoroughness and accuracy, if not always the taste and fairness, of its stories. Some papers have gone beyond respect to cover events that the Enquirer covers. A prime example is the O. J. Simpson trial.

The Diana effect: will anything change? *Columbia Journalism Review* 36:40-1 N/D '97

A number of journalists were asked whether they thought journalism should change in the wake of the Princess Diana tragedy. Excerpts from their answers are provided. Contributors are Jerry Nachman, former editor-in-chief of the *New York Post*; Susan Ellerbach, managing editor of *Tulsa World*; Ellen Hume, executive director of PBS's Democracy Project; David Shaw, media critic for the *Los Angeles Times*; Richard Lambert, editor of the *Financial Times*; Alexis Gelber, managing editor of *Newsweek Inter-*

national; and Louis D. Boccardi, president and chief executive officer of The Associated Press.

What we do now. *Columbia Journalism Review* 36:25-8 Mr/Ap '98

Part of a special section on the White House sex scandal. Regardless of the scandal's outcome, the press will fall in the public's opinion. In a Pew Research Center poll of 844 people taken from January 30 to February 2, almost two-thirds said the media had done only a fair or poor job of cautiously checking the facts before reporting the story, 60 percent said the media had done only a fair or poor job of being objective on the story, and 54 percent thought the press produced another fair or poor performance in supplying the correct amount of coverage. According to Andrew Glass, Cox Newspapers' senior correspondent, President Clinton's increased popularity in the polls is in part a backlash against the press because supporting Clinton is a way people can declare that the press has been too critical.

The erosion of values: a debate among journalists over how to cope. *Columbia Journalism Review* 36:44-7 Mr/Ap '98

Excerpts from a forum involving a panel of five top journalists held in early December 1997 entitled "Confronting the Crisis," which discussed the rise of the tabloid and the trivial on the country's pages and screens, and the growing pressure to conform to the values of corporate owners.

The great pretender: how a writer fooled his readers. Ann Reilly Dowd. *Columbia Journalism Review* 37:14-15 Jl/Ag '98

Stephen Glass's articles in the *New Republic* proved too good to be true. On June 29, following an investigation, the *New Republic* announced that Glass had fabricated all or part of 27 articles that appeared in the publication. Most of the stories were called a "blend of fact and fiction," and misinformation included an account of misbehavior among young conservatives. It is surprising that Glass was not caught out sooner by the *New Republic* and the other leading publications he wrote for.

Pushing the "cure": where a big cancer story went wrong. Michael Shapiro. *Columbia Journalism Review* 37:15-16 Jl/Ag '98 p.

A May 3 *New York Times* report on a cure for cancer was misleading. The front-page article hinted quite broadly that one of two new drugs, angiostatin or endostatin, could begin to cure people of cancer within a year. The reality is that the celebrated breakthrough is only a possibility at the moment, and by inviting overstatement the article undermines the great discovery at hand.

TV news: the great celebrity chase. Lawrence K. Grossman. *Columbia Journalism Review* 37:23-4 Jl/Ag '98

The writer discusses TV newsmagazines' pursuit of celebrity guests. With so many newsmagazines going after so few trophy guests, anything goes when it comes to getting a celebrity to come on a show. For instance, according to *Newsweek's* Ann McDaniel, the lengths to which the networks went in order to court Monica Lewinsky's former handler, lawyer William H. Ginsburg, were unbelievable. The pursuit of big-name guests is probably going to become even more unseemly as TV magazines proliferate.

Killing the messenger. Eve Conant. *Columbia Journalism Review* 37:19-20 S/O '98

Journalist Larisa Yudina was one of the many Russian reporters to perish in 1997 because of their writing. Yudina was murdered by two former aides of President Ilyumzhinov of the Russian Republic of Kalmykia—where the danger to journalists is perhaps greater than that which existed during the Soviet era. Yudina's murder illustrates the lack of press freedom that is found in the outer reaches of the former Soviet Union. The president of the Glasnost Defense Foundation, an organization that monitors press freedoms, points out that by July 1998, six journalists had been killed in Russia, yet not a single case where a journalist has been killed as a result of their journalistic activities has been solved in Russia.

Ten mistakes that led to the great CNN/*Time* fiasco. Neil Hickey. *Columbia Journalism Review* 37:26-32 S/O '98

The writer discusses the errors that gave rise to CNN and *Time's* collaborative TV and magazine "Valley of Death" report on the U.S. military's Operation Tailwind. The debut episode of the newsmagazine, called *NewsStand: CNN and Time*, alleged that the U.S. military used sarin nerve gas on a military base camp in Laos in 1970, killing 100 people, including Americans who had defected to the enemy. An internal CNN study found that the program's researchers' and producers' weak and superficial understanding of the facts begat the sloppy and reckless report. Both CNN and *Time* have issued apologies, acknowledgments, and retractions of their stories. Ten mistakes that CNN and *Time* made in reporting Operation Tailwind are examined.

Just how far is too far? Michael Hoyt. *Columbia Journalism Review* 37:48-9 S/O '98

The writer reflects on the boundaries of journalistic practice and the ethical questions posed by investigative journalist Mike Gallagher's expose of Chiquita Brands International.

CJR poll: after Monica, what next? Neil Hickey. *Columbia Journalism Review* 37:30-3 N/D '98 The writer presents the results of a *Columbia Journalism Review* national poll of 125 senior journalists on the future for journalism after the Bill Clinton and Monica Lewinsky affair. The poll was carried out in conjunction with Public Agenda, a nonprofit, nonpartisan research group. Several journalists discuss their responses to the poll, and charts accompany the text.

Rebuilding trust. Richard Lambert. *Columbia Journalism Review* 37:39-42 N/D '98

By any measure, public trust in the United States' news organizations has been falling for years. The extensive perception that the media are keen to bring down a popular president is a further blow to public trust in journalism. Nonetheless, a mood of ubiquitous self-criticism is abroad, an awareness that things are not as they ought to be. The organizations that transform this into a constructive reexamination of the way they cover the news will have the best chance in the coming years at holding onto and building trust with their audiences. The writer discusses the ways in which news groups can act in concert to help reverse this downward spiral in their relationship with the public.

Why I skipped the scandal. Michael Hoyt. *Columbia Journalism Review* 37:71 N/D '98

The writer discusses how a lack of humanity and restraint in the coverage of the presidential sex scandal involving Monica Lewinsky caused the media to fail in its coverage of the story and consequently lose readers and viewers.

Staged journalism. Tom Case. *Editor and Publisher* 128: 11-12 Mr 25 '95

The decision by the supermarket tabloid *National Examiner* to print staged photos of the murder scene of Nicole Brown Simpson and Ronald Goldman is the most recent example of how the media have begun dramatizing the news. Reasoning that the public should be given an idea of the photos shown to the judge, jury, and attorneys in the O. J. Simpson murder trial, the *Examiner* recreated the murder scene using a stand-in for Nicole Brown Simpson and red makeup for blood. In other examples of staged journalism, the *National Enquirer* ran a computer-simulated picture of a battered Nicole Brown Simpson, *Time* put a darkened mug shot of O. J. Simpson on its cover, *Newsday* published a computer-generated photo that gave the false impression that skaters Nancy Kerrigan and Tonya Harding practiced side by side, and Dateline NBC rigged a GM pickup to explode. Critics say that dramatizing the news hurts the reputation of individual media organizations and journalism as a whole.

Frontier journalism. Fitzgerald, Mark. *Editor and Publisher* 130:10 + Ag 16 '97

For the past 12 years, Paris-based Reporters Without Borders--Reporters Sans Frontieres (RSF)—has endeavored to bring world attention to the conditions of journalists working around the world. Robert Menard, secretary general of the RSF, who spoke at the recent Inter American Press Association conference in Guatemala City on unpunished crimes against journalists, said in an interview that the main objectives of the RSF, which was founded in 1985, have been to devise campaigns and pressure governments and to support and aid those journalists who have become victims of repression. RSF's yearly reports on the status of press liberty across the globe are among the most complete surveys available. In addition, the group established International Press Freedom Day, May 3, which was officially recognized by the UN in 1994.

Death toll down, press freedom up. Leonard R. Sussman & Kristen Guida. *Editor and Publisher* 131:16-18 Ja 24 '98

Although a free press is flourishing globally, homicide, beatings, and jailings still torment journalists, only less than before. Worldwide, journalists were subjected to less violence in 1997 than in prior years, with 26 murders in 14 countries. For the surviving press members, the press was restricted with increasing subtlety, uncertainty, and the abuse of the rule of the law, according to a review of global press freedom by New York-based Freedom House. In 94 of the 186 countries surveyed, the conditions under which journalists operate changed, with press freedom declining in 50 countries and increasing in 44 countries. Compared with their 1996 ratings, 36 countries improved press freedom, 42 experienced declines, and 92 were unchanged.

The world's ten worst enemies of the press. M.L. Stein. *Editor and Publisher* 131:16 My 16 '98 General Sani Abacha, the leader of Nigeria, is the world's worst enemy of the press, according to the worldwide ranking of the "10 Enemies of the Press" by the Committee to Protect Journalists (CPJ). Military dictator Abacha was first on the ranking because of his outrageous assault on Nigeria's once-thriving independent press and because he reneged on his promise to return the country to democracy. The CPJ report was published in conjunction with World Press Freedom Day in May 1998.

Oregon J-schoolers get crash course in hard news. Chris Kenning & Amalie Young. *Editor and Publisher* 131:14-16 Je 13 '98

In the media frenzy that followed Kipland P. Kinkel's high school killing spree in Oregon, journalism school students with minimal real world journalistic experience were suddenly thrown in at the deep end of media ethics and news gathering. A dozen university students were recruited by national news organizations to contribute to coverage of what immediately became the biggest story in the country. They rose to the occasion, but some of them were appalled at the ugly side of news reporting.

Columnist ousted after admitting fabrications. Joe Nicholson. *Editor and Publisher* 131:10 + Je 27 '98

Boston Globe columnist Patricia Smith was forced to resign after she was caught passing off fictional quotes from fictional characters as journalism. The paper's editor, Matthew Storin, said that he tried hard to be fair to Smith, whose career has been marked by recognition of extraordinary talent and recurring questions about whether she fabricated material. The events that led to Smith's resignation and reaction to Smith's actions are outlined.

World marks 50th anniversary of free press declaration. Joe Nicholson. *Editor and Publisher* 131:14 D 5 '98

Although December 10, 1998, marks the 50th anniversary of the Universal Declaration of Human Rights--the world's first commitment to personal liberties, including press freedom--the struggle for press freedom is ongoing. According to reporters group Reporters Sans Frontieres, thirteen journalists were killed in 1998 and almost 100 others remain in prison in 25 countries because they have reported embarrassing facts or refuse to abide by censorship. Indeed, according to the 1998 annual survey by New York-based Freedom House, just 20 percent of the world population enjoy a free press; 38 percent of the global population live in areas with a partly free press, and 42 percent have access only to state-controlled newspapers.

The Magical Medical Media Tour. Gary Schwitzer. *Journal of the American Medical Association* 267:1969-71 Ap 8 '92

The recent increase in presenting news items about medical issues on television has sparked a debate as to the actual thoroughness in reporting on these matters. In particular the role of pharmaceutical companies and their influence over stories involving prescription medicine is examined.

Do Americans deserve a free press? Reuven Frank. *The New Leader* 80:20-1 Je 2-16 '97

Those who believe that the press should not have the level of freedom it enjoys are victims of a grave misunderstanding. Journalism is increasingly being held in low esteem by the public, and the core constituency for a free press is disappearing faster than many realize. The American popular press is no more intrusive than it has always been, however, and it is the rise of television that has revealed its "excesses." The only certain indicator of a free society is an unruly and bad-mannered press, and press freedom refers primarily to the right of all Americans to a press unencumbered by government influence.

The mean streets of Algeria. Anna Husarska. *The New Republic* 215:19-22 Jl 29 '96.

Islamic militants in Algeria, who are conducting a terrorist campaign against everyone and everything that they associate with the state, have targeted the press. The militants' campaign followed the army-supported government's cancellation of the second round of the country's first free elections and installation of Liamine Zeroual as president; the fundamentalist Islamic Salvation Front won a stunning victory in the first round in 1992. So far, some 50,000 people—including 61 journalists, according to lists drawn up by human rights groups—have been killed in the conflict. Journalists are killed not because of the opinions they espouse but because of the attention that their deaths attract, according to Cherif Belkacem, a 62-year-old veteran of the war against the French in the 1950s and a retired government official. Many journalists have chosen to live in high-security residences provided and partly financed by the state, and others are homeless. A very small number try to carry on as though everything were normal.

To tell the truth. Charles Lane. *The New Republic* 218:6+ My 25 '98

The American public appears fairly uninterested in the Monica Lewinsky scandal. Surveys carried out since the start of the scandal have repeatedly demonstrated that at least 70 percent of Americans believe the media are devoting too much attention to it. At the very least, the affair shows that there is a perceptual gap between the U.S. public and the Washington press corps.

What was he thinking? Richard Turner. *Newsweek* 132:57 Ag 17 '98

Columnist Mike Barnicle has been asked to resign from the *Boston Globe* after a recent column of his was found to contain eight jokes lifted almost verbatim from comedian George Carlin's current best-seller, Brain Droppings. Barnicle contended that he had heard the jokes from a bartender and had not read the book, and he was suspended. Soon after, however, a TV tape revealed that Barnicle had recommended Carlin's book for his summer reading list.

The Globe scrapes off Barnicle mess. Claudia Kalb. *Newsweek* 132:56-7 Ag 31 '98

It has been a troubling time for *Boston Globe* editor Matthew Storin recently. First there was the resignation of columnist Patricia Smith, after she admitted fabricating quotes. Then, Mike Barnicle was asked to resign after being accused of plagiarizing material from comedian George Carlin and legendary writer A. J. Liebling, and again after he was unable to confirm the authenticity of a tear-jerker about two young cancer patients. The paper now faces another challenge as the rival *Boston Herald* unveils a more upmarket look aimed at attracting *Globe* readers.

Magazine publishers circling wagons against advertisers. Robin Pogrebin. *New York Times* D1+ S 29 '97

Many magazine executives are seeing a troubling trend toward heavy editorial pressure from big advertisers. What may be the most extreme example of this trend can be seen in a recent incident involving International Business Machines Corporation and *Fortune* magazine. In April, *Fortune* published an article that I.B.M. chairman and chief executive Louis V. Gerstner apparently did not like. In the months since the piece was published, I.B.M. and its software subsidiary Lotus have pulled all their advertising from *Fortune*, business that is estimated to be worth $6 million a year. Such advertiser strong-arming has so concerned the magazine industry lately that editors and publishers are coming together in protest.

At *Los Angeles Times*, a debate on news-ad interaction. Iver Peterson. *New York Times* D1 + N 17 '97

Mark Willes, who became the publisher of the *Los Angeles Times* in September, is pushing the collaboration between editors and advertising executives much further than any major newspaper has done by, basically, removing the majority of the walls that separate the news and business departments. Although Willes has said he will preserve the newspaper's integrity, his moves have been considered controversial by journalists inside and outside *The Los Angeles Times*. While Willes feels that his moves will allow cooperation between the news and business sides of the newspaper to be streamlined, critics think that they have the potential to allow advertisers to gain influence over news coverage.

The press under fire. Mike Wallace. *The Quill* 83:20-3 N/D '95

Part of a special issue on ethics in journalism. The writer argues that in the present climate of declining public trust in journalists, it may be time to reinstitute the National News Council. He explains that this council, which lasted for only ten years, was formed in 1973 "to serve the public interest in preserving freedom of communication and advancing accurate and fair reporting of news." He admits that criticism of the press is nothing new but states that the intensity and volume of criticism from within the press itself is a new development.

'Journalistic nightmare': CNN, *Time* retract nerve gas story. William Kirtz. *The Quill* 86:17-18 Jl/Ag '98

A discussion of *Time* magazine and Cable News Network's (CNN) retraction of a report aired on June 7, 1998. The report stated that the U.S. military used sarin, a nerve gas banned by international law, to kill American defectors during the Vietnam War. As a result of many challenges to the story's accuracy, CNN commissioned an independent study led by Floyd Abrams. It found that the broadcast "cannot be supported." Oliver and Jack Smith, lead producers for the story, were subsequently fired. The senior executive producer of NewsStand, a joint venture between Time and CNN, resigned.

First, we seek truth. Steve Geimann. *The Quill* 86:45 Jl/Ag '98

American journalism has recently been tested as never before as journalists contend with new revelations about misdeeds, mistakes, and missteps in the profession. Each of these lapses, including cases involving the *Cincinnati Enquirer* and the *Boston Globe*, could have been avoided had the reporters, editors, and producers remembered the basics of journalistic ethics.

The CIA-crack story. Thomas Hackett. *Salon Magazine* Online My 30 '97

This article examines the controversial case of Gary Webb, a reporter for the *San Jose Mercury News* who implied a CIA connection to the explosion of crack use in Black urban neighborhoods. After an investigation by outside journalists, several questions about the story arose, leading the newspaper to offer an apology to its readers for "deceiving" them. Hackett discusses the case and examines the role of editors and staff in publishing the series of articles.

I was just thinking. Jack E. White, Jr. *Time* 152:47 Ag 24 '98

The writer discusses the recent scandal involving *Boston Globe* columnist Mike Barnicle. The only reason that anyone cared that Barnicle, a white male, had used a few one-liners from comedian George Carlin without attribution is that a few weeks before, another columnist at the same paper, Patricia Smith, a black woman, had been compelled to resign for making up stories. Although Barnicle's error was far less serious than Smith's, some people thought that the two cases should have been treated identically.

Hot off the presses: pseudo facts, opinion, and fantasy. Joe Saltzman. *USA Today* 125:73 My '97 Traditional print and electronic media are being replaced as sources of information and opinion by less reliable sources. An increasing number of people are now ignoring responsible sources of information and are instead depending on electronic bulletin boards and in-person chats over coffee that foster conspiracies and popular fantasies. The more the public becomes infatuated with paranoid versions of "reality," the more likely America will become a country filled with citizens who base their worldview on legend, gossip, rumor, and fantasy.

The problems with live news coverage. Joe Saltzman. *USA Today* 127:67 Jl '98

The growth of live news coverage has generated a number of problems and concerns for those involved in journalism. The development of portable cameras in the 1970s made live news coverage possible, changing the ground rules of what television news is and how it should be presented. In the 1980s and 1990s, the dominance of live coverage shifted editorial power from experienced producers and writers in the newsroom to less experienced ones in the field, reducing TV news reports and broadcasts to faster, simplistic, one-dimensional, and superficial coverage. The writer discusses several problems and concerns about live news coverage identified by television journalists over 20 years ago that seem even more relevant today.

The media's message. Stephen Budiansky. *U.S. News and World Report* 118:45-7 Ja 9 '95

Public hostility toward the American media is unprecedented. Americans feel that the national press is unnecessarily adversarial, negative, insensitive to the people it covers, irresponsible, arrogant, and elitist. Seventy-one percent say that the media get "in the way of society solving its problems." A growing number of media critics and journalists agree, stating that reporters too often insert themselves into their stories, offer gratuitous opinion, and tailor their reports for insiders or each other. Competition among the expanding outlets for news and the rise of celebrity journalism are partly to blame for this trend.

Nothing but the truth? John Leo. *U.S. News and World Report* 125:20 Jl 6 '98

The cases of Stephen Glass and Patricia Smith, two journalists caught lying by their employers, each represents a different problem for journalism in America. It seems that Glass, who wrote for the *New Republic*, made up material to enhance his reputation. The case of Smith, who wrote for the *Boston Globe*, is rather more alarming, as she does not regard her actions as constituting lying. She seems to be claiming that emotional truth is a justification for using fictional techniques in a column. This reflects a trend in U.S. culture in which the techniques of fiction and nonfiction are beginning to blur.

Are press standards slipping? Paul Glastris. *U.S. News and World Report* 125:22 Jl 13 '98 Despite three recent examples of journalistic sloppiness, journalism itself does not seem to be trending downward. Media critics say the *Cincinnati Enquirer's* firing of reporter Michael Gallagher and the *New Republic* magazine and the *Boston Globe's* sacking of writers caught fabricating characters and quotes cannot be attributed to any single trend. Instead, they are partly the result of the competitive pressure that ensues when an increasing number of news outlets pursue a contracting news audience.

Censorship has many faces. *World Press Review* 44:16-17 Ap '97

The fight for press freedom is seen in its starkest form in dictatorships where the efforts to silence critical voices are brutal and manifest. Elsewhere, however, where less corporations control more media outlets or where the government apportions favors to those who do not come out strongly against it, censorship takes more subtle forms. A roundup of press articles from South Africa, Canada, and America, along with some excerpts from the publication of the International Press Institute in Vienna, outlines various forms of governmental suppression of press freedom in Turkey, Africa, Argentina, Yugoslavia, Mexico, Saudi Arabia, and Indonesia.

Defending the most basic freedom. Larry Martz. *World Press Review* 45:14-16 My '98

By the end of 1997, at least 129 journalists had been jailed in 24 countries, and at least 26 journalists had been murdered in 14 countries in retaliation for their work. Although press freedom continued to extend into formerly closed societies, it was also being attacked and destroyed in countries it had previously infiltrated. The worst development is possibly the increasing subtlety of the curtailment of the press through the distortion of the law.

Index